Explaining Mental Life

Also by James Russell

The Acquisition of Knowledge

Explaining Mental Life

Some philosophical issues in psychology

James Russell

Senior Lecturer in Psychology, University of Liverpool

MACMILLAN PRESS
LONDON

First published 1984 by
THE MACMILLAN PRESS LTD
London and Basingstoke
Companies and representatives throughout the world

ISBN 0 333 34323 9 (hard cover)
ISBN 0 333 34324 7 (paper cover)

Printed in Hong Kong

For Mary and Jim Russell

Contents

Acknowledgements

First of all I would like to record my thanks to Liverpool University for giving me the sabbatical year in which the main body of this book was written.

I am also indebted to a number of people who were generous enough to read and comment on earlier drafts. Here I must thank Peter Bryant, Alan Costall, Howard Robinson, Keith Stenning, Ray Tallis and Ev Thornton, who all read portions of the text, and, in particular, David Hamlyn, who read and made detailed comments on the whole thing. (Needless to say, all remaining howlers and infelicities are well and truly my own.) More distantly, I should acknowledge the excellent teaching of Jim Hopkins, Nick Dent and Harold Cox which fostered my interest in some of the questions discussed here.

Thanks are also due to John Winckler for support in the early stages of preparation and to Steven Kennedy for his sympathetic treatment of the finished article. Finally, I am very grateful to Dorothy Foulds for organising the typing of the final draft.

University of Liverpool, England   JAMES RUSSELL

Introduction: Setting the Scene

Because William James's definition 'the science of mental life' is so frequently trotted out in answer to the question 'what is psychology?', we are apt to forget how radically it diverges from the view of psychology which so many of its practitioners hold today. Not only *is* there such a thing as mental life as distinct from the existence of, say, chunks of metal, flowers and livers, but this constitutes the domain of scientific psychology.

It is behaviourism, of course, which explicitly denies the relevance of mental life to psychology. But despite the fact that behaviourism is now a waning force in the academic discipline, many psychologists, especially those who work in the cognitive areas, take a 'functionalist' view that implies a very similar denial. To explain this: James's definition clearly implicates experience – the experience of remembering, perceiving, using language, intending, believing and so on. However, the prevailing functionalist[1] philosophy in cognitive psychology sets as the focal question: how can the tasks of memory, belief, perception and reasoning be achieved? The mind contains a set of functions or capacities, the assumption runs, and the fact that human beings (and doubtless other species too) have experiences when they achieve memory, perception and so on is at best uninteresting and at worst a red herring. This is a view made explicit in the so-called 'computational theory of the mind', the case against which, and by implication *for* the Jamesian view implicating experience, is the dominant motif of these chapters.

However this is just one theme among others, not the essential task of the book. My primary aim is to highlight some of the issues in psychology that are conceptual issues, that is, not metatheoretical or speculative questions but issues concerning how mental concepts are

1

made to do work for the psychologist. My phrase 'for the psychologist' is perhaps what demarcates this book from those concerned with the philosophy of mind and 'philosophical psychology' as construed within philosophy. This phrase implies that whenever mental concepts like intention, perception and meaning are discussed in the book I try to draw out from the discussion its relevance to contemporary scientific psychology.

People often say that psychology is an ancient discipline, and that it is only experimental psychology that is the recent arrival. There is some truth in this, but not a very illuminating truth because those earlier philosophers who discussed psychological topics had no notion that psychology could be a significantly empirical investigation and were only therefore 'doing psychology' by courtesy of hindsight. Indeed one may well say that psychology has hardly 'arrived' at all because it is not habitually regarded by laymen or by interested parties in neighbouring disciplines, such as philosophy, biology and mathematics, as a science. Mainly for this reason, in my first chapter I try to show that philosophical arguments against the claim that psychology is a natural science are not persuasive. In doing so, I do two other things. First, I argue that human psychology is essentially concerned with the *competence* of the human species. This may look like functionalism but my use of the term is meant to encompass modes of experience and belief for we should be concerned not only with competence in the functional sense of *capacity to achieve X*. Second, I illustrate how nutritious philosophical theses can be to psychology, with special reference to developmental psychology.

In the second chapter on 'mind and brain' I consider the quite understandable ambition of scientific psychology to explain mental life in terms of brain functions. The trouble is that such an ambition cannot be realised, or opposed, without taking up quite definite positions on the 'mind–body problem'. The mere existence of a science of psychology does not make the classic problems in the philosophy of mind go away. I divide the issues here into two. On the one hand there are those which concern the neural causation of emotional states such as depression and the neural conditions for the regulation of behaviour. On the other hand there are the more theoretical questions about how epistemic mental life might have some 'autonomy' from what goes on in the brain. The position that I favour here is the one put forward by the philosopher Donald Davidson. It is that, although mental states are identical to brain states (monism) it is not possible to establish scientific laws of correlation between them. Davidson calls this anomalous (that is, unlawlike) monism.

The bridge to the issues discussed in Chapters 3 and 4 comes by way of the functionalists' claim to have solved the mind–body problem. Indeed it is true that if we take a functionalist view of the mind the problem almost solves itself. Mental functions, because they are regarded as functions and nothing more, can in theory be carried out by any kind of machine and the brain is just one kind of cognitive machine. Thus we construe, say, memory, not as the aspect of our mental life that is concerned with access to our past and our knowledge, but solely as the means of storage and retrieval of information. Machines achieve mental functions by means of representations and the performance of computations on these. What happens inside such machines is the carrying-out of operations with abstract, non-semantic symbols. In this way the mind–body relation can be regarded as one mode among others in which operations are performed on representations. However, the impression that this is a solution to the mind–body problem only lasts as long as the functional construal of the mind goes unchallenged.

In Chapter 3 the principal features of computational modelling of the mental functions are described before I present the sceptical argument that, far from solving the mind–body problem, functionalism is necessarily a form of dualism. It is not as troublesome as the Cartesian variety but it is dualism and troublesome nevertheless. Second, the concern of the computational theory of mind with input–output relationships without any very clear regard for the vast differences that exist between human thinkers and machine 'thinkers' must also result in a form of behaviourism. Continuing the argument in Chapter 4, the case is made that it is not representation that constitutes mentality but objective knowledge, with all that this implies about mental organisation, the active acquisition of data, and location within a social life. There are conditions which must be met if we are to ascribe knowledge to systems and the computational theory of the mind ignores these. The computational approach tries to establish a cognitive psychology of belief when belief is impossible for an entity which does not possess world knowledge.

As I said, what is essential to the computational approach is the assumption that it is representation that constitutes the domain of the cognitive. So in the next two chapters representation is our main concern. In Chapter 5 I principally discuss the sense in which perception cannot be said to be representational and I do this in the context of the late James Gibson's radically anti-representational theory of perception – the 'theory of direct perception'. For Gibson regarded the notion that sensory access to reality depends on some kind of representational medium as an epistemological disaster. Whilst supporting some features of Gibson's thesis this chapter also indicates the ways in which the theory of direct perception cannot be a complete account of perceptual experience and belief.

There is, of course, a quite uncontroversial sense in which *thought* is representational; but can this representation be formal and computational in the way in which the computational theory of mind suggests? More fundamentally: is representation the *medium* of thought or might we say that natural language and sensory imagery representation *constitute* thought? In Chapter 6 I argue for the latter case. This emphatically does not mean that thought is something that is open to us and quite 'knowable' by introspection, because the causes of thought – both genetically and in the stream of mentation – are unconscious.

Finally, in Chapter 7 the psychology of meaning and the implications of the previous proposals for language acquisition are explored. Predictably, the arguments are quite opposite to those favoured by computational theorists, and their strongest conclusion is that, as language is acquired, thought develops. We do not require a form of proto-language or 'language of thought' to acquire language in infancy. In a sense language *is* thought – frozen thought – and to have words and the ability to group them implies knowing so much about human life and the material world. The great mistake is to regard language as nothing more than a representational and expressive medium. The partial and paradoxical nature of this conclusion is accepted, somewhat reluctantly, at the end.

As the reader will discover, there is quite a lot of prejudice in this book, but, as the reader will I hope allow, most of it is inevitable given the type and range of topics covered. My main prejudice is towards the view that human competences cannot be made fully intelligible in psychology without studying their acquisition through experience. The important word here is 'through'. Knowledge cannot come *from* experience and, about this, old-style empiricism was surely mistaken. Moreover, as I argue in Chapter 1, psychology is hardly possible at all unless we accept that we bring with us into the world something that may be called 'human nature'. But I believe it is a very fruitful prejudice indeed and one for which some conceptual arguments are available: that a condition of our knowing anything is that we have had experiences of a certain kind, because we have lived and continue to live a mental life.

1
Philosophy and the Science of Human Nature

Many would take the view that human nature has properties which render its scientific investigation impossible. Are not human beings, after all, conscious, wilful, responsible, imaginative and capable of being both rational and irrational within the space of a few seconds? Are they not unfit material for any science? Sometimes the objection takes a more romantic turn: each person is unique and free and every generalisation about individuals is dehumanising. Even as students of psychology we may well have slipped into this way of thinking in our more nihilistic moments or at least had to suffer this kind of plaint from sceptical laymen. One of the things I will try to demonstrate in this chapter is that there is no such property or set of properties.

Of course, if scepticism about the scientific status of psychology were found only in querulous laymen and jaundiced practitioners it could easily be dismissed. But it is not. It is frequently the prerogative of philosophers to argue that the scope of psychological explanation is de-limited by the nature of man. So one of my principal tasks will be to deal with the most pressing of these arguments, and in such a way that they are shown to be founded on a fundamental misunderstanding of the nature of psychology. My thesis, then, will be a negative one; but only in the sense that ground-clearing is a 'negative' enterprise. With the ground thus cleared the necessity of philosophical argument to psychological practice will be brought into sharp relief. But first we must consider what is the nature of psychological explanation.

The questions to ask of human nature

The psychologist looks at people (of course he looks at animals too, but human psychology is our concern here) and sees them talking, reasoning, remembering, laughing, making moral choices, behaving in and out of character, being aggressive or submissive, and asks how this came about; he asks what determined that this should be so.

We can consider such determination by posing six main questions. As we shall see, there is a natural break between the first two and the remaining four because the last four are recognisably hypothetico-deductive and therefore most reminiscent of the other natural sciences. The second question shows most clearly psychology's dependence upon philosophy and the remaining four stake psychology's claim for scientific status. It is with these last that we shall therefore be concerned in this chapter.

1. The *performance-descriptive* question: What is the nature of the behaviour under consideration? We may wish to know, for example, what is the structure and content of children's play, how much of it may be called 'rough-and-tumble', of what rough-and-tumble play typically consists, whether it is more common in boys than in girls and so on. In contrast, we may wish to investigate what may be called the 'ecology' of thinking: the kind of things that people think about and their actual beliefs. We may even collect data on people's description of their own mental processes; though, as we shall be discussing in Chapter 6, the relation between people's descriptions of their own mental processes and those mental processes themselves is extremely difficult to conceptualise. In general, because accurate description must necessarily precede appropriate explanation (for example, what are the functions of play in development or of mental imagery in efficient thought?) performance-descriptive questions are often in the foreground.

2. The *competence-characterising* question: What is the nature of the competence that underlies this behaviour? In this spirit Chomsky (see Chapter 7) and Piaget produced models, respectively, of the human grammatical system and of the stages of mental development. However such models are not exclusively formal and abstract, for we may also include in this category James Gibson's theory of 'direct perception' (to be discussed in Chapter 5) which tells us what it is to be a competent perceiver. The claims made by theorists of this kind are too general and too fundamental to be called 'hypotheses'. Although they *generate* hypotheses of course they represent hybrids between philosophical analysis and empiri-

cal psychology. In general psychology cannot be a very congenial environment for the purist.

3. The *genetic* question (genetic in its original meaning, concerned with the development of the species and of the individual rather than with genes): How has the evolutionary history of the human species and the developmental history of human beings determined that we can do *X*, *Y*, or *Z*?

4. The *performance* question: What is it that people do when they do *X*, *Y* or *Z*? Here we are asking 'by what procedures?' If introspection were incorrigible, answering this would be a matter of simple observation because all the psychologist would need to do would be to reflect on his or her own performance. But, of course, not only is introspection highly problematic, but also for many mental processes it is not even *possible*: performance is wholly, and perhaps necessarily, unamenable to conscious inspection.

5. The *mechanistic* question: What is the physical realisation of humans' capacity to do *X*, *Y* or *Z*? The ultimate answer is regarded as taking the form: because the brain *works* in this way. Genetic and performance questions can be answered without prejudice to mechanistic questions, and vice versa.

6. The *differential* question: Why do persons *A* and *B* differ in their capacity to do *X*, *Y* or *Z*? This question has relatively separate descriptive and explanatory aspects. The descriptive aspect – which shades into question 1 – is the more superficial because it is that concerned with 'sorting' people into categories. Thus we may answer: because *A* is an unstable extrovert and *B* is a stable introvert; or because *A* has an *IQ* of 140 and *B* has one of 95. But *why* do they differ in these respects? When we seek explanations for these differences we may pose genetic, performance, or mechanistic questions, or questions that are a mixture of these.

Let me illustrate this schema by an example. Psychologists want to explain how it is that people can reason deductively, can perform inferences of the kind $A > B$, $B > C$, therefore $A > C$. The genetic question is: How are we able to acquire this ability? First, we can make such inferences because we are human beings and human beings have the potential to acquire the ability to make logical inferences in language. So here we are asking about the nature of the native competence of human beings: what has evolutionary history produced? There have, of course, been many characterisations of this potential for competence: that humans have a capacity for constructing models of the world through action of which the transitive inference is one fundamental feature (Piaget); that inferences are an acquired feature of basic perceptual competence and that logical inferences are an elaboration of these (Helmholtz), that inferences represent an innate law of organisation (the Gestaltists) and that humans have the behavioural capacity to benefit from positive reinforcement of spontaneous emissions of such inferences (behaviourism).

Typically the answer to the *phylo*genetic question is a working assumption on which the *onto*genetic question is posed: what takes place in development to cause such a competence? Piaget, for example, proposed the theory that the infant's actions on the world eventually become organised to the extent that he or she can comprehend transitive arrangements of objects; this process then becomes interiorised so that around the age of seven years the child can make transitive inferences in language. Others[1] take an opposing view: competence is the result of the child being able to organise perceptual information serially so that $A > C$ can be 'read off' from the series $A > B > C$, plus the rule 'bigger to the left'. Here the developmental task is seen as acquiring the appropriate mode of representation.

Turning to performance questions ('by what procedures?'), according to one worker in the area[2] there are four main candidates for these procedures: (i) linguistic encoding; (ii) spatial representation via mental imagery; (iii) a mixture of these; and (iv) the application of a series of mechanical or algorithmic steps. These may be investigated by varying the method of presentation against cueing conditions and recording the speed with which subjects produce solutions. The detailed models which each theory allow are, in essence, flow-chart representations of human 'computer' programs (discussed in Chapters 3 and 4)

Questions 1 and 2 assume the presence in the brain of some 'machinery' by which perceptual input, for example of a pair of sticks blue > red, then a pair red > green, can result in the output 'blue is bigger than green'. Any detailed answer to the question is more in the realm of science fiction than science fact, but there are a number of lines of investigation that the physiological psychologist might follow. He or she may investigate, for example, whether there is some unique feature of the human brain which supports the inference at a sub-verbal level. Classic studies of transitive performance in rats[3] have suggested that there may not be any such unique feature. Alternatively we may look for forms of brain damage in which transitive deduction is impaired and investigate whether certain loci are typically involved, what cognitive malfunctions typically accompany such impairments at such loci and what cognitive functions are unaffected. We may look at the differential contributions of each hemisphere to this capacity.

Finally, the differential question may be: how is it that Jones typically makes the inference swiftly and accurately, whereas Smith does not? When given a genetic caste the question would concern the developmental history of Jones *vis-à-vis* Smith. Smith may have been cognitively impaired from birth or may have been a highly extroverted child with little interest in formal schooling; or Jones' parents may have encouraged what has been called a 'contemplative'[4] attitude to life or may have played reasoning games with him. On a performance interpretation we may ask whether Jones is a 'high imager' relative to Smith. On a mechanistic interpretation we may ask whether being a 'high imager' is a function of the extent or mode of lateralisation of Jones' brain relative to Smith's.

Clearly, a relationship of mutual dependence exists between these questions. This is clearly true in 4; but it is easily appreciated for 1, 2 and 3 also. The explanation of development, first of all, is frequently attempted by searching for the different procedures and strategies which children have at their disposal at different age-levels. This is, in fact, the guiding assumption of the so-called 'process' theories of development.[5] Similarly, brain development may itself govern certain aspects of psychological development directly. It has been claimed,[6] for example, that the reason children make egocentric errors in the performance of spatial-location tasks is that the frontal brain of the child is undergoing a growth-spurt at the time these errors are common – given that the frontal brain may well be responsible for spatially egocentric performance. Moving to performance questions, we may ask how adults perform as they do. Our answer can take either a genetic form, where we ask how certain procedures were necessitated, encouraged or facilitated in development, or a mechanistic form by which we try to translate conceptual 'black boxes' ('decision centre', 'comparator', etc.) into neural units ('medial hypothalamus', 'hippocampus', etc.).[7] Finally many of the questions we ask about brain structures and processes are straightforwardly genetic or performance questions. It is not just that psychologists do, in fact, study brain development, but that brain functions may actually become more intelligible by looking at their development.[8] Additionally, it is impossible for any neuro-anatomy of (say) cognitive processes to get under way without there first being a model of what these processes actually are, of what goes on between input and output, and indeed of the social determinants of cognition.

Because psychologists are not exclusively concerned with such bloodless capacities as that for deductive reasoning this may seem incomplete or at least too austere. But one might in fact go through the same exercise for any aspect of the emotional life. Even the capacity to love can be studied by genetic, performance, mechanistic and differential strategies. At first blush it would seem that genetic and differential questions were the only appropriate ones in this area, but the relevance of performance questions becomes more evident when we acknowledge that falling in and out of love sometimes can involve complex conscious and unconscious processes of rationalisation, denial, selective and constructive memory, hypothesis construction and the like – of the kind analysed by Proust in his great novel. Similarly, sensual love is related, at some remove at least, to sexual arousal and attraction, the neuro-anatomical mechanism of which physiological psychologists have been studying for the past fifty or so years.

Another objection to this schema may be motivated by the sound intuition that central to any psychology must be an account of man's 'inner life' – consciousness, ego, whatever we wish to call it. This is not a capacity in the sense that deductive reasoning or interpersonal attraction are based on capacities; it may not even be construable as a set of capacities. But the fact that people have egos, that on awakening in the morning we emerge as the person we were yesterday, *is* a natural phenomenon. This is the case because we started as humans, developed within a human culture, came to perform certain cognitive operations, possess a mental 'organ' and because the difference between our own ego and those of others is explicable by these three kinds of process. So we deny the objection by insisting that anything people do can be considered as a capacity. I will employ the broader term *competence*.

Thus, we may regard the business of the psychologist as investigating the determinants of human mental competence. In an analogous sense the physicist studies the determinants of the 'competence' of material bodies, the chemist those of substances, the biologist those of organisms. Indeed I intend the broadest possible interpretation of the term competence here, as 'what X can do'. This differentiates a scientist from a non-scientist who is interested in what goes on in the world, because it pin-points the fact that the scientist does more than study phenomena for their own sake: he or she studies why the material, chemical, organic or mental world is as it is, what *determines* that it is this way. If the scientist were somebody who studied phenomena for their own sake then the historian and the student of literature could also be regarded as scientists.

It may seem somewhat peculiar to apply the term competence to some aspects of human behaviour and mental life, particularly when asking certain kinds of differential question. How, for instance, can we apply the competence framework to explaining the fact that some individuals have levels of anxiety so high that they cannot function normally in social situations or cannot prevent themselves from repeating meaningless routines? Similarly, where is the competence element in 'low self-esteem' or 'affectionless character'? Such differential questions sort themselves into two kinds. First, we may regard the mental incapacity as the over-supply of a kind of competence. In this way, having made the safe assumption that a degree of anxiety is necessary for normal functioning, we can study the reasons why some people are too prone (or insufficiently prone) to manifest this competence. Alternatively we can regard a disability as the result of individuals' failing to develop a criterial level of competence in maintaining self-esteem throughout the set-backs and rebuttals of everyday life, or in establishing personal relationships – and study the determinants of this failure.

One further caveat: the term competence is not a very happy one because it implies skill and therefore that humans are characterised by a kind and degree of skilfulness. I can only insist here that my use of competence is meant to comprise what we may call ways of experiencing, believing and knowing that 'something'. There is a sense in which knowing is *more* than a skill,[9] a sense to which we shall attend in Chapter 4. But the fact that we can know at all is explicable, if not reducible, to competences. (I also cover this point under 'conceptual indeterminacy' below.)

In general, it is essential to recognise the fundamental divergence between the layman's and the psychologist's interest in explaining behaviour. The psychologist is not a layman who happens to know more facts in a more systematic way. Unlike the layman he explains on the level of the species, not on the level of individuals and individual behavioural episodes. He does not ask why Jones crossed the road on Thursday, May 14, at 2.30 p.m. Unlike the layman he is concerned with competence, not with what people do with their competences under normal circumstances. That human beings can do such things as road-crossing *at all* fascinates the psychologist, not that Jones happened to do it. It is in the failure to recognise this divergence of interests that scepticism about the scientific status of psychology principally originates – as we shall see in the next section of this chapter.

What I have done then is to admit that people are just as wilful, imaginative and so on, as the sceptic claims them to be, but then to cast the basic psychological question as 'How are they able to be so?' However, it is very unlikely that this would completely satisfy the sceptic. For he could accept that the competences involved in being fully human are determined in some way, but deny that they are *tightly* determined in the way that the magnetic attraction between bodies is determined or the formation of crystals in a saturated solution is determined. Relative to these kinds of determination human behaviour is indeterminate. It is a very innocuous assumption, the sceptic might say, that *something* determines human behaviour in some way or other.

There are, I think two kinds of indeterminacy with which the sceptic might charge the psychologist. One I shall call *empirical indeterminacy*, and the other *conceptual indeterminacy*. Empirical indeterminacy arises when, for a given phenomenon, there is more than one way that it could have come about. For example, salt dissolves in water, and there is *one* reason for this. On the other hand, the argument may run, children acquire their native language, but we cannot be at all confident that they all acquire it by the same developmental steps: the differences in style of acquisition which some workers[10] have found may actually be differences between *modes* of acquisition. Similarly, for performance questions, people may differ fundamentally in the strategies they employ, for example, to re-member things, so fundamentally that we can hardly expect a determinate answer to the question 'How do people store and retrieve lists of words?' any more than to the question 'How do people store and retrieve cotton reels?' As for mechanistic questions, it may be impossible to make firm generalisations about the way grammar is represented in the brain, because the mode of representation in the brain may vary to a large extent across individuals. Finally, there may be a high level of empirical indeterminacy in the study of individual differences in emotionality and extroversion because these are essentially behavioural styles which people select for all kinds of reasons: humans are essentially actors. Thus we must expect a highly indeterminate answer to the question 'How is it that Jones is an unstable extrovert?', in the way that we would to the question 'Why does Jones wear checked shirts at weekends?'

The charge of empirical indeterminacy is, then, that human nature is indeterminate *material* relative to the rest of nature. How do we answer this? The best answer is to accept, first of all, that the indeterminacy of the kind described *does* exist in psychology. The four sceptical suggestions are fairly reasonable. Indeed, considering the recent burgeoning literature on 'metamemory'[11] the second suggestion has some force. But having accepted the possibility of a high level of empirical indeterminacy we can still defuse the implied objection of principle to the notion of psychology as the study of the determination of human mental competence. There are two ways this can be achieved. The first is by pointing out that the question of the degree of empirical indeterminacy that exists in human 'material' is an *empirical* question to which there can be given a determinate answer. For there to be 'degrees of freedom' in the manifestation of competences there must also be 'degrees of constraint'. The only assumption the psychologist needs to make when studying language development, memory, personality and the neural mechanisms for language is that these competences do not come about in an *infinite* number of ways. There can be a perfectly determinate answer of the form: these are the constraints and these are the possible ways in which competence comes about. In fact the situation is rather like that of the differential questioner: why one mode of acquisition/memorial strategy/locus of representation/'choice' of personality and not another?

All the charge of *empirical* indeterminacy really amounts to is the indication that, in psychology, one outcome can be achieved in a number of different ways. So our second answer to this charge must be that the same is true of the other sciences. There are a number of ways in which the temperature of a body can be increased; but the physicist is not troubled by this fact – his question is about its atomic and sub-atomic nature. Similarly the student of language acquisition may be happy to accept that there may be more than one route to full competence, but his or her questions are about the necessary conditions for language development (whatever the route) and about what happens to the child cognitively when the acquisition is taking place. Like other scientists the psychologist must believe in necessary conditions for an outcome; like other scientists he need not be troubled by the fact that a number of conditions may be sufficient for the outcome once these necessary conditions have been met.

The charge of *conceptual* indeterminacy is more difficult to dispose of however. Indeed it cannot actually be 'disposed of' at all. Rather what we must do is to re-construe it as a statement of the particular nature of psychological science, whilst dismissing the term 'indeterminacy' as inappropriate. The charge is centred on certain key concepts employed in the explanation of intelligent behaviour, concepts such as intention, belief, knowledge, expectation. In dealing with it I will be presenting a bridge between the discussion of the nature of psychological explanation and the discussion, in the next section, of philosophical objections to a science of human behaviour.

The objection would run that, up to now, I have been discussing competences that are either essentially skills (transitive reasoning) or that are amorphous but reducible to skills (possession of an ego may be 'reducible' to a set of memorial skills and the like). But what of the ability to have an intention, to hold a belief, or to know X? These are absolutely fundamental to human nature, but they are not skills in any simple sense because they cannot be characterised in a theoretically neutral way, and, principally for this reason, the characterisation of them is the business of philosophy. They are 'slippery' concepts. What the objector is saying, then, is that before the psychologist can study such concepts he has to be able to say what they are – and this is philosophy. Anglo-Saxon philosophers, at least, have reached some degree of consensus over the years about the quality of some arguments, but nobody would actually call philosophy a cumulative exercise which will eventuate in a set of agreed definitions of notions such as 'intention' and 'belief'. Almost certainly, the great day of consensus will never come, so the psychologist is going to be denied this essential grist to his mill.

It does, indeed, make sense to say that psychologists cannot study the development of certain beliefs, for example without some guiding theory about the nature of these beliefs; but there is no inescapable circularity here. The psychologist must begin his investigation with a working theory of the nature of the belief under study. This theory may then change during the course of the investigation or when it is complete; indeed we may even say that the theory has been improved upon by this encounter with data. Let us consider the following fictitious case. A psychologist wishes to study the development of knowledge of causality by studying the beliefs that the child holds about causality at different periods of development and how the changes from one kind of belief to another are determined. He may begin with a theory of causal beliefs after David Hume: that all we know about causal connections between certain Cs and certain Es in the world is that the Cs typically precede the Es; there is no necessary connection between the two; all we have is the experience of 'constant conjunction' which leads to the habitual belief that E will follow on C. The psychologist looks for the development of this 'habitual expectation' based on the experience of constant conjunction. He studies infants and discovers that they take a very long time even to acquire the concept of an *object* as a thing existing apart from their perceptions of it. The world of objects is not 'given' to the infant: he develops object-knowledge by a gradual process of dissociating his own actions from sensory data. One necessary process in this is the differentiation of perceptual sequences *caused by his own actions* (for example, the infant looks at a door, turns his head to the left and sees the wallpaper) from perceptual sequences *independent of his actions* (whilst he looking at a door it opens and Mum walks in). This causal knowledge is a necessary prelude[12] to the object-concept which is in turn a necessary prelude to understanding causal relations between objects. By such a process the psychologist decides that his theory of causal knowledge was mistaken or at least inappropriate: the differentiation of self-caused from self-independent perceptual sequences is causal knowledge preceding the habitual expectation that *event E* will follow *event C*.

What has happened is that the data have persuaded our psychologist that a Kantian[13] account of causal knowledge is more appropriate to his work than a Humeian one. You may well say 'Doesn't this just show how reliant upon philosophical characterisations the psychologist is – conceptual indeterminacy!' No, all this admits is that psychology must proceed with *a* philosophical characterisation, and suggests that the better the philosophy the more coherent, pertinent, heuristically fertile, and so on, the work will be. But this is true of all science, not just of psychology.[14]

Like the psychologist the physical scientist has to construe the world, and this business of construing is highly problematic. The world does not lie there before the scientist in ready-labelled pens and pre-constructed hierarchies: the scientist must start with *a priori* assumptions. The more philosophically sound these assumptions are the more empirically fruitful the work will be. Of course science is essentially empirical *vis-à-vis* philosophy, but it must begin with decisions of principle about the kind of questions to ask and how to frame them. For example, before pre-formationist theories of embryo development could be replaced by epigenetic theories, the *a priori* assumption had to be abandoned that development must proceed by simple enlargement. This simple philosophy of development actually determined what people saw: they imagined they could see through the earliest microscopes tiny men swimming around in the seminal fluid.[15] So the conceptual advance had to be made that development may be a sequence of qualitatively different but not discrete changes governed by the principle of increasing differentiation and integration. This was not an empirical discovery: it was a conceptual advance for which we owe much to the work of the philosopher Leibniz. True, it resulted in a biological theory *empirically* different to preformationism, but its origin was not in observation but in reconceptualisation – philosophy.

If this example is not philosophically 'pure' enough, let us take the case of Einstein's development of the theory of relativity. This theory – which I am not competent to do much more than refer to – involved not only the generation of empirical predictions from mathematical equations, but a fundamental alteration in our concept of time. Einstein tackled what must surely be called philosophical problems of how we should construe the simultaneity of events at vast distances. In fact, Einstein has described[16] how he was helped towards this conceptualisation by reading Hume – so maybe Hume is more nutritious for the physicist than for the psychologist! In any event, nobody is likely to level a charge of conceptual indeterminacy against physics.

What I am claiming, then, is that indeed psychology *is* dependent upon the philosophical analysis of concepts; but in this respect it is no different from any other science. The charge of conceptual indeterminacy does not stick because this quality of conceptual, or what would be a better term *opacity*, is shared with other sciences. However one thing which must be accepted is that psychology is far *more* dependent upon philosophical analysis than are the other sciences. It is only the theorist in the very vanguard of his or her science who must wrestle with the nature of ontogenesis or time as concepts; but for the psychologist conceptual questions are the very bread and butter – or rather, a necessary and substantial hors-d'oeuvre and diet supplement.

But what of philosophy? Is there just a one-way traffic from philosophical analysis to psychology, such that the philosopher's relation to the psychologist is that of a generator of arguments in splendid isolation from psychological data? There is much to be said on this issue, and much of it will be said in other parts of this book. However, I will only make one point before passing on. Like the psychologist, the analytical philosopher deals in data, in the sense that he backs up his arguments with examples of what people do and what people say about what they do. One way of construing the nature of psychological practice, on the other hand, is as systematically casting this net more and more widely. Thus the psychologically-informed philosopher when discussing intentionality need not restrict himself to examples such as that of a man's walking upstairs as being intentional and a man's jumping when he suddenly sees a face at the window as not so being. He can consider the proto-intentionality of the three-month old infant reaching for an 'object', the informational constraints on intentionality studied in reaction-time experiments, the status of the relation between neural firing in the parietal cortex and an intentional action, or the schizophrenic's lack of intentionality *qua* autonomy. It is very unlikely that the philosopher's thesis will remain unaffected by these new kinds of data.[17] Consider, for instance, the challenges to traditional accounts of rationality that have been posed by recent advances in artificial intelligence (to be discussed in Chapters 3 and 4). Even if the challenges can be met, our notion of rationality will have been tempered and refined in the process.

The first sceptical case: explanation as interpretation

So far we have only been considering the sceptical case against a science of human behaviour as a possible response to some very general claims about the nature of psychological investigation. But there are more radically sceptical points to be made which arise out of the philosophical analysis of human action.

Essentially this sceptical case places a dilemma before the psychologist, a dilemma which is almost as old as the history of philosophy itself.[18] For psychology to be a science, the argument might run, it must deal in the *causes* of behaviour. But a defining characteristic of intelligent behaviour is that it is not caused, because when we act, rather than just respond, we act from knowledge out of rational considerations. All action can be justified – so where is causal analysis to find a foothold? Here now is the dilemma . . . it is no good for the would-be scientist of human behaviour to claim that *intentions* cause behaviour, for one grouping of philosophers will try to show that intentions are not the causes of behaviour, whilst another grouping of philosophers will accept that intentions cause behaviour whilst denying that such causes bring about behaviour in a determinate way, in contrast to physical causes. What I will be discussing in this section is whether this is a genuine dilemma for the psychologist or just an anomalous but interesting feature of the conceptual system employed in describing intelligent behaviour which has no restrictive implications for psychology.

To begin with one horn of the dilemma, what of the suggestion that intentions do not cause behaviour? That intentions *do* cause behaviour, in some sense, has been an assumption deeply engrained in philosophical thinking.[19] It was probably the philosopher Ludwig Wittgenstein who made the first fundamental challenge to the thesis. Wittgenstein[20] pointed out that voluntary action is marked not by the presence of certain prior, determining mental events but by the absence of them. When we lift an arm to signal or to pay the milkman we do not will or intend that we should do it at time t_1 and observe whether we have succeeded at time t_2. What constitutes intentional action, Wittgenstein said, is that it is 'marked by the absence of surprise'. Intentions, then, are not mental causes. Other philosophers[21] have followed Wittgenstein by claiming that to say something was an action is essentially to rule out causal explanations of it. When explanations of actions are requested what is really being required is the appropriate description of the action as an action of a certain kind such as saluting, waving, beckoning and so on. An explanation of an action does not cite a cause. On this view explanation of behaviour is an hermeneutical or interpretive business which must proceed by placing an action within a social context. To say that an action was 'a pass', 'a challenge' or 'a joke' goes as far as we can go towards explaining it.

But surely some aspect of action is caused; we are organisms in a physical world after all. The solution of the philosopher A. I. Melden[22] to this problem is that bodily *movements* and *actions* are often identical; but that only movements require causal explanation. Melden's often-quoted example is that of a car-driver signalling to turn as he approaches a junction: the arm movement is an anatomical event determined by a physiological event, but the *action* must be explained by citing its characterisation as the kind of action it was for the agent – a signal.

Now, it may be apparent to the reader that we have moved from Wittgenstein's important intuition about voluntary action towards what would be a very negative view of psychological explanation if it were generalised to scientific psychology. Indeed everyday explanations of why Jones did *X are* often of the form given above, that is, as descriptions of the action as a kind of action, or as following a particular rule. But I hope that my earlier delineation of the types of psychological question has made it clear why psychological explanation is different in kind from the explanation of individual behavioural events by people within the stream of everyday behaviour.

The first important difference is that the person who explains the behaviour of another *person* typically explains why the individual actions took place, whereas the psychologist seeks to explain how *people* can do that kind of thing at will and why some kinds of people are more likely to do it than other kinds. This is not to deny, of course, that interpretation and description are of central importance to psychology – indeed they are encompassed by questions 2 and 3 (see p. 7 above). But they are necessary as preliminaries to explanation, and are usually relative to the kind of explanation required by the theorist. To illustrate: a social psychologist, for example, must characterise the social episode in which he is interested as, say, 'ritualised aggression'; indeed he must characterise the states of mind that it evinces (for example, 'desire to display virility') before he can go on to explain the determination of these desires. But in all this, interpretation and description are relative to the kind of explanatory interest which the psychologist has.

It would be wrong to pass on without encountering the view expressed in some quarters of psychology that, indeed, interpretation *is* the be-all and the end-all of psychology, because psychology is an 'hermeneutical science'. The motivation behind such a view is a kind of pessimistic conservatism which carries the assumption that because all behavioural interpretation must be on the basis of the system of interpretation enshrined in the human conceptual system then, being, as it were, victims of this system, we can never do more than appeal to it in our explanations. Moreover Shotter[23] has elaborated on the view expressed by the philosopher Charles Taylor[24] that the hermeneutical sciences are also moral sciences, in the sense that the scientists' interpretation of behaviour is relative to a view about how to live.

There is, indeed, something undeniable in Taylor's claim that there exists an 'hermeneutical circle' and that in attempting to understand human behaviour 'we cannot escape ultimate appeal to a common understanding of the expressions of the "language" involved'. But is this not really just another way of putting – though more elegantly – the point I made above about the necessity for philosophical analysis in the practice of psychology? That is, *philosophy* is an hermeneutical discipline (at least in part) and we require philosophy to provide coherent, intelligible, heuristically fertile characterisation of behaviour. The fact that the psychologist then conducts experiments from this basis shows, to my mind,[25] that there is a way out of this hermeneutical circle.

Now some cognitively-orientated psychologists would pounce on the Wittgensteinian thesis as a kind of behaviourism and repudiate it, not just as applied restrictively to psychology, but also as a characterisation of action. Their justification for this would lie in the fact that one of the main planks in B. F. Skinner's radical behaviourism[26] is the thesis that intentions do not cause behaviour. However the fact that Wittgenstein and Skinner are at one on this issue does not make Wittgenstein's thesis behaviourist, any more than the fact that Adolf Hitler and Marilyn Monroe believed that two and two equal four makes Hitler a sex symbol or Monroe a Nazi. The thesis is a characterisation of the concept of intention, but what constitutes behaviourism is going *beyond* this to the empirical claim that the causes of behaviour lie in the environment, given that they do not lie 'in' the organism. So the thesis is certainly a stepping-stone to behaviourism, but it is a stepping-stone to other kinds of psychology as well.[27] As I said earlier, any valid characterisation of behaviour will prove heuristically fertile for the psychologist.

But there is another, more insidious, way that the explanation-as-interpretation thesis may lead to behaviourism. Rather than taking

Skinner's route some psychologists concerned principally with mother–infant interaction, argue that if what people are doing when they explain the behaviour of another is interpreting behaviour then the *genesis* of intentionality must reside in the process of social interpretation. Again the name of Shotter[28] is associated with such a thesis. The assumption appears to be that if intentions are not mental *causes* then it is not *within* the individual that we should look for the determinants of intentionality (a fallacious inference). What develops therefore is not a kind of competence in behaving intentionally but a belief in one's personal efficacy, a belief which originates in the caretaker's (usually the mother's) treatment of the infant's actions (crying, reaching, turning, etc.) *as* intentional. Movements are mirrored back to the baby as actions and thus the baby develops a belief in his or her own autonomy. Leaving aside the logical problems of such an hypothesis (the infant must recognise this maternal interpretation as of an intentional action prior to developing the concept of intentionality) and the empirical problems (much work has shown the *infant* to be the controlling partner in mother–infant dyads),[29] what must be appreciated here is its essentially *behaviourist* nature.[30] Shotter[31] has used the expression of the 'baby becoming human' to describe such a process.

Nobody would deny that the mother must play a crucial role in the development of autonomy. Indeed R. D. Laing's[32] case-studies have graphically demonstrated the consequences for the child of a mother's behaving as if her child lacks autonomy. But the notion of our becoming human by way of having our actions interpreted by others as intentional is a monstrosity, not just morally but psychologically. In fact, I believe it is a monstrosity that is made almost inevitable through the neglect of one of the six principles of psychological explanation already outlined (pp. 7–9). The principle – assumed in question 3 – was that human nature inheres in human beings from the outset; it is not something that is caused to happen to us; humans are born not made. I must admit that such a principle has a pseudo-empirical flavour, and one may justifiably ask 'How do you know?'. My point is that once we abandon this assumption we find ourselves on the slippery slope to behaviourism. Now of course some psychologists *are* behaviourists, wish to remain so, and would repudiate the present interest in competence; but others, such as Shotter, who are keenly anti-behaviourist may if they neglect this principle find behaviourism happening to them whilst they are intending something else entirely.

I will keep to the issue of the relation between the 'explanation-as-description' or 'interpretation' thesis and behaviourism as a means of approaching the discussion of another way in which this thesis can be used to restrict the scope of psychological explanation. The most obvious way of utilising the thesis is as an anti-behaviourist argument. This was essentially what Richard Peters attempted in his important monograph *The Concept of Motivation*.[33] It was a timely book because at the period of its publication (the late 1950s) psychological explanation was bedevilled by the notion of 'drive'. The concept of 'drives' did sterling work in Clark Hull's mathematical, architectonic animal-learning theory, and Hull's theory was taught in detail as the mainstay of many courses and presented to students as the paradigm of scientific psychology. Indeed 'drive' entered into many other areas of psychology: monkeys had 'needs to know' and personal growth was explained by needs for love and tendencies towards 'self-actualisation'.

Peters's book succeeded in doing two things. First, it employed essentially Wittgensteinian arguments to show that the stream of normal human behaviour must be explained by means of a 'purposive rule-following model'. Positing a series of stimuli and responses (Hull's view) could not explain human behaviour because human behaviour is typically action in accordance with consciously formulatable procedures constituted by norms of correctness and appropriateness. What Jones does when he crosses the road to buy tobacco (Peters's example) is only intelligible on the assumption that Jones is following a known convention, that is, waiting his turn for service, asking for a brand, paying, getting change and so on. Moreover, behaviouristic explanation deals in movements, whereas 'paying', 'marrying', 'promising' and the like are rule-bound procedures which cannot be delineated in terms of a set of necessary movements.

Peters's second achievement was to show that the explanation of human behaviour by reference to drives involved a confusion of levels: the causal level on which basic drives (for food, sex, warmth, etc.) and stimuli move the organism in a Hullian fashion, and the level (already discussed) on which people have reasons for what they do which they can articulate. Thus it may be possible to explain some feature of Jones's behaviour as expressing a 'need for approval' or a 'drive to assert himself over inferiors' in a clinical fashion, but theories which assert that such needs and drives are general features of human behaviour are hopelessly doomed in so far as they run together causes of and reasons for behaviour.

However, the assumption running through the book is that this reasons–causes distinction which Peters drew with great thoroughness (leaving only motives as hybrid cases) was actually demarcating the causal area as the only one amenable to scientific treatment and the reason-governed area as that which was amenable only to piecemeal, informal investigation.[34] Unfortunately such an implication seems rather well grounded when we consider that many psychological theories of personality are essentially clinical: they generalise to all human behaviour from what happens when normal behaviour *breaks down*. For Peters was arguing that human behaviour can principally be said to be caused when it is abnormal or driven in quite a simple way. He gives the examples of a married man who suddenly makes an advance at a choir-boy[35] and that of a starving man devouring a plate of food[36] as cases of behaviour being causally determined.

Not surprisingly Peters strongly approves of a demarcation made by Freud in his later writings between primary and secondary processes in the mental economy, because such a distinction closely parallels Peters's own. Primary processes essentially explain the disruption of normal behaviour in terms of unconscious promptings from the id and the superego; secondary processes belong to the ego and the conscious aspects of the superego and encompass the agent's living according to beliefs and principles. In fact Freud was the psychologist *par excellence* who generalised about human nature on the basis of the causes for its breakdown. But it was Freud himself who said that he was only studying those aspects of mental life that psychology typically ignored. My point is that a model of psychological practice derived from Freud's procedures and Peters's prescriptions is not going to be of much relevance to the psychologist interested in explaining *normal* intelligent behaviour. Must the psychologist just take intelligent behaviour as the conscious following of conventions and leave it at that – a kind of micro-sociology?

Peters's own conclusion seems to suggest precisely this:

> The difficulty about developing a science of psychology is that, in a sense, we already know too much about human behaviour, albeit

in a rather unco-ordinated manner. Common sense, which is incorporated in the concepts of ordinary language, has creamed off most of the vital distinctions. Psychology has the task of systematising what is already known and adding bits of special theory to supplement common sense e.g. Freudian theory and theories about conditions which facilitate learning.

So we find ourselves back with Taylor's hermeneutical circle or some approximation to it.[37] Of course the optimist would say that in the quarter of a century or so since this was written psychology has advanced so prodigiously (computer modelling, psycho-linguistics, the dissemination of Piagetian psychology, etc.) that Peters has been simply proved as wrong about the scope of psychological explanation as he was right about the doomed nature of general theories of motivation. Maybe, but this optimism must be tempered by attention to the fact that many psychologists take very seriously indeed the distinction between so-called 'hard' and 'soft' psychology. Although the parallel does not hold in detail between hard/soft and causally-determined/reason-governed it holds in spirit. 'Systematising what is already known and adding bits of special theory to supplement common sense' – what better description could there be of 'soft' psychology from the vantage point of the hard-nosed computer modeller, animal-learning theorist or physiological psychologist!

What has gone wrong therefore? First, Peters makes the familiar error (which we will re-encounter many times before this chapter is out) of taking the explanation of *individual behavioural episodes* as the paradigm of psychological explanation. Jones's crossing the road to buy tobacco is an acquired competence which can be explained genetically, mechanistically, differentially or as a performance:

1. *Genetic*: the child must acquire the behavioural self-regulation, planning functions, the concept of payment and its conventions, and much more besides.
2. *Mechanistic*: the person's brain must support such performance.
3. *Differential*: we may ask what determines that Jones does this even when he has been told that continuing to smoke will, in his case, lead to almost certain death from lung cancer.
4. *Performance*: the person must be able to select a brand by visual search, compute the amount of money to hand over and so on.

The second problem is that the reasons/causes distinction does not hold in anything like the hard and fast way that Peters intended it to do. Indeed Stephen Toulmin[38] has argued that this distinction, which has run through the history of philosophy, has done more to obscure the explanation of behaviour than to clarify it. Toulmin illustrates his thesis by focusing on the fact that acting for reasons is something that we *learn* to do. There are *stages* in this learning and there are *degrees* (almost as many degrees as our imagination can construct) between behaviour that is essentially caused and that which is reason-governed.

Toulmin chooses the convenient number seven to describe levels in the gradation from personal events that are physiologically determined (such as heavy drinking leading to hangovers) to the critical appraisal of rules (for example, deciding between alternative methods of making a mayonnaise). He then suggests that we may view human development as the progression from the relatively causally-determined to the rational. Thus in terms of the schema sketched in the previous section he is discussing the genetic species of psychological investigation. In another paper[39] Toulmin argued that the causal mode of explanation in terms of neural processes does not come into conflict with explanation by rational processes. So in terms of our present taxonomy Toulmin is saying that for a given phenomenon we may attempt genetic or mechanistic explanations of it; but that these modes of explanation are not conflicting nor mutually exclusive, and one theory or hypothesis may make reference to both levels (we might add the performance and the differential).

All this may strike the reader as rather bland if not actually obvious. But this impression should dissolve on recalling the context in which the points are being made: as a rebuttal to the charge that in so far as intelligent behaviour is the product of conscious, rule-following ratiocination rather than mechanical causes its determinants are not scientifically explicable.

The second sceptical case: the ideographic nature of mental causes

We have now dealt with one horn of the dilemma introduced at the beginning of this section: that because intentions do not cause behaviour and because the explanation of action should be descriptive/interpretive, psychological explanations of action cannot be causal and thus scientific. We explored the ramifications of the original piece of philosophical analysis and concluded that it can only be adapted to make a negative point about the scope of psychological explanation by assuming that this explanation is on the level of individual behavioural episodes and not on the level of explaining the determinants of the competence of the species, as was outlined in the previous section.

The other horn of the dilemma grows from a contrary assumption: that citing reasons and intentions is a species of causal explanation. The thesis is then developed that although mental events can cause actions, unlike physical causes of the kind encountered in physics, chemistry and biology, these do not permit *scientific* explanation. This line of argument is primarily associated with the work of the philosopher Donald Davidson, although Davidson was neither the first nor the only philosopher to oppose the neo-Wittgensteinian philosophy of action.[40]

In the classic presentation of the thesis Davidson[41] began by defining such causes as a species of reasons: *primary reasons*. These consist in two things. First, the agent must have a certain 'pro attitude' to the action, that is, he must at the time of acting *want* the result; he may have a desire or urge towards the outcome or he may just be deeming it fit to fulfil the social conventions which the action represents. He may not regard the act as morally admirable, or even desirable – he may just *yield* to the desire one day whilst believing quite the opposite. Second, he must believe that his action is of a certain kind and that the appropriate relation exists between the action and the outcome. Thus (i) the man runs upstairs because he *wants* the brief-case, and (ii) he believes that he is *in fact* running to its location.

Davidson rejects the explanation-as-description thesis for two main reasons. First, because explaining how *physical* events come about – giving their causes – can also be the same as describing them appropriately. This is the case, for instance, when someone asks 'What are the marks on your legs?' and is told 'Burn marks'. If explanation and description *are* closely related then this is not so because of the logical features of human action-concepts but because of a not-very-interesting feature of explanation in general. Second, if we place the agent's action in a certain social context and give the reason then it is not clear how this reason is supposed to bring about the behaviour. To place the action within a pattern of conventions does not explain the action 'since the relevant pattern or context contains both reason and action'.[42] This is an important point to which we shall be returning. To illustrate: in Melden's example of the man in a car who raises his arm to signal when approaching his turning, if all we can do is say that he had a reason to signal and he raised his arm, which was the signal, then this does not explain *what the connection is between having the reason and raising the arm*. There is a gap: between *having a reason* for doing X and *doing X*. At least, says Davidson, a scheme which, following Aristotle, stresses the parallelism between physical and mental causes will move some way towards filling the gap, by equating the primary reason for the action with the cause of the action.

This gap which Davidson and others[43] have shown to be consequent on the explanation-as-description thesis demonstrates the essential respect in which such a framework is hopelessly inadequate for scientific psychology. For if it were not possible to say *something*, however indeterminate, about the connection between the reasons people have for doing things and their then doing them, how could we ever conduct experiments on rationality? The experimental psychologist must answer Toulmin's question 'May not a man's accepting a consideration (*recognising* its force, *acknowledging* it as a reason) cause him to act as he does?'[44] in the affirmative. Of course, for reasons on which Davidson later elaborates a man may *not* act as we expect him to in the light of his desires and beliefs. But because, all things being equal, intelligent behaviour does have a degree of predictability, psychologists can establish experimental and control groups when rational behaviour is the research topic.

Because we are concerned here with the philosophy of action only in so far as it is relevant to the scientific status of psychology we need not linger over the complexities of Davidson's defence of his thesis. Rather we will now discuss how two supporters of the thesis develop it towards restrictive implications for psychology and then how Davidson himself does so. In every case we re-encounter the misconstruction of scientific psychology as the attempt to explain and predict individual behavioural episodes.

Philip Pettit[45] has argued that a science of human behaviour must be founded on the common-sense scheme-of-action explanation as described by Donald Davidson. This scheme is grounded in the assumption that men are rational. But this very assumption of rationality invalidates any attempt to mount a serious scientific psychology of human action because of the following logical loop. If we predict what somebody will do on the basis of the assumed generalisations or laws about the grounds for rational conduct, and then the person does *not* act as predicted what do we do? What we do *not* do is then alter our ideas about the nature of rationality, as would a scientist testing a theory about the nature of X. We assume instead that either we were mistaken about the degree to which that agent was in a rational state of mind prior to the action, or that the agent changed his mind between our correct reading of his mental state and his performance of the act. Why do we proceed like this? Because, says Pettit, 'the assumption of rationality is so deeply embedded in our habits of thought about action'.[46]

Indeed the assumption of rationality is. But what Pettit's argument does is to indicate a crucial feature of our mental orientation towards the status of rationality – that rationality is 'no respecter of persons'. Clearly this is of relevance to psychology because, in so far as psychology aims to explain how rationality (*qua* a competence or set of competences) is determined, it must characterise its logical nature; but the point is simply irrelevant to the question of the scientific status of this aim.

Some may object, however, that we are escaping too lightly by this dismissal of prediction: is not the prediction of outcomes essential to any science? Certainly it is what experimental psychologists spend much of their time doing. Indeed, but there is a basic difference between predicting what Jones or Smith or Brown will do in situations x, y, or z and predicting what one group of experimental subjects will do relative to another group. The difference is not, I must emphasise, *numerical*: it is not captured by saying that the philosophers' examples have $n = 1$ whereas experimental psychologists employ grouped data. After all, single-subject experimentation is sometimes appropriate and even if we want to predict what Jones, Smith *and* Brown do in one situation the case has not been altered. The difference may appear subtle but it is crucial nevertheless. It resides in the fact that when we are predicting what Jones will do in situation x we are making a prediction about Jones *qua* Jones, about this man with a relatively unique life-history and set of dispositions and competences. But when we predict what an experimental subject (more commonly: *subjects*) will do we regard the subject as representative of humanity and predict not in order to test an hypothesis about that subject's unique nature, but about human nature. One aspect of the art of designing experiments in science is making the uniqueness of the materials irrelevant to the outcome, be it saline solutions, strains of rats or people. The experimental method, like rationality itself (cf. Pettit's argument), can be no respecter of persons.

I said that the difference between the everyday prediction of behavioural episodes and psychological prediction is not merely numerical; but the difference is more evident when we consider why the psychologist makes predictions about groups and assesses the experimental outcome in terms of performance averaged across the group. The fact is that psychologists use groups or subjects typically because individuals *are* relatively unpredictable, as Pettit indicates. But this is not to admit that they are infinitely unpredictable, that there is an infinitude of processes by which an outcome can be achieved – as I mentioned (p. 14) under 'empirical indeterminacy'. If, for example, we are asking the performance question as to whether skilled readers decode text to sound in order to make it intelligible by the route that speech is made intelligible, we may well have two kinds of 'problem' subjects: those who simply do not concentrate on the task for whatever reason and those who have idiosyncratic reading-strategies perhaps through having taken 'speed-reading' courses. The first set of subjects just produce 'noise' which the use of fair-sized group should tune out. But those in second group are not problems at all because, although atypical, they tell us something substantive. Thus we find[47] that skilled readers do decode to sound but that some exceptionally skilled readers do not appear to, or at least do so hardly at all. In this way our conclusion is that there are 'choice points' or some degree of 'plasticity' in the acquisition of reading skills.

What reinforces this mistaken impression that reliance upon grouped data implies lack of scientific precision is the resulting dependence upon statistical techniques and therefore on probability levels. Thus, there is popularly taken to be a kind of magic line of $p = 0.05$ above which a result is 'not significant' and below which it is 'significant'. That this line is wholly arbitrary does not inspire respect for psychology's scientific exactitude. Moreover psychologists tend to use phrases such as 'highly significant' for (say) $p < 0.001$ but just 'significant' for $p < 0.05$, even 'weakly significant' for, say, $p < 0.07$. If this significance is a matter of degree then surely the prediction must be very peculiar indeed: a prediction cannot be 'slightly fulfilled' or 'very fulfilled'.

This scepticism arises out of simple ignorance of the nature of statistical prediction. The level of significance refers not to the degree to which our prediction has been fulfilled but thè degree to which we as experimenters can be *confident* that it has been. I borrow the following analogy from Bernard Singer.[48] The psychologist looks at his or her data and wants to know whether there is anything there, rather in the way in which a coastguard looks out to sea where he thought he saw a rescue-flare go up. If the weather is clear and his point of focus not too far distant he can be certain that he saw a flare and set forth; in fog and at great distances he is less certain. But the degree of uncertainty is the coastguard's: there either *is* a flare or there is *not*.

To return now to the question of predicting the behaviour of individuals, we may ask what is the role of the psychologist *vis-à-vis* the layman when it comes to this? If we assume that a given layman and a given competent psychologist have about equal acquaintance with Jones and have about equally sound 'intuitions' about people then the psychologist should be more successful at prediction. He will be more successful because Jones is human and the psychologist (if that is his speciality) knows facts about human behaviour which the layman does not; he may also be sceptical where the layman is not and should be. So, such predictions are made about Jones on the basis of generalisations from (typically) grouped data, that is, by deduction.

It is interesting to witness the muddle that results when the direction is assumed to the opposite: the *in*ductive sequence from the behaviour of individuals to generalisations about all individuals. Colin McGinn[49] seems to be assuming this in his expression of another Davidsonian negative thesis about the scope of psychological explanation. He recalls, first of all, Davidson's claim that there are two conditions for mental causes: (i) having certain 'pro attitudes' (roughly: desires) and (ii) having certain beliefs. The problem is that when we state what these are we find them disclosing a penumbra of further beliefs and desires. This is due to what Davidson calls the *holism* of mental states. For example, we explain Jones's rudeness to Smith by (i) the desire to humiliate him; (ii) the belief that Smith will in fact find such action humiliating. But (i) may depend upon further 'deeper' and more general desires, say, to establish his superiority over working-class people like Smith, and (ii) may depend on the further belief that Smith will not retaliate with such skilful viciousness that Jones will end up with the worst of it. In this way, argues McGinn, we can go on and on with the desires becoming more and more general. But as they approach a sufficient list, if there could be one, the prospect recedes of our ever generalising *across people* on the basis of what Jones does, because this list becomes *more peculiar to Jones alone* the more accurate it becomes.

McGinn refers to the distinction between *ideographic* and *nomothetic* laws in science in order to place his conclusion. Nomothetic explanation holds in general and enables precise predictions to be deduced from laws (for example, deducing the deceleration of a body from the laws of mechanics); whereas ideographic explanation helps us to understand how it is with individuals. Thus the conclusion is that 'ratiocination is ideographic, not nomothetic', and so psychology cannot produce laws to explain rationality. But none of this damages the prospect for a scientific explanation of rationality at all, because the argument is based on the false but familiar assumption that the methodology of psychology is ideographic: that psychologists try to do the impossible, namely derive nomothetic laws from ideographic cases by induction.

Finally in this section I wish to consider a major paper by Davidson himself in which he sets forth a series of arguments which are supposed to demonstrate that there is something in the logical properties of rational action which renders a scientific psychology of conduct impossible of attainment. Significantly, the title of the paper is 'Psychology as Philosophy'.[50]

The paper begins with the now familiar misconstruction of the goal of psychological explanation. Davidson asks 'Can intentional human behaviour be explained and predicted in the same way that other phenomena can?'[51] This looks harmless enough but, as emerges later, it is the explanation and prediction of intentional behaviour by individual agents with which Davidson is concerned. Davidson goes on to argue that the logic of intentionality shows us that deterministic laws of the kind that exist in physics cannot hold for behaviour. Throughout, physics is equated with science.

The reason it is important to consider the argument further despite the fact that its premiss violates one of the central principles of psychological explanation is that Davidson claims to have shown how intentionality *defines* the psychological domain and at the same time puts that domain beyond the reach of scientific laws. We can agree with the former whilst rejecting the latter.

Davidson says:

> When we attribute a belief, a desire, a goal, an intention or a meaning to an agent, we necessarily operate within a system of concepts in part determined by the structure of the beliefs and desires of the agent himself. Short of changing the subject, we cannot escape this feature of the psychological; but this feature has no counterpart in the world of physics.[52]

The first sentence is, in fact, what we have just been discussing in McGinn, and Davidson's claim a little later that psychology is 'nomologically irreducible' is the same as McGinn's. (I am, of course, reversing the order of influence: it was McGinn who, as I said, borrowed this thesis from Davidson, not vice versa.) But the second sentence does hit on an important difference between the physical and the psychological. It is possible to predict the behaviour of an object under controlled conditions with 100 % accuracy, whereas it is not possible to predict the behaviour of a person with anything like a comparable precision under conditions as controlled as they can be and with theory and technology as advanced as they could be, because human beings act out of desires and beliefs which are not 'fixed' in the way that object properties are. To say that a species has intentionality is, in fact, to say that at the level of the individual behaviour has a degree of unpredictability. We can view this as a characterisation of a fundamental *species-competence*; and we have already discussed this. It is also true to say that the laws of physics obtain their quantitative precision through this exact prediction of event outcomes. As Davidson says, psychology can never attain this precision.

What this is telling us is the respect in which psychology and physics differ. *If* we define 'science', as Davidson appears to be doing, as meaning not just 'physics' but this particular aspect of physics (exact outcome prediction) then indeed Davidson has succeded in showing that psychology lacks something essential to a science. But there is no justification for such an equation.

I said earlier that a broad definition of science would be the study of why the material/organic/mental world is as it is – what determines organic and inorganic competences. Because the physicist deals with the competence of objects he is able to study determination via strict laws and exact predictions whereas the psychologist who may wish to explain how it is that people have the competence to be *radically unpredictable* cannot proceed in this way. The onus is then on the sceptic to say why such explanation must be radically indeterminate. One does not encounter such arguments in Davidson's paper. We have discussed on page 14 the matter of empirical and conceptual indeterminacy and concluded that they do not undermine the scientific status of psychology. What the sceptic must be able to demonstrate is that psychology entails a kind of indeterminacy beyond these.

Two other issues that emerge from Davidson's paper require discussion: (i) the assumption that the data of psychology must be probabilistic and unlawlike relative to those of physics, and (ii) the claim that in psychology there can be no 'psycho-physical' laws relating brain events to psychological events.

First, Davidson says that what emerges in psychology are not

the strict quantitative laws embedded in sophisticated theory that we confidently expect in physics, but irreducibly statistical correlations that resist, and resist in principle, improvement without limit.

We have already discussed this dependency upon statistical analysis. All we need to say here is that in psychology – to recall the coastguard metaphor – the weather conditions are typically poor due to the fact that humans have the competence to be unpredictable. In physics the weather is typically clear. Admittedly psychology is not *as* exact as physics; but this is a rather unexciting conclusion given that nobody would deny that some sciences are more exact than others.

Davidson is also correct, of course, when he says that the psychology of rational conduct has no strict quantitative laws. In fact he illustrates this point by an experimental study of decision making which he co-authored[53] and which produced the result that subjects' preferences were sometimes intransitive (that is, preferring *A* to *B*, *B* to *C*, but *C* to *A*). Indeed, conduct does fall short of perfect rationality but then psychology does not aim for strict laws of rational *conduct* but for laws – or at least generalisations across humans – about the necessary and sufficient conditions for competence in a given aspect of rational behaviour. Davidson could then, of course, ask us to produce these laws. Well, we could say, experimental psychology is about 100 years old and physics is about as old as civilisation itself. This is *an* answer, but we should also be able to point to some generalisations or at least speculations that could reasonably be regarded as being in the running for lawlike status. Here is an example chosen almost at random (in that it comes from the paper which I finished reading whilst writing this).

The author, A. J. Marcel,[54] describes some complex experiments demonstrating that the presentation of polysemous (having more than one lexical interpretation) words below threshold (subjects report having seen *nothing*) facilitates the recognition of *both* the lexical associates if the presentation of the polysemous word is pattern-masked.[55] However when the same word is presented above threshold (subjects are conscious of seeing it) then recognition of only *one* of the lexical associates is facilitated. Thus, presenting *ball* subliminally will facilitate the perception of both *throw* and *dance*, but presenting *ball* above threshold so that the subject 'knows he has seen it' facilitates the recognition of either *throw* or *dance*, not both. This implies that stimuli access a range of lexical entries nonconsciously; but that what happens in conscious perception is the selection of *one* of these. Some writers[56] have suggested that the role of consciousness in this context is to inhibit all alternative associates except one. The author then finally speculates that action on the basis of perception must involve the conscious selection from the finite set of associates accessed through perception represented nonconsciously. Marcel writes:

Perception without action can be infinitely ambiguous. It is when action is required that selection between alternatives must be made. It is this selection, which is the perceptual pre-requisite for action, that is the goal of focal attention and thus consciousness.[57]

This is a statement about the empirically rather than logically necessary conditions for intentional action. There is nothing *a priori* about it because the world could be otherwise: we may act whilst retaining such ambiguities in consciousness, or we may act nonconsciously and only reflect consciously on what has happened to us and so on. At present the claim is necessarily vague and the data which suggested it may prove either unreplicable or of limited generality. Nevertheless, claims of this kind may adumbrate lawlike statements about the necessary conditions for intentional competence. As to the question of how 'quantitative' such putative laws may prove to be it is difficult to say, but it is not at all evident that they are logically debarred from quantitative formulation.

I said earlier that experimental psychology is 100 years old; in fact the kind of cognitive research just described belongs to a tradition that is less than 40 years old.[58] My point is that we should give no significance to the fact that laws expressing the necessary and sufficient conditions for competence in intentional behaviour or any other aspect of rational conduct have not emerged *yet*.

We can now turn to Davidson's claim that there cannot be what he calls 'psycho-physical laws'. By this he means that despite the fact that psychological events *are* physical events (that is, intending to ψ is also our brain undergoing process ϕ) psychological events do not fall under psychophysical laws. On the one hand psychological events are physical events; on the other hand, as he has just argued, 'events do not fall under strict laws when described in psychological terms'.[59] It would take us very far afield into the mind–body problem to discuss the full implications of the thesis, and in any case psychophysical reductionism will be discussed in the next chapter. Nevertheless the irrelevance of the claim to the scientific status of psychology needs signposting.

Let us take an example to illustrate Davidson's claim. Suppose somebody is deciding where to go for his holidays. At time t_1 he is undecided and at time t_2 he decides on Italy. We can call his brain state at time t_1, B_1 and at time t_2, B_2. Similarly we can call his mental states M_1 and M_2 respectively. What Davidson is saying is that the processes which determine the change from B_1 to B_2 are lawful physical events – physiological changes ultimately reducible to the laws of physics. But the determination of $M_1 \rightarrow M_2$ is not lawful because explanation by reference to beliefs, desires and the like cannot be lawful, as we have just been discussing. Obviously there is a paradox here: psychological events are physical events and when so construed obey physical laws, but when construed as psychological events they cannot be termed in hybrid 'psychophysical' laws. Davidson calls his position 'anomalous monism'.[60]

A caveat: I have deliberately refrained from giving Davidson's full argument because to do so would mean introducing a major distinction which will be the motif of the remainder of the book beginning with the full discussion of the thesis in Chapter 2. Now is not the time for its introduction. But I hope this sketch is sufficient for the reader to appreciate Davidson's denial: that although brain-states and conscious states may be identical in fact, it is impossible in principle for us even to construct laws which relate the mental to the physical. Why? Essentially because our characterisation of mental states is hampered by the holism and dependency on a rational framework of explanation that we saw discussed in Pettit's and McGinn's papers.

But let me assume that Davidson *is* correct. Does the argument show our conception of 'mechanistic' questions in psychology to have been mistaken? No, and for a very familiar reason: the psychologist is not concerned with the relation between mental *events* and physical *events*. He seeks to explain how brain mechanisms make competences possible. Why should we not call generalisations about the type of complexity required in (say) frontal lobe function or degree of lateralisation for a person to perform syllogistic reasoning, 'psychophysical' laws? Obviously this is far in advance of anything currently on the horizon of physiological psychology.

It is, in fact, possible to adopt a more radical attitude towards Davidson's assumption that physics represents the paradigm of scientific status, with psychology even failing to attain that status. Psychology is the least exact of the sciences and physics the most exact but this only makes psychology 'less' of a science if our sole criterion for scientific status is exactness. Similarly, we may assume (if we are materialists at least) that all mental and organic processes are physical processes and thus reducible to physical descriptions. But this only makes physics the paradigmatic science if we also assume that there is only one direction in which reduction can travel. For it is also possible to mount an argument for all the sciences being reducible to *psychological* processes. Are not all sciences, after all, dependent upon perception, planned observation, hypothesis formation, deduction, induction, categorisation, etc? – psychological processes all of them. There is, of course, something blustering about this claim; but it is not without cogency. Perhaps the most defensible kind of view – one associated principally with Piaget – is that there exists a circle of sciences where mutuality of reduction is the case.[61] Indeed it is one of the main platforms of Piaget's 'genetic epistemology' that experimentation with children may foster new perspectives on problems in theoretical physics such as temporal duration and contiguity. (He mentions that it was Einstein who suggested that he study the child's notion of simultaneity.)[62]

Finally let us not forget that Davidson's influential paper is called

'Psychology as Philosophy'. In the printed discussion after the paper Davidson seemed to withdraw from any actual territorial claim on behalf of philosophy,[63] but the title is a revealing one because it coins the epigram for an attitude to psychology not uncommon among philosophers. The attitude is that because psychology deals with traditionally philosophical topics such as intentionality, perception, rationality, memory, belief and the like the philosopher must have the last word. Davidson's paper can be read as a defence of this right.

To summarise this section, we have been discussing the apparent dilemma for psychology which has arisen out of philosophical discussions of human action. On the one hand there was the claim that intentions do not cause behaviour, that intelligent behaviour is not explicable by causes, and as 'cause' is the key-concept of science[64] this was seen as restricting the scope of a scientific psychology merely to description and interpretation. On the other hand there was the claim that 'mental causes' determine behaviour but that because mental causes are constituted out of an agent's desires and beliefs the explanation must make reference to these; this process must involve a degree of unscientific indeterminacy given the nature of desires and beliefs. We saw that although both theses contained important conceptual truths about behavioural description they floundered as objections to scientific psychology because of their common mis-construction of the nature of psychological explanation, as described in the previous section. Philosophers often take the model of psychological explanation to be the common-sense, everyday schema by which individuals explain the actions and mental states of their fellows. This is not, however, the model of psychological explanation, which is the quest for the determinants of the mental competence of the human species.

From philosophical analysis to empirical psychology

In the previous section I ended the discussion of Davidson's views on the relation between philosophy and psychology by implying how it is mistaken to believe that philosophy should have the last word in the investigation of rational behaviour. However I also pointed out in the discussion on conceptual indeterminacy (p. 15) that philosophers frequently do and should have the *first* word. But perhaps philo-sophical arguments are of the greatest use to the psychologist as agents for (i) the disciplining of his intuitions so that they can be made public and corrigible, and (ii) revealing the theoretical commonalities between disparate bunches of data. What I will do in the final section is to give an illustration of how a thesis offered by a philosopher solely as a piece of conceptual analysis can achieve that grand-sounding pair (i) and (ii). This is presented partly as a trailer for a discussion of similar issues in Chapter 7, partly as an illustration of how I intend the phrase 'philosophical psychology' to be taken (as the study of the utilisation of philosophical ideas in psychological practice) and partly as a means of balancing the negative force of the previous section.

In fact this negative force will be counterbalanced very thoroughly because our example of a psychologically nutritious piece of philosophy will come from Davidson. The first piece of psychological research to be discussed will be some of my own work on the development of logico-mathematical concepts in the child. (Doubtless there are better illustrations of the canalising and disciplining effects of philosophical analysis on psychological research, but as I know the motivating agencies behind my own research better than I do those behind anyone else's I have taken this chauvinistic course.)

Two philosophical theses have affected this work (or my conception of it) on the development of logical understanding. About the first, which is in fact the more influential, I will say practically nothing because it has already been discussed at length in my book, *The Acquisition of Knowledge*.[65] This is the notion, derived from Wittgenstein and discussed in a developmental context by David Hamlyn,[66] that concept-acquisition must necessarily involve the process of coming into agreement with others about criteria for the truth and appropriateness of judgements. Among other things, therefore, the child's concept of *truth* must change with increasing intellectual maturity. This is emphatically not to claim, *à la* social behaviourism, that the child acquires this conceptual intersubjectivity through social transmission, although this may be the case. But it does imply that the acquisition of knowledge is, in an important sense, the acquisition of knowledge about how the currency of thought is adapted to certain ends. Logical thinking is rulebound thinking and rules, by definition, are held in common. Moreover the child must not only *learn* rules he must appreciate the function and force of them, and as Hamlyn has said more recently 'It would make no sense to suppose an individual could acquire an appreciation of the force of a norm by himself.'[67] Thence my concentration on the child's interpretation of rulebound linguistic terms[68] and on dyadic interaction between children.[69]

Hamlyn has indicated to the student of cognitive development the crucial role of truth. Davidson too has emphasised the role of truth in meaning but in the context of the mental attitude of *holding a sentence true* in contrast to Hamlyn's interest in truth as normative. Although their philosophical positions are quite divergent, from the psychologist's angle important commonalities emerge which overshadow the differences. So let us now turn again to Davidson.

The point which Davidson has brought out in a number of papers on meaning is this.[70] The task of interpreting what somebody means by what he says cannot be accomplished without our knowing under what conditions the speaker holds a sentence to be true. For example, we may be ignorant of what Herr Braun means by '*Schnee ist weiss*', but if we know he holds the sentence to be true if, and only if, snow is white then we have evidence for what he means by it. But sentences are held to be true because of two things. First, because of what is believed: Braun must *believe* that snow is white when he says '*Schnee ist weiss*', otherwise it cannot mean that snow is white for him. Second, Braun must take '*Schnee*' to refer to snow and not just any cold substance, and so on; that is, he must *mean* the words in a certain way. Our problem, therefore, when faced with the task of interpreting the meaning of others' speech is, as Davidson says, of 'abstracting simultaneously the roles of belief and meaning from the pattern of sentences to which a speaker subscribes over time'.[71]

Davidson then goes on to indicate the logical constraints on the success of this translation. Our task is essentially to 'pair up sentences the speaker utters with sentences of our own that we hold true under like circumstances'. But the problem is then that we cannot allow for *errors* in translation (caused by divergences in belief and in word meaning) unless we have a 'base of agreement', and we cannot establish this base without some awareness of error. Thus, in Davidson's phrase, translation of another's sentences into our own 'must necessarily warp the evidence to fit the frame'. In the paper 'Psychology as Philosophy' this argument is employed in support of the sceptical case against the scientific status of psychology. For if the interpreter is the psychologist and the speaker is the subject then we appear to have a justification for the claim that psychology can never attain definitive characterisations of what the subject says. There is not, of course, such an indeterminacy of translation to be found in physics.

This problem of interpretation is an especially acute one in developmental psychology because in order to understand how children think we have to talk to them and listen. But how are we to interpret the child's language or translate the child's sentences into our own, as Davidson would put it? The chief difficulty is that the child's beliefs are different from our own (his knowledge-base is different) and (one can safely assume) his semantic system is divergent as well.

What Davidson's thesis offers the developmental psychologist is not a solution to a problem but a characterisation of a problem. The psychologist must do two things at once: (i) get at the child's meaning-system by investigating his beliefs, whilst (ii) employing semantic interpretation to reveal these beliefs – both things being attempted by studying the 'pattern of sentences to which the [child] subscribes over time'. But far from spelling pessimism this thesis does a clear service to developmental psychology by stating rigorously what some developmental psychologists have been struggling to express for many years:[72] the essential interdependence of the child's cognition (*qua* belief system) and his linguistic usage. They have, in fact, been struggling to make the point against the prevailing Piagetian orthodoxy which assumed that, in Bertrand Russell's phrase, language is 'transparent'. On the 'transparency' view the child's judgements can be regarded as a more or less direct reflection of his 'cognitive structures', if the judgements are interpreted carefully enough.[73]

Here then is my example of the way such an insight can canalise theorising about how development actually takes place. Piagetians argue that the child's failure on tasks such as conservation illustrates the lack of 'reversibility' of the young child's thought in the following way.[74] Thinking about the logico-mathematical properties of arrays becomes 'centrated', or stuck, on uni-dimensional attributes of these arrays, so that the child will say that 'amount to drink' changes when orange squash is poured into a taller, thinner glass. Reversibility in this context means the acquisition of the ability to 'decentre' or prise thought free of the uni-dimensional property and focus on the other uni-dimensional property of width decrease and on the possibility of reversing the process. On Piaget's account the child's problem resides in his basic cognitive operations, or lack of them, not in his ability to understand crucial linguistic terms such as 'amount'; or rather that such linguistic understanding presupposes cognitive operations of the kind Piaget was describing.

In this situation the 'simultaneous abstraction' of belief and meaning meant the following. On the one hand there was the examination of beliefs about changes in amount across perceptual changes *when conservation terms are not being employed.* On the other hand there was the study of the young child's interpretations of conservation terms *when beliefs about quantity were not being tested.* As regards the former question, non-verbal procedures for testing length and number conservation produced the result that children as young as four years of age succeed whilst failing the standard verbal task.[75] As regards the second question, research has shown that phrases such as 'same amount of room for . . . ' are interpreted as meaning 'same shape' when a comparison to a standard has to be selected and as meaning 'same height' when the comparison has to be produced by manipulation.[76] Thus the 'non-conservation' answer may not be reflecting a divergent belief about substances but may be reflecting a divergent semantic system.

The next move in the attempt to separate and study beliefs and meaning is posing the question: 'If a child interprets the instruction inappropriately what kind of divergent beliefs about the adult system of meaning does this evince?'. The answer, I think, lies in the difference between stating beliefs about appearance and stating beliefs about reality. Some years ago Martin Braine demonstrated that children of 5 to 6 years of age interpret questions about size and shape phenomenally,[77] that is, as questions about appearance, although they *can* distinguish between the two kinds of interpretation. Thus, they will interpret 'Is it bigger?' as 'Does it look bigger?' although they can respond in terms of actual size when asked 'Is it really bigger?' Therefore might not the non-conserver be talking about *appearance to him* not a reality that he already knows to be unchanging (cf. the non-verbal studies of conservation)? Certainly, a large proportion of children above five years[78] who give non-conservation of liquid answers will assert that it is not really more, it just looks more.

We must then ask how the development of conservation can then take place. Why does the child come to answer in terms of a known reality rather than in terms of subjective appearance? Principally, we might propose, because the child believes at one time that judgements about logico-mathematical principles in terms of subjective appearance are more appropriate than judgements in terms of objective reality. For development to take place therefore non-conservers must attain the belief that the objective judgement is 'preferable'. Studies of dyadic interaction in logico-mathematical tasks[79] and studies of story completion have tended to support this conjecture.[80] So on the basis of this we might propose that there are two major stages in the development of the kind of knowledge tapped by conservation tasks:

1. the ability to distinguish judgements about subjective fact (or appearance) from judgements about objective fact (or reality)
2. the ability to regard the latter as more appropriate within the logico-mathematical domain.

The research programme outlined here was not inspired by Davidson's theory of meaning; Hamlyn's work, as I said above, was more influential at the outset. Indeed I only came to read Davidson seriously when the majority of the studies were complete. The situation was rather that the kind of non-Piagetian approach to development, emphasising the role of language, belief and truth concepts, which many of us have been trying to develop contained a host of hidden assumptions about the way language relates to mental states.[81] The encounter with Davidson's thesis revealed the conceptual problems inherent in the original assumptions but also, of course, signposted the reasons why a consideration of the relation between belief and meaning when trying to make a true judgement (for example, when answering an adult's question) must be accommodated within any serious theory of the development of knowledge. And this is more than the process of elevating some sceptical theorising above mere 'Piaget-bashing', more than the provision of a different 'conceptual framework' (a hackneyed and, by now, almost meaningless phrase): it is the promise of a coherent alternative to the Piagetian view that language more or less directly reflects things called 'cognitive structures'.

Now this may appear as a piece of naive optimism when we remember that the conclusion of Davidson's argument was that such a translation of utterer's (child's) sentences into interpreter's (experimenter's) sentences is impossible in principle – or rather that we can never know if we have succeeded. But this need not trouble us at all. As Popper has pointed out,[82] we should never regard truth in the physical sciences as an absolute goal which is attainable in principle. Similarly in the psychological sciences, we should not assume that *absolute* correctness in our attributions of beliefs and semantic systems to children (or indeed to adults) is possible.[83] The main thing is to move in the right direction.

I will now move down the age-scale for another example of the role of philosophical analysis in psychology; this time the topic will be language acquisition. Davidson's theory of meaning will be re-encountered but first another theory of meaning will be considered which, to date, has been far more influential, and which is radically divergent from Davidson's – that of H. P. Grice.[84]

Students of the growth of meaning now generally accept the view that before the child ever produces anything recognisable as a word he *means* – principally by manual and vocal gesture. Now there are a host of what are generally described as 'functionalist' philosophies of language which promise the conceptual tools for the analysis of such sub-linguistic meanings. They all assume an intimate association between non-verbal intentions and linguistic meanings: 'The traditions of . . . Mead and Dewey, of Wittgenstein and Grice' Davidson has called it.[85] Grice holds that sentence meaning can be expressed ultimately in terms of the utterer's meaning and the utterer's meaning is not merely the utterer's intention to get the audience to believe that *p* by saying *s* but also his meta-intention to *induce that belief via the audience's recognising that intention*. Given Davidson's position on the relationship between belief and language it is to be expected that he would reject such an approach; principally because without a theory of the semantics of the sentence 'we cannot answer the question how we know when an interpretation of an utterance is correct'.[86] Or as Hamlyn would put it: the language system is normative in a way that a functionally-based dyadic gesture is not, because meaning is 'institutional' as well as intentional. Platts has recently reviewed the case against Grice's theory as being a complete theory of linguistic meaning.[87]

However, the approach does at least do justice to one necessary feature of linguistic meaning, the communicative or 'pragmatic' aspect as it is usually called. Indeed a case can be made for saying that in this early, pre-verbal stage of cognitive development such a theory might express a sufficient account of utterer's meaning. For the theory does an important thing: it specifies the meaning of 'meaning' so as to de-limit and determine empirical theories about what develops.

What the psychologist gains from the philosophical formulation is a criterion for the arbitrariness or non-naturalness of the symbol – the criterion of meta-intention. To illustrate: it is tempting to say that whenever the pre-verbal infant 'gestures' with the result that the mother interprets the gesture as 'meaning' something then *ipso facto* we have meaning. Some would indeed claim, basing their claim on little more than a well-chosen quotation from G. H. Mead,[88] that the fact of adult interpretation is not only the crucible of language acquisition, it is the royal road to it. (There is an obvious commonality here with Shotter's willy-nilly behaviourism discussed above.) Now, Gricean theory does more than sensitise the psychologist to the sloppiness of such an approach: it states sufficiency conditions for communicative behaviour attaining the status of behaviour of the kind '*A* means *p* by *g*'. Without such sufficiency conditions where is the psychologist going to stop in his ascriptions of 'meaning' to the child's pre-verbal behaviour and how is this meaning going to be regarded relative to meaning in language? The meta-intention condition entails that the child's behaviour should not only be *characterisable* as 'child intends mother to believe *p* by *g*' but that the child should intend to induce the belief via her recognition of the intention. There must therefore be behavioural criteria for the child's wanting his mother to believe that *p* in this way: not just choosing *g* because he thinks it will do the trick (for example, get him a drink) but because he wants the trick to be done via the mother's recognition of his intention as such-and-such. It is as if the child is saying 'I want you to recognise that I intend you to take "Johnny wants a drink" as the meaning-for-me of my vocal gesture "eekle" and not just by any behaviour that works'.

Hence the gesture is not arbitrary at all for the *child* but it is highly arbitrary relative to a purely *natural* (in Grice's terminology) gesture such as holding out an empty cup. Thus *g* must have some degree of inter-subjectivity if Grice's meta-intention condition is to be met; it must be produced because the child believes that the mother believes that for both of them *g* means *p*, not because of some material, natural association such as that between wanting a drink and holding out an empty cup. To take an example of the latter from a recent paper by Denkel on the relevance of studies of pre-verbal communication to Gricean and Davidsonian theories of meaning:[89] the mother's

> interpreting the infant as simulating a cry in order to stop the mother from giving it more food, this being a cry simulated with the intention to stop discomfort by getting an effect on another social agent.

But, as we have already noted, Grice's thesis may not be very useful when we come to analyse the acquisition of full linguistic meaning. A Gricean analysis seems to work well for meaning that is, as it were, non-institutionalised, but when utterances approximate to the regnant semantics and syntax the situation is altered. Not only Davidson but also Wittgenstein[90] and indeed functionally minded developmental psycho-linguistics tell us that linguistic form and meaning *qua* intention are logically indissociable.[91] At the very least Gricean theory as applied to linguistic meaning is highly controversial.

One way in which developmental psycho-linguistics has framed the problem of the relation between non-verbal meaning and language acquisition is: 'What are the cognitive structures necessary for the child to acquire our semantics and syntax?' However excessive concentration upon cognitive *structures* of the kind implied by an object concept or sensory-motor knowledge of causality leads us to ignore the fact that when the child speaks he is expressing beliefs about the world (as we saw for Piaget's theory of logical development in middle childhood). Thus, following Davidson, we cannot explain the transition from pre-verbal to verbal meaning without a theory of how belief in language is acquired, and we cannot have a theory of how this is acquired without an account of what beliefs are expressed by early one- and two-word utterances. In order to achieve the latter we must investigate under what conditions the child behaves as if certain utterances hold true. As Davidson puts it in quite another context:

> behavioural and dispositional facts . . . on which a theory of interpretation is based will necessarily be the vector of a theory of meaning.[92]

Naturalistic studies or experimental manipulations of the environmental conditions within which utterances or assertations come to be made are by no means common in developmental psycho-linguistics. When such research is done the aim is to tease out the cognitive or linguistic structures underlying simple one- and two-word utterances.[93] What is being stressed here is that such utterances also express beliefs about words and the world.

Unfortunately these final remarks represent more of a hopeful gesture than a flourish; but my aim has been to illustrate how philosophical analysis might be (and in the case of Grice *has* been) enormously nutritious to psychology (in this case to developmental psychology). The very least we can say is that by attending to the fact that interpreting any language, no matter how primitive, necessarily involves studying the mutuality of semantics and a belief system in the context of holding utterances to be true we discover a previously neglected facet of language development.

In conclusion, I hope that two unambiguous proposals have emerged from all this. First, far from the natural science paradigm being deeply inappropriate to human psychology, psychology *is* a natural science if it is anything at all and does not even have to graduate as one when some criterial level of precision has been attained. Second, although philosophy should be denied the last word on psychological topics (i.e. being decisive in empirical isolation) which it has been granted since ancient times, the role of philosophy in providing not only adequate characterisation of the *explicanda* of psychology but actually in inspiring the formation of theory and canalising the interpretation of data must be recognised. The way in which philosophical theory may be influenced by psychological data has also been touched on. This interplay between the philosophical and psychological studies of man will be the subject of the following chapters.

2

Brain and Mind

The pancreas is the organ which secretes insulin into the blood and digestive juices into the duodenum; the brain is the organ of the mind. But can we reduce mental functions to physical functions in the same way that we can reduce a flow-chart description of the jobs done by the pancreas to the actual bio-chemical processes undergone by the organ when it does them? Can we reduce psychological theories to physiological theories; can we, indeed, *replace* psychological theories by physiological theories? The questions I will be asking in this chapter – and, in good company, failing to answer – all concern the issue of whether there is something special about the mental functions which ensures that they can never be fully explained in terms of processes going on in the brain.

It is not, of course, uncommon for psychologists to adopt highly stereotyped positions when the issue of psycho–physical reductionism is raised. One psychologist may say:

'All psychology which does not take neurological processes as its explanatory terms is *descriptive* and *provisional*. Explanation which does not include reference to brain-processes is no more explanation than are accounts of blood-sugar regulation which make no reference to the pancreas and its secretions.'

But others would reject the implication that, what we have called, genetic, performance, and differential hypotheses are mere tokens awaiting physiological cashment. The reply might be:

'I admit that all mental events are also electrical events in the brain and that all mental structures are also chemical structures in the

48

brain: they have their material aspect. But even if we were able to relate mental types to neural types in some systematic way (and where is the proof that we can?), would this really *add* anything to the psychological account? Moreover, when we carry out this reduction we do so by virtue of psychological concepts. Because accounts of the brain's function must depend on psychological theory and data no psychologically neutral characterisation of brain-structures is possible. If no psychological neutral characterisation of the brain is possible, where then is this purely 'neural' level to which psychology can be reduced? This whole notion of 'reducing' is confused.'

But before the reader becomes confused with this trailer for battles to come let us just consider why these positions are so entrenched. They are entrenched because they represent different philosophies: one basically materialist and the other basically anti-materialist. The materialist believes that the world is a purely physical world, that mental entities do not really 'exist' at all. The resulting view of mind is that because all aspects of consciousness (belief, knowledge, intention, etc.) are only there by virtue of material events in the brain such mental entities have no autonomy and therefore no efficacy in this material world. The strong implication from this for psychology is that the terminology of psychological theories can be rendered obsolete, as, for example, Richard Rorty has argued:[1] all that we at present cover by psychological terms could be covered by material terms with no loss of any meaning that is significant to us.

Idealism is the philosophy symmetrically opposed to materialism: the view that the world is a mental construct and that we really are 'such stuff as dreams are made on'. But it is dualism that, in the mind-brain context, presents the natural alternative. Dualism is the position that there are two distinct kinds of entity in the world – mental and material. Descartes claimed, famously, that these two interacted in the brain of man. 'But *how?*' we are entitled to ask. The fact that no possible answer could be forthcoming (for how can the immaterial affect the material or vice versa?) seems to force some kind of monism on us: namely the position that mental and physical processes are identical. Now, it is important to bear in mind that it is possible to be a monist without being a materialist: we can accept that indeed mental and physiological processes are one and the same kind of process but refuse to accept that the former are reducible to the latter in any sense, let alone accepting that the former can be utterly eliminated in favour of the latter. One can be a monist, therefore, whilst arguing for 'autonomy' of the mental both in ordinary language and in the construction of psychological theories. Later sections will flesh out what 'autonomy' means here.

It is apparent, then, that what we require before proceeding further is some working assumption about the mind – body relationship which avoids the logical horrors of strict dualism without resting on a hard materialist platform. Let us just assume, as surely must be the case, that the mind exists by virtue of brain-processes but assume this entirely without prejudice to the question of whether the world of psychological discourse is in any degree autonomous. I will call this provisional position 'psychological monism'. That done, we can go on to discuss three issues in this chapter:

1. The status of purely physiological accounts of motivational and affective states, with particular attention to the neurochemical model of depression.
2. Can the eradication of psychological terms in favour of physiological ('eliminative reduction') be achieved with psychological terms as primitive as those employed in animal learning theory?
3. The logical, and therefore explanatory, autonomy of the higher mental processes.

The neural causation of motivational and affective states

Psychological explanations are frequently contrasted with physiological explanations in the following manner. The psychological explanation of such phenomena as depression or schizophrenia or individual differences in temperament may make reference to learning histories, the cognitive evaluation of self or social milieu, the state of the unconscious mental economy, and the like. Physiological explanations, on the other hand, describe how neural malfunctions lead to mental malfunctions or how individual differences in neural structure lead to temperamental differences.

Let us begin with the last-mentioned: temperamental differences. Perhaps the clearest and best-known example of such a theory couched in physiological terms is the differential conditionability theory of Eysenck, after Pavlov. This states that differences in degree of extroversion exist because of differences in levels of 'cortical arousal'. Introverts have high levels with the result that they screen out experiences and are easily conditionable (because this cortical activity allows CS–UCS connections to be easily cemented). Extroverts have lower levels of arousal and therefore seek stimulation and are not readily conditionable. These differential levels are hypothesised to exist because the ascending reticular activating systems (RAS) of introverts and extroverts are structurally different: the introvert's RAS 'gate' is relatively wide and allows more incoming stimulation up to the cortex; and vice versa for the extrovert. Is this theory reductionist?

If we adopt the strict view of 'reductionist' – that the term can only apply to attempts to replace psychological terms by physiological terms – then the theory is *not* reductionist. But the theory is, of course, reductionist in the sense of positing a physiological *cause* for psychological phenomena. It does not claim that extrovert/introvert behaviour and brain-structures are logically identical nor that one implies the other; it says that the brain-structures are, in fact, genetically prior to the utilisation of the experiences which lead to the behaviour. It is – recalling the terminology of Chapter 1 – partly a genetic and partly a mechanistic theory.

I think it is well to point out that such a species of reductionism, if it is even worthy of the name, is really very unexceptional and even regarded by most of us as undeniable. To explore this proposition we might call into a pub on the way home one evening, order three double whiskies and drink them in rapid succession. Lo and behold, a change in temperament has taken place, a mood-change – for better or for worse. Who would deny that this mood-change has as a condition the alcoholic content of the blood affecting our central nervous system (CNS)? Now obviously the degree or manner in which alcohol changes our mood itself interacts with a host of other factors, such as whether the drink is celebratory, consolatory or to deaden a toothache; but none of this can cloud the fact that in the short term imbibed chemicals affect temperament. If we accept this then we should also be happy to accept that brain-structures may affect temperament in the long term. (Sometimes, of course, the label 'reductionist' is pejoratively applied to theories of the Eysenck type as meaning something like 'mechanistic in a crude nineteenth-century manner'; *that* is another question.)

But all this is only by way of *introducing* the problem of the status of physiological explanations of motivational and affective states. Our main task will be to try to conceptualise this 'interaction' between *CNS* states and other factors to which I referred in the previous paragraph; in particular we will consider the relation between the neurochemical model of depression and the social and experiential conditions for depression.

People may become depressed because of something in their personal life – unemployment, marital breakdown, bereavement, social isolation, physical disability – and to explain how the personal condition leads to the mental state would appear to be a definitively psychological task. Of course, as psychological monism entails, any psychological state is also a brain state, but what might be the status of an explanation which short-cuts the psychological and goes straight to the brain?

The neurochemical account of depression is not an unqualified success story but it does provide a realistic empirical context for discussing reductionism; and in discussing it I will consider the views expressed in a recent book by Austen Clark entitled *Psychological Models and Neural Mechanisms*.[3] Essentially Clark endorses the case that indeed what we have now *is* a neurochemical explanation of depression and that although the empirical story may not all be told there are no conceptual barriers against the proposition that a theory of the *kind* that Clark discusses should be the theory of depression. Yet Clark couples this with the view that psychological terminology, for example 'reinforcement', is *not eliminable* in favour of physiological terminology, as we shall be discussing in the next section. I believe that both these views require a good deal of modification if not actual rejection.

A problem arises from the fact that in producing an account of the success story which does not proceed far beyond its first chapter Clark gives the impression that reductionist accounts are more definite than they really are. This is not, as we shall shortly see, a matter of empirical completeness alone: the complexities influence the way we should construe the task of psycho-physical reduction.

The thesis to which Clark refers is that depression is caused by the depletion of certain brain-chemicals which facilitate synaptic transmission within the pathways of the limbic system. To explain this I must now make a brief digression into the chemistry of neurotransmission. The original thesis cited by Clark is that antidepressant drugs (ADs) are effective because they facilitate the action of certain neurotransmitters, that is, chemicals which are released from the presynaptic axon into the synaptic cleft (the functional interface between neurones) in order to make possible the passage of electrical potential from one neurone to another. The principal neurotransmitters which have been discussed are noradrenaline (NA) and 5-hydroxitryptamine or 5-HT (also called 'serotonin'). The ADs increase the concentration of neurotransmitters at the synaptic cleft in two ways.

1. The so-called tricyclics block the 're-uptake' of transmitter substance. To explain: the 're-uptake' of a transmitter chemical is the process by which it is re-absorbed into the presynaptic axon where it is stored for future use.
2. Drugs may increase the concentration of neurotransmitter substance by inhibiting the action of the enzyme monoamine oxidase (MAO) which metabolises the neurotransmitters (that is, changes their chemical structure so that they become ineffective). These ADs are called the MAO inhibitors. (Storage of the neurotransmitter in the synaptic vesicles normally protects it against such enzymes.)[4]

But within the past few years the evidence has become greatly complicated in the following principal respects.[5]

1. Other AD drugs have appeared which neither inhibit the uptake of NA or 5-HT nor inhibit MAO – the so-called 'atypical' ADs.
2. Some of these atypical ADs, such as mianserin, actually exert a blocking effect on 5-HT.
3. The atypical ADs form such a chemically heterogeneous group that it is very difficult to generalise about how their effects are achieved.
4. It is in 'acute' studies (single dose administration and recording of immediate effects) that these findings regarding AD effects on amine uptake have been produced.

However therapeutic effects in humans only appear in 'chronic' studies (repeated administration over a period of at least two weeks), and data on functional changes induced by chronic administration of ADs suggest the effects are more complex and often support the opposite hypothesis that they decrease the functional response of neurones to monoamines. When coupled with the fact that no common mode of functioning has ever been discovered in acute experiments the explanation of chronic therapeutic effects is simply not forthcoming. Indeed some workers have been led to claim that it is NA *overactivity* which occurs in depression and thus ADs (and also electro-convulsive therapy) produce a decrease in sensitivity.[6]

What, you may well ask, has all this got to do with the *conceptual* issue of whether a reductionist account of a phenomenon like depression is possible in principle? Is not all this just to complicate a picture without actually changing its major features? To an extent, yes. A recent review ends:

> It is hard to resist the conclusion that monoamines are involved in some way in the pathogenesis of depression and that antidepressant action is reflected in mechanisms involving monoamines.[7]

But we now know that how this involvement is mediated is not by one type of chemical causing depletion in a predictable way at a particular locus, but by the disruption of a *system* containing a vastly complex set of checks and balances: this is what the evidence tells us. Moreover it is not merely that the original hypothesis is empirically inadequate; but a hypothesis of that *kind* lacks the conceptual resources for explaining depression. For it makes poor sense to conceptualise the physiological basis of depression as merely impaired neural transmission at certain loci because the obvious follow-up question is 'How does that impairment then cause depression; that is, what system for maintaining mental equilibrium is being disrupted?'

I will illustrate this point about disruption of a system by reference to another way in which the evidence is complicated. Some ADs have the following kind of contradictory effects: a pre-synaptic effect on uptake inhibition (i.e. facilitatory) along with a post-synaptic effect on receptor blocking (i.e. inhibitory). In fact a number of other agents in addition to ADs have such effects. This leads researchers to look beyond the synaptic cleft either for a second order system which is determining the action that the agent has at the synapse or to examine elements downstream from those changed by monoamine activity.[8] Indeed it is very likely that once this higher system has been uncovered still higher systems may need to be postulated. But is this not just what we should expect given the kind of syndrome that depression is? The symptoms of depression are many and varied and it really is more like a 'state of mind' than a tendency to produce or inhibit specifiable responses. Behaviourally and phenomenally depression is a loss of mental equilibrium – the tendency for the scales to bang down on the side of irrational pessimism rather than hover, as normal, between this and irrational optimism. So, in general, the notion of the state of depression being reducible to the action of a finite set of transmitter substances at a definite locus is conceptually distorting as well as empirically untenable. Indeed the logic is the same with a system as simple as a carburettor: disruption can come about by turning a screw one quarter turn – but we cannot explain the effect on the engine's performance by simply focusing on the place where the screw was turned.

A final caveat: the foregoing should not be confused with the notion of 'loose localisation of function' where one psychological function such as that of being a 'reward centre' may be mediated in different loci or where one locus may have a number of functions (see below). There is nothing *loose* about the kind of system which research is uncovering. Quite the opposite: greater and greater specificity in the different actions of chemical agents with sometimes only slightly different molecular structures is what we find. Moreover, none of this adds up to anything 'anti-reductionist'. For if we can describe a system within the limbic region consisting of a set of neurochemical functions which have to remain in a certain state of equilibrium if there is to be mental equilibrium then we have a reductionist theory of the *neural conditions* for depression. But the discovery of an association between depression and certain kinds of chemical depletion is only the first step towards such a theory.

Let us now return to the question of the relation between 'psychological' and 'physiological' theories of depression. There are, of course, social-psychological theories of how social isolation, unemployment and so forth may lead to depression,[9] but let us take a theory derived from animal learning because (i) it promises to uncover basic commonalities between the different social aetiologies and (ii) because its concern with reinforcement makes it more favourable to the reductionists' case. This is Martin Seligman's theory of learned helplessness.[10] Seligman and others have observed that when dogs are exposed to unavoidable electric shock they will later fail to avoid electric shock that can be terminated by simply moving to another part of the chamber – the animals just lie there whimpering as the shock is delivered, as if they 'believed' that nothing they might do could affect the situation. The analogy with depression in humans is a very powerful one: depressives are people to whom the world has – either suddenly or over a period – delivered pain which they were powerless to combat. Then when matters arise that fall well within their competence 'learned helplessness' obtrudes and makes failure a self-fulfilling prophesy. As is to be expected with all theories that extrapolate from animal studies to human life, Seligman's theory has attracted its share of brickbats.[11] Nevertheless it *is* a powerful theory because it exploits a feature which I would suggest lies at the heart of all social determinants of depression: they are experiences that make the individual feel personally impotent. Plain old-fashioned unhappiness, in contrast, need not involve any negative personal evaluations at all.

Now there are two clear differences between the 'learned helplessness' account of depression and the neurochemical account, quite apart from the psychological nature of one and the physiological nature of the other. One of these differences is fundamental. The less important of the two is that although they both utilise learning-theory concepts there is all the difference in the world between saying that depression *is* the inability to find rewarding events rewarding, as derivatives of the neurochemical account have done,[12] and saying that depression arises because of expectations about the efficacy of one's own behaviour in obtaining reinforcement. Seligman's theory implicitly denies (*pace* Clark's *Psychological Models and Neural Mechanisms*, p. 11) that depression is the inability to benefit from rewarding events.

But the fundamental difference between the accounts is that Seligman's theory is concerned with *aetiology* (causation) whereas the neurochemical account describes how the mental state of depression is mediated by the brain. Indeed the neurochemical account also diverges from other 'physiological' explanations such as Eysenck's conditionability theory. The Eysenck theory is one of aetiology because it claims that differences in neural structure are prior to behavioural differences (p. 51): it does not need to say that life events caused the neural structures to diverge. However the neuro-chemical account of depression still has to say what caused the chemical imbalance – unless, of couse, it is claimed that it is due to congenital differences in neural structure.

Some, however, would object that environmental aetiology is

simply not relevant to the explanatory power of the reductionist theory because the development of depression *through experience* is only one route to depression. It is, after all, possible to suffer from depression as an effect of drug treatments[13] (and through hormonal imbalance, jet lag, and other wholly non-cognitive, non-experiential agencies). Some may go so far as to say that the existence of such depressions bolsters the claim that 'psychological' explanation of it is wholly inappropriate.

This does not make the question of how depressive disorders are determined by experiential factors go away. What it does, in fact, is to reinforce the suspicion that by concentrating solely on the physiological determinants of depression we are describing the *result* of a process which has already taken place. Are we not justified in expecting something more from a 'theory of depression' than an account of how depression is realised physiologically and how depression can be elicited by tinkering with blood content and circadian rhythms. To take an analogy: there are a number of competing explanations of cot death in babies. As theories of aetiology they still compete when there is agreement in the data regarding the immediate causes of death as revealed in post mortems. Evidence about the immediate causes of death is just more evidence, not the *explanation* of cot deaths. Just as we wish to know what led to death being precipitated in these ways we wish to know what led to the chemical imbalance which is the precipitating cause of depression. The fact that chemical imbalance can lead to depression is only to give a precipitating cause, the final link in a chain of events of which a full theory of aetiology should be able to provide an account. What we require, therefore, are theories which link environmental events with eventual chemical imbalance.

Given this, it would seem that all that the theorist advancing a physiological explanation of depression needs to do is to supplement the neurochemical account by placing such terms as 'non-contingent punishment', 'loss of love-object' and the like on one side of an arrow and the limbic mechanisms on the other side. But this would be hopelessly inadequate as a 'physiological' theory of depression because all that is to be explained by 'experiences → chemical disequilibrium' resides in the arrow. That is to say, a fully physiological theory of depression must spell out the brain-mechanisms that enable experiences to be assimilated in such a way that they lead to the hypothesis of personal impotence (or some other form of cognitive antecedent) and how these mechanisms lead in turn to chemical imbalances within the limbic system.

What we must be very careful not to allow, because it violates our basic assumption of psychological monism, is the suggestion that this dependency upon, let us call it, 'the cognitive appreciation of events' (including Seligman's dogs in this) enables us to discard the notion of behaviour being grounded in physiology. Of course, it does not because what we really have here is not an arrow between appreciation of events and brain-processes – indeed between mind and body – but between two levels of brain process; or more realistically multiple double-headed arrows between multiple, hierarchically-organised systems within the brain.

Our conclusion in this section must therefore be that a full-blown physiological theory of the aetiology of depression is a very long way off, depending, as it must do, on some neural explanation of the perceptual and cognitive functions implicated in learning and their relation to limbic processes. But this is a conclusion that leaves absolutely intact the claim that chemical mechanisms in the limbic system sustain equanimity and can cause depression when they are caused to malfunction.

Eliminative reduction and learning theories

Having sounded some caveats regarding reductionist theories of depression in the previous section I now wish to suggest how a standard argument *against* the reduction of learning-theory concepts to physiological terminology may be mistaken. Our concern in this section will be exclusively with the vocabulary of animal learning and our question will be:

> If we have a behavioural theory and a physiological theory which both explain the same data, and if we assume via psychological monism that the phenomena encountered in the former exist by virtue of phenomena referenced by the latter, then does the former (psychological) theory become redundant?

In trying to answer this I will be making an assumption, for which I have argued in detail elsewhere,[14] namely, that classical conditioning and the associative elements in instrumental conditioning can be given a purely causal (that is, non-cognitive and non-intentional) explanation. It is these elements whose reduction we will be considering. Obviously this is a big claim to make, but given the conclusion of the previous section we cannot proceed without it, because it allows the working assumption that some learning phenomena are explicable without reference to cognitive processes that presumably take place in higher, cortical areas.

The principal candidates for such reduction are the so-called 'black box models' which represent or analogise physiological reality in terms of flow-charts. This is not to say, of course, that they are mere descriptions, because they do generate empirical claims about which brain loci mediate which psychological functions. Among the earliest attempts at such an enterprise was Sokolov's model of habituation, and among the most elaborate and challenging examples in recent years have been J. A. Gray's models of conditioning and of anxiety.[15]

It is very difficult to 'dip into' such a complex activity as model-building whilst retaining intelligibility; nevertheless as some characterisation is necessary, here is a précis of Gray's model of a two-process learning system.[16] At the top of the flow-chart are descending arrows described as 'signals of reward or of non-punishment' in one case and as 'signals of non-reward or of punishment' in another. These travel, respectively, to boxes labelled 'reward mechanism' and 'punishment mechanism', which both send signals to the 'arousal mechanism' and to the 'comparators' for reward and for punishment (to be re-encountered later). They travel downwards to the 'decision mechanism' and thence to the 'go' or 'stop' boxes respectively which receive input from the arousal mechanism. The output from these goes to the 'motor system' which produces or inhibits a response.

Feedback begins by the consequences of the response being recorded by comparators for either reward or for punishment. Depending on how the comparators assess the input from the environment the information is thence relayed as a signal of either reward (or non-punishment) or of non-reward (or punishment) and the whole process begins again. In classical paradigms the comparators assess consequences once expectancies have been formed on the basis of CS + UCS links. In this way the model can explain avoidance-learning, for example by claiming that safety signals (CSs of non-punishment) are assessed by the comparator and then reinforced, so generating a repetition of the behaviour.

In terms of our present concern it is not necessary to understand how the model functions as a whole and what its explanatory power is, but the next step is highly relevant. Gray then goes on to say to what brain loci these boxes might refer on the basis of anatomical, lesion, stimulation and drug studies. The 'arousal mechanism' becomes the reticular activating system, the 'decision mechanism' the medial hypothalamus, the 'comparator' the amygdala, and so on.

The reductionist's claim is, therefore, that such 'black box' models are only aids to conceptualisation and that once workers are agreed about the equivalences between given psychological functions and physiological structures we can dispense with the psychological. Henceforth psychologists would not talk about the 'comparator' but about the amygdala; they may even drop the term 'reward' and talk about the loci in which reward is mediated. In a similar way we use the structural term 'heart' rather than the functional concept 'blood-pump'.

The term 'reward' is generally agreed to be one of the most troublesome candidates for reduction in this context, so we will consider Clark's argument for the indispensability of this psychological concept. But let us first encounter a useful analogy that Clark introduces towards the end of his book: the relation of a sentence in a language to its use (or 'pragmatics') is analogous to the relation between a 'structural' and a 'functional' account of behaviour. The structural aspect of behavioural explanation encompasses the terms employed in the theory and the way they are related to each other (semantics and syntax); the functional aspect encompasses the explanatory purpose of 'terms plus formal arrangement' (what we 'say' with these). Therefore we can have what I shall call a *grammatical isomorphism* between psychological and physiological accounts in exactly the sense in which Gray's model of learning proposes an isomorphism between terms like 'comparator', 'reward-mechanism for approach-behaviour', etc. and their interrelation, and terms like 'amygdala', 'septum', 'medial forebrain bundle', 'lateral hypothalamus', etc. and *their* interrelation. Yet it is possible to allow this whilst denying that the psychological and the physiological accounts are adapted to the same purpose, that is, denying that they are *pragmatically isomorphic*. Clark accepts that there can be grammatical isomorphism between a term such as 'reward-centre' and whatever brain locus is suggested for it (psychological and physiological sentences can be derived from each other); but he denies pragmatic isomorphism because the physiological concepts *cannot do the work* of psychological concepts. It is important to bear in mind that only in the case of pragmatic isomorphism do we have eliminative reduction, because only here can the psychological terms be rendered redundant.

Clark points out that the barriers against grammatical isomorphism are not logical but empirical, because they arise from the fact of the 'loose localisation of function' in the brain. That is, one psychological function may be carried out by a range of alternative physiological structures and one physiological structure may mediate a number of different psychological functions. Moreover the brain is a very 'plastic' organ, in that if one centre becomes inoperative its job is usually taken over by another – especially before maturity. Therefore the physiological sentence to which a psychological one is being reduced (that is, to which it is grammatically isomorphic) may well be *disjunctive*: psychological function X is carried out at loci a or b or c or . . . (This has already been discussed under 'empirical indeterminacy' in Chapter 1.) However, as Clark argues, contrary to Fodor,[17] this diffuse or disjunctive localisation of function does not make sentence–to–sentence reduction (grammatical isomorphism) impossible. It is simply an unwarranted *ex cathedra* prescription to make it a condition for the success of psychophysical reduction that the psychological and the physiological terms be co-extensive (that there should be a precise one-to-one mapping between the two). This is, we may add, to state *empirical* conditions for the success of a logical argument.

And so we now turn to the issue as to whether a term such as 'reward' can actually be replaced by reference to an activity at a physiological locus (pragmatic isomorphism). Clark's answer is negative, both to a 'weak' version of the replaceability thesis and to a 'strong' version. The weak version states that 'physiological theory will *logically imply* all the observation statements currently derived from psychological theory' (*Psychological Models and Neural Mechanisms*, p. 158), that is, if we knew enough about the physiological state of the organism we could strictly deduce its behavioural state. Loose localisation of function rules this out, Clark argues, so the weak version fails empirically.

But this is strange because yet again a claim about logical connections between kinds of theory is assessed in terms of empirical features of the brain. But even if we say 'predict' rather than 'logically imply' the fact of loose localisation of function still fails to bolster any important negative conclusions about the replaceability of psychological by physiological terms. What 'loose localisation' actually refers to is the inability of researchers at a point in time to narrow down neural responsibility for behaviours as well as they wish to do; it is an historically relative concept. Imagine if a book on a similar topic to Clark's had been written in the distant heyday of Lashley's equipotentiality theory (total 'looseness of function'); it would have dismissed even the possibility of such reduction out of hand. If one function can be performed at alternative loci or if one locus may have more than one function should we not assume that this is explicable by reference to the larger system within which the locus is operating? Pure chance (were there such a thing) would not determine how psychological functions are mediated. *Something*, we must assume, determines which locus is being utilised and which function a locus is mediating and this 'something' must be in the brain: the fact of 'loose' localisation of function must be the result of brain-governed principles. In short, the degree of looseness in localisation is something of a red herring in so far as the replaceability of psychological terms is concerned.

But perhaps it is well to do as Clark does and assume fixed localisation of function for the sake of argument in a hypothetical example and then pass on to a discussion of the strong version of the replaceability thesis. This is the claim that we could entirely replace a psychological term by a corresponding physiological one with no loss of intelligibility. What Clark aims to show is that it is precisely intelligibility that would be lost. Why? The example that Clark takes is the hypothesis[18] that the principal locus for reward is the site of the noradrenergic (NA) pathways in the medial forebrain bundle (MFB). The 'psychological' explanation of why rats self-stimulate when electrodes are implanted in this centre is that 'the electrode activates their mechanisms of natural reward, and so the probability of the rat pressing the bar increases, just as it would for any instinctual response' (p. 159). The reducing explanation would be that the rat self-stimulates because 'the current releases NA in the MFB'.

Clark denies that the latter could replace the former because 'the purely physiological description does not make clear the connection between the physical process and the behaviour in question. It provides an explanation of self-stimulation only if one knows that NA pathways of the MFB are the reward pathways' (p. 159). This is true, but it is true in the sense that physical concepts can never do the job of psychological concepts without taking on the character of psychological concepts: this is what 'doing the job of' means in this context. Indeed 'release of NA in the MFB' would inevitably come to inhabit the logical space of the term 'reward' and in so doing assimilate its functions. But the physiological term does not just come to mean 'reward' in the trivial sense in which the Chinese word for reward means what we mean by 'reward'. It is not just a semantic change because as the physiological expression comes to inhabit the logical space of 'reward' it will acquire a hybrid status (at once physiological and psychological). It will not just mean 'reward', but something larger. So surely Clark is wrong to call this 'elimination only in name' (p. 175) because the physiological term will be changing its character. Is this not what 'replacement' means, and is it not something very substantial?

But if this seems like rather a trivial dispute over whether or not something should be called a 'semantic' change let us consider the more crucial point that the psychological account amounts to no more than a terminating tautology. The physiological account, however, is a terminating empirical statement. Should not the scientist prefer the latter; and is this preference not a form of replacement? Of course explanation of a behavioural episode by saying that the organism does x because it is rewarding is not tautologous in itself because organisms behave for other reasons than to obtain rewards. But once we have established that the organism does x because it is rewarding we have only categorised the behaviour as requiring a certain kind of explanation. As Clark himself says, 'reward' is defined 'by its relations to behavioural change' (p. 159).

Behavioural theories compete with each other about the mechanisms responsible for the establishment and maintenance of responses, not about something that we may call 'the behavioural nature of reward'. So this indissociability of the concept of reward from a certain class of behaviour (such that the behaviour defines the term rather than being evidence for the process to which the term refers) is the aspect of the concept of reward which Clark exploits in order to disclaim its replaceability by a physical term. It is the very tautological nature of reward-explanation that makes it 'irreplaceable', in a paradoxical sense. So what we can see the physiological account enabling us to do in the present context is to break out of this tautological circle.

All this entails, of course, that 'reward' should not be the only eliminable term, given that many concepts employed in animal-learning are relatives of this base concept – 'non-reward' and 'punishment', for example, as well as some others from Gray's model. Moreover what is the barrier against extending these arguments to the independent variables of classical conditioning, 'CS' and 'UCS'? Certainly there is a close association between these and the concept of reward – so close indeed that sometimes both instrumental rewards and UCSs are referred to as 'reinforcement' even though this reinforcement may be an electric shock. But is there not a difficulty here encountered through running together cases of stimulation and cases of reward? Although I will deal in some detail with the close logical association between the concept of reward and that of stimulus in the next section it would be well to indicate now that the 'stimulus' must be eliminable if 'reward' is eliminable. In a nutshell this is so because reward *is* stimulation – rewarding stimulation.

This leads to the conclusion that any model of psychological functions which can be expressed in terms of 'reward', 'stimulus' and closely cognate terms is potentially eliminatively reducible to physiology: it is pragmatically as well as grammatically isomorphic to brain structures. Now I have already touched upon some of the reasons why a psychological theory of depression may not be expressible in these terms (principally because there are ineluctably cognitive elements even in processes such as learned helplessness, processes that cannot be construed as the elicitation and maintenance of behaviour by rewards and stimuli). But what of anxiety? Certainly the causes of anxiety can be defined, and have been so defined by Gray,[19] wholly in terms of their classical activation by stimuli associated with punishment or frustration or by novel stimuli (the behaviour being constituted by inhibition, arousal and orienting), a definition which enables us to speak of anxiety in such lowly creatures as fish. Therefore we can regard Gray's account of anxiety in rats (in terms of neurochemical activity in the dorsal ascending noradrenergic bundle – septo–hippocampal system) as being able to perform the same task as the psychological concepts that it explains – as being eliminatively reductionist.

But are we not being somewhat arbitrary here in the deployment of scepticism – directing it against reductionistic accounts of depression and withholding it from reductionistic accounts of anxiety – particularly as they are almost synonymous in common parlance?

This may appear so because our capacity for envisaging that which is not present and that which may come about enables us to be in 'states of anxiety' comparable to 'states of depression'. But 'anxiety behaviour' makes sense in the absence of the state whereas the same, I would submit, is not true of depression. The elicitation of depressive behaviour by stimuli through classical procedures stretches the meaning of the term 'depression' to breaking point.[20]

The 'autonomy' of the higher mental processes

In this final section my topic will be the autonomy of the mental relative to the physiological, the autonomy of what is usually referred to as the 'higher mental processes' as opposed to the motivational and behavioural processes with which we have been concerned up to now. The most uncontroversial thing that one can say about the quality of being 'higher' is that once language is involved we are in the realm of higher mental processes. In doing this we will be moving away from live empirical issues, because these are processes which no right-minded neuro-physiologist would dream of attempting to reduce. Nevertheless the issues to be considered still have psychological relevance, for they have implications for accounts of the function of consciousness.

The first thesis, which we have already encountered, comes from Donald Davidson.[21] It claims an autonomy for the mental whilst assuming monism and takes the form of a demonstration that the physical and the mental cannot be related to each other in a lawful fashion – that there cannot be 'psycho-physical laws'. However to appreciate fully the point of the argument it is necessary to understand two properties of the linguistic system, *intensionality*[22] (note spelling) and *extensionality*; hence a digression.

Although there is no general agreement on the definition, the most commonly discussed acid test for something being an intensional context is whether truth-value is preserved through the substitution of co-designative terms. This means that intensional sentences typically contain verbs such as 'believe', 'hope', 'expect', and so on, or imply them. Additionally, 'modal' contexts are said to be intensional: that is, 'necessarily p' and 'possibly p'. It is possible to argue that there is also a believer here, implied in the sense of a difference between ways of believing, because to say and mean 'necessarily *p*' implies a different mental orientation to *p* than to say and mean 'possibly p'. However I should say that this is not a widely-accepted position.

Here is an illustration: *A* says to *B* 'Hawkins is going to obstruct my proposals at the meeting this afternoon'. (Let us assume that they both know a lot about Hawkins.) *B* then replies 'So you believe that a person whose mother wore a hideous purple hat to his wedding will . . . etc.' Now although *A* is aware that 'a person whose mother . . .' secures reference to Hawkins he will deny that B's version is a true characterisation of his belief, whose content had nothing of purple hats in it! However the original statement and *B*'s version have the same extension: they both denote the same entity. It is precisely because the intensionality of a sentence is a measure of the belief that it expresses for the speaker that intensionality may be called a quintessentially psychological property. However in extensional sentences the possibility of there being a speaker and thus a believer is bracketed off, as in 'Hawkins obstructed some proposals for staff redundancy at yesterday's meeting'. We can substitute any term that denotes Hawkins in the example and the sentence remains true.

Now, if intensionality implicates belief it must also implicate knowledge. Thus, if *A* finds that his car has been scraped in the car park by another car, and notices a little bright red paint on the scratch we can say '*A* thinks that somebody who drives a bright red car is responsible'. He does not know that Hawkins was the culprit, so we cannot say '*A* thinks that *Hawkins* is responsible'.

A famous example is one of Bertrand Russell's: 'George IV believed that Scott was the author of *Waverley*'. 'The author of Waverley' of course, denotes Scott, but substitution of this co-designate certainly changes the truth value – 'George IV believed that Scott was Scott'. This was not what the king was believing.

Armed with this distinction let us assess the following argument. Jane sees a spider at time t_1, which, by monism, is identical to a physical change in Jane's brain also at time t_1 that we will call *B*. Additionally, we must accept that for every physical event in the brain there was a prior event in the brain that was its condition; we make this assumption because the brain is a physical system obeying physical laws. Let us call the prior physical condition for *B*: *B'* at time t_{-1}. The $B' \rightarrow B$ succession is explicable by a physical law. The conclusion is that there must be a psycho-physical law which explains the seeing of a spider at time t_1 by Jane in terms of the prior physical event in her brain B' at time t_{-1} which was its cause.

But, Davidson says, we cannot accept the conclusion from these premises because laws hold not between the extensions of terms, the events undescribed, but between events described in a certain way. So there is a parallel with the foregoing cases of the following kind:

> if there is a causal law connecting event a described as X and event b described as Y, it does not follow that if event b can also be described as Z that there is a causal law connecting a described as X and b described as Z.

But if it is the case that laws hold between events or processes *under descriptions* not between the events themselves, why does this create problems when psychological characterisations are involved and not create problems when both of the events are physical? The reason is that mental events, unlike physical events, cannot be objectively specified. In characterising mental events, says Davidson, we run up against certain fundamental problems (discussed in Chapter 1). The main problem is that of holism:

> any effort at increasing the accuracy and power of a theory of behaviour forces us to bring more and more of the whole system of the agent's beliefs and motives directly into account.[23]

A related problem is that such characterisation is not purely 'empirical' because we 'impose conditions of coherence, rationality, and consistency' on to the account which have no kind of echo in physical theory. In Chapter 1, you may recall, I argued that if such problems do arise then they have no negative implications for the power of psychological explanation because the laws which psychology seeks to establish concern competence not the stream of mentation.

Let us consider Davidson's proposals with reference to Figure 1.

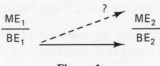

Figure 1

1. ME_1 (mental event) is identical to BE_1 (brain event) and ME_2 is identical to BE_2 working on the assumption that all mental events are physically instantiated.
2. There are lawlike causal relations between BE_1 and BE_2.
3. There cannot be a strict causal relationship between BE_1 and ME_2, however, because of (i) holism and (ii) the necessity for characterising mental states within a given rational framework. Davidson calls this position 'anomalous monism', with 'anomalous' here meaning literally 'not falling under any law'.

Is this not also a very *paradoxical* kind of monism? On the one hand, it seems, Davidson is saying that ME_2 *is* BE_2 whilst denying that ME_2 can be objectively characterised. How can there be something which is enough of an entity to be something physical and yet not enough of an entity to enter into causal laws? In fact there is no real problem here. It is quite possible to claim as a matter of principle that all conscious happenings – howsoever described – are physically instantiated whilst at the same time claiming that we are logically debarred from giving them a description adequate to our purpose. Sure enough, we can always give mental events *a* description but that is not good enough.

Let us now consider some objections to the proposal that it is not possible precisely to specify mental events so as to enable them to enter into causal laws. The tactic adopted by Honderich, for example, is to develop an account in which 'occurrents' (o) (that is, mental events distinguishable as being of a certain character by the subject) are regarded as being in lawlike 'correlation' with physical processes (pp). What Honderich does is to present this as a coherent theory and then defend it against Davidsonian and other varieties of objection. As against anomalous monism he asks:

> What reason is there for thinking that an item which falls in one domaine, and whose description there depends on X [the physical] cannot be in lawlike connection with an item in another domaine, whose description depends on Y [the mental]. There is no clear truth to the effect that there cannot be lawlike connections between items whose descriptions have different necessary conditions.[24]

The problem here is with 'depends on Y'. Let us take Honderich's example of a person seeing olives on a table (o_1), deciding to have one (o_2) and then taking one. Thus, o_1 and pp_1, and also o_2 and pp_2, are taken to be in lawlike correlation. But what we have here between our *o*s and our *pp*s is not a difference between two *descriptions*, or even between two levels of description. It is a difference between two entirely different kinds of activity. In the physical cases there are neural processes 'over and above' whatever characterisations physiologists decide to give. In the mental case, however, what sense is there to the claim that there are mental occurrences o_1 and o_2 'over and above' the subject's regarding his thoughts as having such-and-such a content? There is a largely Wittgensteinian body of thought (see later this chapter and Chapter 6) which rejects any such division and Honderich has rather an easy way with such scepticism. To anticipate: in the physical case there is clearly a *something* plus a description of it, but in the mental case *is* there a something which we describe when we describe our mental states? Is it not more satisfactory to say that the 'object' of our descriptive attention and this descriptive attention are *one*? Is this not what having *experiences* amounts to?

The related Wittgensteinian point that Honderich does consider is that any characterisation of an occurrent by a subject must be relative to the history of the social life and learning experiences of that subject.[25] This is in turn closely related to Davidson's objection from holism that any occurrent can only be characterised relative to a vast penumbra of beliefs and desires. To illustrate both, imagine that an English philosopher and an African tribesman were both viewing the olives. The tribesman believes that olives are actually petrified snakes' eggs which have aphrodisiac properties and so his intention to eat one is not brought about through a simple desire for a taste-treat. Note how their consciousness of the olives will differ and how difficult it is to separate the 'olive-consciousness' from culturally relative beliefs.

The first objection Honderich dismisses by claiming that the notion of an occurrent need *not* imply any particular socio-historical ancestry – only 'whatever can be distinguished by an individual from other things in consciousness'.[26] Is this good enough? Stich[27] has argued that if occurrents are construed in this way then they are not worthy of the appellation 'thoughts'. Presumably in our example Honderich would say that there is some occurrent property that is *common* to the consciousnesses of the two people which is worthy of the name 'thought' -awareness of edibility or even some wholly non-semantic awareness of the olives. (Cf. the 'over and above' point in the paragraph before last.) This is a troublesome assumption, which we will touch on a little later. Suffice it to say for the time being that many would take the view that a necessary aspect of what we properly call 'thoughts' is not accessed by immediate consciousness, that this unaccessed aspect is a determinant of the nature of immediate consciousness and that nothing in consciousness escapes this determination. One way of regarding this unaccessed property is as 'a background of beliefs'.

So what of holism? Honderich's argument against holism is that background beliefs are dispositions that can be correlated with physical processes in the brain and that therefore dispositions 'do not complicate the mental side of things'. This is strange because Honderich seems to be assuming here that these beliefs only have physical not mental causes and effects, which clearly goes against his own principles. Although it would be false to imply that there are neat knock-down arguments against Honderich's programme, clearly if Honderich is concerned with anything more mental and contentful than non-semantic mental 'flashes' (that is, the argument may work for pure *sensation*) then holism is going to be a problem. In general, despite the fact that the argument from holism is powerless against the scientific status of psychology, it applies with a vengeance against any attempt to 'box up' mental events into neat correlatable units.

The second objection is, less radically, concerned to demonstrate the limitations of anomalous monism. All Davidson can show, it suggests, is that we cannot *say* anything – given the intensionality of the mental – about lawlike connections between mental states and neural states, but that such lawlike correlations may nevertheless *exist*. As Mackie puts it: 'It is vitally important whether we think of laws (or lawlike correlations) as statements which connect *descriptions* or as relations which hold *objectively* whether or not they are ever discovered, formulated and so on.'[28] He goes on to say that because Honderich's occurrents 'were not defined in a way that would pull them into line with [holistic] psychic descriptions' they apply to the latter case of 'objective' psychophysical laws rather than psychophysical law statements. There is, of course, a strong intuition at the back of this which many share – that *surely* the relation between the mental and the physical domain is not arbitrary: 'psychic terms must arise out of physical ones, and it would be quite implausible to suggest that they do so in an utterly chaotic way'.

What is this notion of 'objective' psychophysical regularities about which no lawlike statements can be made? It seems quite mysterious how there can be lawlike correlations between two processes one of which *cannot* be (not just 'is not presently') characterised objectively. Mackie assumes that it is possible in principle to discover regularities between mental and physical events. But how are we ever to make such discoveries except by characterising mental events in some objective manner? So this brings us back to square one. Moreover Davidson's claim is not that laws hold between descriptions but between *events as falling under descriptions*; so there is no warrant for this bifurcation between 'descriptions' and 'objective events'.

Two points need to be made about this 'chaotic' relation between the mental and the physical which Davidson's thesis is supposed to be suggesting. First, Davidson is arguing against the view that there should be what are usually called *type identities* between mental and physical events: that physical event type x is lawfully correlated with mental event type y. But, as a monist, he is not denying *token identity*: that a mental state at time t_1 is identical to the constellation of the brain at time t_1. Holism implies the impossibility of type identity between mental events at different points in time and between different individuals and thus denies that mental events are 'sliceable' in such a way as to be characterised as types that can enter into lawful statements about correlations between mental types and physical types. But there is still token identity, so to this extent Davidson is not inviting us to regard the mental/physical relation as chaotic.

There is a second sense in which anomalous monism does not entail, in Mackie's term, a 'chaotic' relationship between the mental and the physical. The point which I laboured at length in Chapter 1 was that psychophysical laws are about the relation between mental *competences* and brain-functions and structures, not between events like thinking about olives and neural processes in real time. In the former case we do indeed assume a lawlike character to what has been sometimes called the 'causal powers' of the brain. But in the latter, stream-of-behaviour case, I have been suggesting that we accept anomalous monism as a healthily sceptical position.

Before passing on from anomalous monism I wish to bring out a major difference between mental and physical 'objects of description', a difference I have already exploited in the previous discussion. This distinction appears to bolster the case for anomalous monism.

In the case of physical objects (such as chairs and brains) there is clearly an object of perception or belief that is publicly accessible.

Although there is an infinite number of ways in which the object can be characterised there is, nevertheless, a 'something there'. What of mental objects however? (Again by 'mental' I mean 'cognitive', and am excluding sensations.) Certainly it is possible to distinguish between the chair *qua* public object and my mental chair or the 'chair-for-me' – perhaps the chair-for-me is cognised as 'something to stand on' or 'a bargain'. We may want to call this an intentional[29] or mental object. But the use of the word 'object' is very misleading here. In the case of the physical object the relation between the subject's perception or belief and the object is clearly a dyadic one: mental orientations can vary around an object 'core' in this case without the core being affected. But for the subject to be characterising (or generally having a mental orientation towards) his mental 'object' is in that act to *constitute* the mental object – there is no unchanging core towards which different mental attitudes may be adopted. And why? Because the content of a mental event is exhausted by what the subject believes about the content (that is, when you have said what he believes then you have described the object). Moreover the relation is not a dyadic one because you cannot have two different orientations to the same content in the purely mental case. This is essentially the point which I was making when I said that it is difficult to regard mental content as being something 'over and above' a description of it.

If this is so, then ME_1 and ME_2 are not really possible objects of characterisation, but are rather something *between* acts of characterisation and their goals. Ordinary language lets us down when we want to say what mental events are. Wittgenstein said about mental content: 'It's not a *something*, but not a *nothing* either!'[30]

But how is this point supposed to bolster anomalous monism? It does so by placing certain unacceptable alternatives in the way of any attempt to argue for psychophysical laws. The essential problem is that if the subject's mental characterisations of his mental contents exhausts the contents, then the specification of mental contents must be ineluctably from the subject's point of view. But of course, as Honderich points out, there are not supposed to be different psychophysical laws for different people:[31] the laws must hold *across individuals* just as do physical laws. If this is the case then we require some means of specifying when two individuals are in the same mental state and when one individual is in the same mental state at different times. This is the problem of type identity again. If we cannot produce some programme for making the quest for such type identities intelligible then the case for psychophysical laws must flounder. How can we at once admit that there is no such thing as the objective content of a subject's characterisation of his mental state and yet assume the existence of such identities?

One solution is to take a behaviourist line, which some have claimed to be the view of Wittgenstein. Here we would say that ME characterisations are essentially verbal acts, so if two people truthfully say that they see a bowl of olives on the table then that's good enough grist to the correlational mill. The immediate problem here is that this assumes that all mental events are verbally infused. But what of mental images, upsurges of directed anger, sudden unverbalisable flashes of insight – and what indeed of animals and very young children?

An alternative view which consists in rejecting this kind of behaviourism could run as follows. Although being in a cognitive state is not a private experience to the extent that the language of belief and knowledge is necessarily acquired through public processes (Wittgenstein's 'private language argument' will be discussed later) a degree of subjectivity or person-centredness is present in the case of mental events such as beliefs and intentions. This is because, as I argued above, in the case of intensions the mental content is constituted by the subject. The reason why it makes little sense to talk of two people experiencing exactly the same kind of mental event is emphatically not that we can never *know* whether they are, because there is no object of knowledge here, no content over and above what they believe about these mental events. But, you may say, if these two people speak the same language why should they not communicate these 'constitutions' of their mental life to the extent that a psychologist might say that they are in the same mental state? The reason is that to accept such a possibility entails that the meanings of words are fixed to a sufficient extent, or at least that a word has a certain semantic essence or core. So we are, in fact, merely dumping our paradox about the contentfulness, yet lack of objectivity, of mental events on to language. As we shall see in Chapter 7, essence-ism in linguistics is at least as troublesome as it is in the philosophy of mental life – where it is usually referred to as 'Essentialism'. In general my conclusion here is a Davidsonian one, albeit reached by a non-Davidsonian route: it is a statement of the *ideographic* nature of mental events (see McGinn, in Chapter 1).

The history of the mind – body problem is a history of failure. What has contributed greatly to this failure is our reluctance to abandon the prejudice that the mental and the physical are separable in such a way that it makes sense to talk about one being the cause or correlate of the other. Anomalous monism does not actually tell us how we should regard the physical basis of mental life (or the mental basis of physical life – it comes to the same thing), but it points us away from one source of problems and paradoxes.

How then does anomalous monism bear on the present issue of the autonomy of the mental? In the interests of consistency with the previous section, we must now examine why it is that we cannot apply these arguments to mental events of which the object is a 'stimulus' rather than a colleague, spider, chair . . . In so doing I hope to be able to justify being reductionist about such terms as 'reward' and 'stimulus' whilst accepting the autonomy of the mental in intensional contexts. Related to this, are my foregoing hints that anomalous monism may not be true for sensations – non-intensional mental occurrents.

The fact is, if the term 'stimulus' means anything definite at all outside the context of a particular experimental manipulation (and some have doubted that it does)[32] then it is as an environmental event that impinges on an organism (human or otherwise) with the result that it is registered, whether or not this registering leads to overt behaviour. Now, for something to be a stimulus and nothing more, this registering must not be registering *as* anything. Thus, for there to be classical conditioning the CS must not be registered, as it were, 'intellectually' as a signal for the UCS; nor in the autoshaping of a pigeon need the illumination of the stimulus key be registered in any cognitive sense as a signal for reinforcement: the stimulus causes or evokes a response. It *is* construed as a 'signal' by the psychologist performing the experiment however. (I am not excluding the possibility that such non-intellectual registering should exist in human performance; but to give human examples here would mean dragging in questions of the relation between sensation and perception and of the status of 'non-epistemic' seeing – both of which are to be covered in Chapter 5.)

So I hope it is apparent that through deliberately denying that a stimulus can be the object of anything psychological, any more than a *trigger* is the object of anything, the context in which we talk of the registering of stimulation is not intensional. This, therefore, leaves open the possibility that lawful relationships should be proposed between prior states of the nervous system and an organism's responsivity or susceptibility to stimulation. And indeed this is precisely what animal-learning theorists do attempt, with some success.[33] Probably Davidson himself would deny that these are really strict causal laws, which relate brain-states to the efficacy of stimulation, because he equates 'strict' with 'of an equivalent precision to physics', as we have already seen. But is even *this* degree of precision very far off? After all, neuro-psychologists investigate the chemical state of the synaptic cleft and this molecular approach promises literally *molecular* reduction. It is not reduction of the total brain state as a sufficient condition for the stimulus being registered and possibly responded to, but it is reduction to the kind of synaptic events or states which are *necessary* for this registering.

How does the concept of reinforcement relate to all this? All that I said above about 'reward' (pp. 60ff) and its relation to 'stimulus' applies to reinforcement: reinforcement *is* stimulation, reinforcing stimulation. Therefore a reinforcing event can be non-intensional because it can be efficacious without the organism adopting any psychological relation to the event. The self-stimulating rat, for example, does not register the stimulation as reinforcing, it just *is* reinforcing.

Finally, I wish to consider another anti-reductionist argument which appears on the surface to be a variant of anomalous monism – in fact it is not monist. The argument – actually two related arguments – comes from Hilary Putnam.[34] The reason why it looks like anomalous monism is that its conclusion is that mentation is indeed 'realised' materially but that there is no physical explanation of thought. What it refuses to admit however is the *identity* between psychological events and physical brain events. Why?

Putnam's argument rests on the notion of 'functional isomorphism', a concept that we shall be considering in the next chapter and which is very closely allied to the pragmatic isomorphism between theories, already discussed. 'Two systems are functionally isomorphic', writes Putnam, 'if *there is a correspondence between the states of one and the states of the other that preserves functional relations.*'[35] This is best understood in relation to computing machines where two different kinds of machine, one electronic and the other clockwork, are functionally isomorphic if state S (example, copy all digits in the left-hand column) is followed by state B

(example, add digits to memory m_1) in one, and state S is followed by state B in the other: they perform the same tasks with different physical realisations. For example, if we assume for the sake of argument that Gray's black-box model of conditioning is correct, then running a computer program based on the model would produce a relation of functional isomorphism between the electronic states of the computer and the neurochemical states of the rat's brain. Functional isomorphism is, in fact, the root assumption of the computer modelling of mental functions.

Now, although Putnam casts a sceptical eye on the claims of the computer modellers, he places great emphasis on the fact that functional isomorphism entails that physical realisation (brain tissue, cogs, electric circuits) is irrelevant to the success of a system. But what of the objection that we know everything about computing machines (because we made them) and practically nothing about how computational procedures are realised in the brain? He admits that it is 'sloppy' to 'apply the notion of functional isomorphism to systems for which we have no detailed idea at present what the normal form of description would look like . . . [but not] fatally sloppy'.[36] Be that as it may, the conclusion is: therefore mental states *cannot be identical* with brain states or any *particular* physical state because 'the realisation is in a sense quite accidental'. We have, in short, strong reasons for believing that the jobs done by our brain could be done by systems made of quite different material. This is a far greater degree of autonomy of the mental than that allowed by anomalous monism.

The difficulty with this position is that it tends towards a kind of dualism as between 'the functions of mind' on the one hand and 'any kind of physical realisation of them' on the other hand. Anything of that kind gives itself the problem of explaining how the two are related – how one affects the other. This comes into clearer relief when we consider the piece of science fiction that Putnam uses to defend his thesis. He imagines the inhabitants of another universe who have 'good, old-fashioned souls, operating through pineal glands perhaps' and compares them with ourselves as construed by monists, i.e. material minds.

And suppose that the souls in the soul world are functionally isomorphic to the brains in the brain world. Is there any more sense to attaching importance to this difference than to the difference between copper wires and some other wires in the computer?[37]

Rather than answer this question one way or another, we should reflect on why such an analogy is even possible at all. It is made possible because deploying the notion of functional isomorphism in the way Putnam does reifies mental functions as free-floating entities – 'memory', 'attention', 'pain', conceived not as functions *qua* aspects of human mental life as functions *per se* which can be realised (or conjured up) in any way we please. This is not to say, however, that memory, attention, pain, or whatever, are uniquely human, that Martians, for example, with entirely different brain structures could not have these functions more or less as we do. But in ascribing memory, attention, and pain to Martians irrespective of the fact that their brains differ from ours we assume that they are identical to *Martian* brain-states; we need not assume that human and Martian memory, attention, and pain are the same *entities*.

But why, you may ask, can we not say that computer machine states are identical to computer mental states? Because (to anticipate the next two chapters) we need some warrant for saying that computers have sensations; because our Martians are organic such a problem does not arise. (Those who bristle at this will just have to wait for further discussion.)

We are not denying here that human mental functions can be modelled on computers; but what is being modelled is not the mental functions themselves but what we may call the functions *of* the functions, that is, not human memory itself but the job that a memory does for us.

Indeed – and to anticipate a little more – the functional isomorphism argument has great appeal to those who regard the brain as essentially a computational entity, as something which performs operations by manipulating symbols. As any computational job can be carried out, in principle, by any computational machine, functions can be prised away from particular realisations. But all this is predicated on the assumption that the computational model of the mind is the only possible model.

Much of the remainder of Putnam's argument is concerned with illustrating how nonsensical it is to attempt the reduction of cognitive states to microscopic brain processes. It is as ridiculous, he argues, as trying to explain why a peg passes through one hole and not through another in terms of the molecular structure and dispersal of particles in the board *vis-à-vis* the peg, rather than just saying that the peg goes through one hole that is larger than its cross-section. Agreed: the above discussion of anomalous monism was supposed to provide some of the reasons for this nonsensicality.

Putnam's anti-reductionist arguments – as were Davidson's – are directed against the reduction of psychological *states*, of mental events such as being about to say 'three' or to tell a secret. And this is because philosophers typically take the stream of mentation as the 'psychology' that has to be reduced. But as I concluded in the discussion of anomalous monism, this is relevant only to the general question of the autonomy of our mental life and has no negative implications for the mechanistic approach to psychology. For the whole burden of Chapter 1 was that it is competence, not the stream of behaviour and mentation, the states in the stream and the passage between the states, that psychology seeks to explain. Clark endorses this: Putnam's argument, he says (in *Psychological Models and Neural Mechanisms*, p. 153) '*holds for terms in ordinary language*, but perhaps this is because no developed models use such terms, and because investigators do not use them in their theorising' (my italics).

The psychologically-relevant face of the question of whether cognition can be reduced to brain processes is to ask: 'Can cognitive competence be explained by reference to the brain as a total system *and by reference to nothing else*?' For the brain theory to which the reduction of cognitive processes is a serious possibility is a macro-theory about interacting systems, not a micro-theory about synaptic transmission. To such a macro-theory we may take two kinds of route: 'top down' from large-scale theorising about the general principles on which the brain functions and about levels of brain function[38] to the testing of specific hypotheses, and 'bottom up' in which we initially focus on one synaptic system and then study the dependency of this system on higher and higher supervisory systems. Eventually, one hopes, empirically competing macro-theories will emerge. Well, *could* cognitive competence be explained wholly in these terms? I would suggest not, because any account of how cognition goes on must also makes reference to what lies outside the brain – and this for reasons not unconnected with the logical intensionality of mental sentences and with the related property of the intentionality of the mental. The presentation of my reasons for taking this view, must, however, wait till the next chapter on computer modelling because they rest on assumptions about the nature of psychological explanation by reference to *any* form of mechanism, organic or non-organic.

It would, however, be foolish to claim that psychological explanation can be complete – or can even proceed very fruitfully – without reference to brain mechanisms. Although one may wish to deny the sufficiency of mechanistic explanation its necessity must be admitted. For all that has been said here about the autonomy of the mental is about the autonomy of our mental life *vis-à-vis* physical processes in our brains. It is not an autonomy of purely mentalistic explanation in psychology.

3

The Computational Theory of Mind: Old Problems for New Paradigms

It is difficult not to be impressed by the capacities of computers. Not only can they simulate actors, language-users and object-perceivers – as well as chess-players and psychiatrists more particularly – some of them are making inroads into the literary *avant-garde*. RACTER writes:[1]

> I was thinking . . . as you entered the room just how slyly your requirements are manifested. Here we find ourselves, nose to nose as it were, considering things in spectacular ways, ways untold even by my private managers. Hot and torpid, our thoughts revolve endlessly on a kind of maniacal abstraction, an abstraction so involuted, so dangerously valiant, that my own energies seem perilously close to exhaustion.

In fact exhaustion is unknown to RACTER which can write a short novel of pulp standard in around 5 minutes. The sceptic would say 'The speed is not at all surprising when you consider that the machine doesn't need to think'.

To a purist student of artificial intelligence (AI)[2] the sceptic's last comment would be a compliment rather than an insult. For this person AI is not a field of psychology but the study of the performance of computational machines on tasks that we would say required intelligence if they were given to people. The fact that human beings perform by what we call 'thinking' is regarded as deeply irrelevant to the business of designing machines and writing programs, indeed the purist may even say 'So much the worse for human beings. This explains their inefficiency as performers'.

But not all members of the AI community are purists; indeed in many cases they are indistinguishable from cognitive psychologists. The AI–cognitive scientist has quite a different philosophy, albeit a deeply ambiguous one. The argument for the psychological relevance of AI is this: experimental cognitive psychology is necessarily fragmentary, it produces data in paradigm-driven and problem-driven research that pertain to relatively isolated pockets of enquiry. It is – in the modern jargon – 'bottom-up'. But what cognitive psychology requires are highly disciplined and systematic 'top-down' theories about the nature of thought. Rather than looking at the input-output regularities of experimental subjects and inducing models from the resulting data we can ask 'What kind of system could perform such a task at all?' Designing such a system should provide us with clues to the nature of the human system.

Now here is the ambiguity. When such a cognitive scientist writes a program to model human performance, is he or she testing the internal structure or consistency of a theory of performance or is he constructing a system *that is performing like a human being*, which we may even say 'understands', 'believes', 'perceives'? In the first case a theory may be written as a flow-chart, then as a program to be run on a computer. If the theory contains insufficiently specified assumptions or hidden inconsistencies then the program will fail to run. If the program runs successfully however then we can say that a system of the kind proposed by the model *works*.

John Searle[3] has called this 'weak AI' and contrasted it with 'strong AI'. In strong AI the program simulates mental process in a way that is more than metaphorical because the machine is taken to be doing what humans do and by essentially the same kind of processes. So, this is not only top-down psychology, it is a *synthetic* kind of psychology in which you build the system as a means of understanding the system. But as would be expected, in practice there is a continuum between these two positions. For example, the psychologist may write a program to perform like a human being in the sense of making the same kinds of errors and generalisations to new tasks.[4] If the model realised as a program produces human-like performance then *possibly* these are the procedures by which humans perform such tasks. We do not actually have to assume here that the computer understands anything but some assumptions are necessary about the commonalities between information-handling by a machine and by a mind. In fact most researchers appear to take the position that the more constraints that are written into programs so as to make them reflect what we already know about human performance then the more 'psychological reality' they will possess and thus the more likely they are to be strongly analogous to human performance. But this process is a very difficult one indeed to conceptualise, as we shall see.

My concern in these two chapters will be solely with the claims of *strong* AI, with the position that the mind is a computational system in the way that a computer is. I shall use the broader term 'computational theory of mind' (CTM)[5] to refer to the underlying philosophy of strong AI. My orientation to CTM will be a highly sceptical one, but – I cannot overemphasise – this does not involve a Luddite orientation to the use of computers in psychology in the weak AI sense (perhaps 'constrained AI' would be a less insulting term). For one may take the position that computers may be prodigiously useful media in which to frame theories of performance whilst rejecting CTM. Conversely – and paradoxically – many supporters of CTM (see Chapter 7, note 1) are highly sceptical about the empirical benefits to be gained from computer modelling in psychology. In fact, CTM is a metatheory–cum–philosophy of mind; and it is as *that* that it will be discussed here. Long may the computer flourish in the psychological laboratory.

Why spend two chapters on CTM only to show its weakness? Because in considering the claim that the mind is *essentially* (not just in one of its many functions) a computational system we gain insights into *how* it is not, and thus into what it may be, and therefore into some of the explanatory tasks for psychology. Our first step will be to consider what it is, in fact, that computers are supposed to model and what assumptions about human cognition are grounded in the attempt.

The what and the how of modelling

We may ask what are the *levels* of mental process that may be simulated by a computer program. Here are just four possibilities:

1. conscious thought
2. unconscious thought (i.e. in the psychoanalytic sense of being amenable to revelation in consciousness),

3. non-conscious mental processes (not amenable in principle to revelation in consciousness),
4. brain processes.

Conscious thought

We may model on a computer the processes that we know we undergo in thinking because we can introspect on them. Indeed this is one way in which theorists have sought to lend psychological reality to their systems.[6] Additionally some programs, such as CONNIVER for example, have recursively 'introspective' planning functions which mimic what happens when we consciously run over the possible consequences of our doing so-and-so. However, one may well say that if these processes are open to consciousness why model them? We already know a large amount about conscious thought as, what is sometimes called, 'folk-psychology'.[7] The modeller might reply that the process of developing the system tells us what are the mechanistic conditions for conscious thought; but how are we to know that these are anything like the mechanistic conditions for 'real' consciousness?

Unconscious thought

According to Freud, unconscious thought-processes of the kind he considered are amenable to revelation in consciousness. There is considerable divergence within Freudian scholarship around the issue of whether Freud intended the unconscious to be a kind of second, hidden mind or a set of causes[8] (see pp. 24–5 above); either way, if it is potentially open to consciousness a better strategy for studying the unconscious would appear to be to try to lay it bare – assuming this to be possible – by analysis rather than construct computer models of it.[9] That is, much the same goes here as for conscious thought.

Non-conscious processes

It is possible to regard thought as the *result* of processes that have gone on within us:[10] that we are aware of the end-product of thinking but not of thinking itself. (These processes should be called *non*-conscious to distinguish them from unconscious processes

because they are not amenable to revelation in consciousness.)
Developmental psychologists often quote Binet's dictum in this
context that 'thought is the unconscious process of the mind', while
physiological psychologists are more likely to cite Lashley's 'no
activity of the mind is ever conscious'. But to say that thought is non-
conscious is not to make an empirical generalisation: it is to
emphasise the logical status of the concept 'thought'. For if we could
become aware of the causes of our thoughts then these too would be
conscious thoughts with their own causes, and so on, and when this is
added to the assumption that thoughts cannot be undetermined we
have the Binet/Lashley position. As we saw in Chapter 1 (pp. 8–9) it
is precisely this feature of thought that necessitates our asking
performance questions of the kind 'By what procedures do we do X?',
and, clearly, answering such questions is the province of AI. But it is
important to distinguish these performance questions from mechanistic questions about the actual neuronal processes which support
conscious thought. Performance questions are about the general
procedures or strategies that the brain – construed as an
information-processing system – employs. Taken this way it is easy
to see that procedures can be realised on machines other than the
brain (see pp. 75–8 above); so we may regard the task either as that
of modelling theories of these processes (weak AI) or as *realising the
same processes by other means* (strong AI).

There is another kind of non-conscious psychological process that
AI is ideally adapted to investigate. These are the processes which
support particular domains of skill such as perception in three-
dimensional space, sensorimotor co-ordination and sentence pars-
ing. One of the defining characteristics of skill – and of certain kinds
of creativity – is that we cannot say how we did it, suggesting thereby
a form of knowledge which Michael Polanyi called 'tacit knowledge'.[11] Indeed it is strange that Polanyi himself and those heavily
influenced by him such as Dreyfus[12] regard tacit knowledge as
precisely the kind of knowledge that is *not* amenable to computer
simulation. So the great promise of (weak and strong) AI is that it
may enable us to generate in a disciplined way models of the processes
that make ratiocination and performance possible when the
piecemeal nature of human experimental psychology and the relatively under-developed state of neuropsychology makes it unlikely
that such general theories will come from any other source.
Moreover, modelling non-conscious processes rather than know-

ledge and belief-governed processes *may* be undertaken without the assumption that the computer really understands anything.

Brain processes

If we adopt the weak AI assumption that it is psychological theories that are being modelled then theories in any branch of psychology may in principle be modelled. So there are no conceptual barriers against doing a kind of theoretical neurophysiology on a computer. With regard to the visual system, although the interests of pattern recognition theorists have diverged sharply from those of physiologists since the 1960s,[13] computer modelling is certainly a very useful supplement to standard techniques such as single-unit recording when theories of mechanism for quite atomistic processes such as feature-detection are constructed.[14] This is weak AI, but real philosophical problems inevitably arise because this shades into theorising about the intensional process of perception itself;[15] which leads us to the general problem of how we should regard the relation between psychological models of non-conscious processes and models of brain-function. All I will say for now is that such problems come to the fore when workers in AI regard the constraints that must be placed on their models to make them psychologically realistic as being, at least in part, physiological, but more of this later.

One may say then that AI holds the promise of providing a set of intelligible pictures of mental processes that are hidden from the subject by virtue of being non-conscious or neurological. If this is so, what then are we supposed to do with consciousness?[16] Essentially the tactic of CTM is to ignore the question of consciousness, or rather the question of how that which is hidden from us relates to that which is open to us,[17] and to say that the basic function of the mind is to represent the world and to perform 'computations' on these representations. If computer models can do this also, then they have captured what is essential to mental activity. Moreover, because the notion of a representation of reality implies an intensional context (supporters of CTM claim)[18] it shares logical features with the intensionality of natural language.[19] Therefore if a computer has a representation of reality then this is strongly analogous to a person with beliefs about reality. Obviously these claims need close examination.

Before we pass on to the major assumptions about the *how* of modelling it is well to indicate for future reference that there is reason to feel a deep dissatisfaction with so easily sloughing-off the problem of consciousness. Dennett has put the matter in terms of the relation between two levels of explanation: on the 'personal' and on the 'sub-personal' level. He originally used the distinction in the context of sensation. Pains, for example, have a personal aspect because although our claims to be in pain are not absolutely incorrigible[20] having a pain is not like having something that can be rendered objective. To take Wittgenstein's analogy,[21] imagine that the word 'beetle' was learnt by each person carrying around with him a beetle in a matchbox which he inspected but never showed to anybody else. (This is on the analogy of a pain as a private 'object'.) Because the beetle is a private object it has 'no place in the language game at all; not even as a 'something': for the box might even be empty'. Similarly there is a kind of nonsense in claiming that we acquire the concept of pain by inspecting our own 'mental objects'. Wittgenstein almost certainly would not have put the matter this way but, because there is not a dyadic relationship[22] between person and sensation object, and because the sensation is indissociable from the person having it, sensations like pain are 'personal'. But if this is the case how is the psychology of pain to go beyond the personal level into some more objective realm? Of course, neurologists can take the explanation, if not beyond the personal level, at least *beneath* it to the neural structure and to the events responsible for pain experience – the sub-personal level. However, as Dennett says, 'when we abandon the personal level in a very real sense we abandon the matter of pains as well . . . pains are feelings felt by people and they hurt'.[23]

So our question might well be 'If AI is carried out at the sub-personal level does CTM not imply a retreat from truly psychological territory to the land of mechanism?' The proponent of CTM would answer: 'Indeed it is carried out at the sub-personal level but it is not carried out at the *physical* level of metal, plastic, glass, silicon and fibreboard. Computer programs perform *functions*; and if we could build a robot that behaved just as a human being does when we bash it with a mallet, then the onus would be on *you* to say why we should deny the ascription of pain experiences to this robot'. It is a measure of the power of the computational metaphor that Dennett has now come to accept something close to this argument.[24] Indeed, it is not difficult to see from this exchange why some would claim that CTM enables us to resolve traditional philosophical issues such as the 'mind–body problem'. This too requires close examination.

In the remainder of this section I will describe four concepts which are basic to AI because no discussion of the status of CTM can proceed without acknowledgement of them. They are:

1. the division between hardware and software
2. representation as data structures
3. the manipulation of symbols
4. the syntactic as opposed to semantic nature of programs.

Hardware and software

The software consists of sets of instructions to the hardware to perform certain operations on data. Although even the hardware–software distinction is not entirely clear-cut we will not go far wrong if we regard the program as the software and the machine itself (memory, central processing unit, peripheral equipment, input-output facilities) as the hardware. Another way of viewing this distinction is in terms of two kinds of language, the machine code and the programming language. The machine code is an abstract language of commands which directly control the machine by telling it to perform particular electronic operations and containing such simple terms as 'add' and 'store'. It is usually expressed in binary notation. The programming languages on the other hand are instructions at a level of abstraction closer to ordinary language. Thus the different programming languages (for example, LISP, FORTRAN) stand for complex series of machine code instructions. Between these two are the special programs called 'interpreters' or 'compilers' that translate programming languages into the machine code of a particular type of computer, so that one language can be used with different kinds of machine and vice versa. We can see, therefore, two reasons why the hard–soft distinction is somewhat blurred: (i) because a machine code is 'soft' in that it is abstract, yet 'hard' in that it directly refers to electronic processes, (ii) because of the consequent necessity for interpreter programs. Indeed this blurring of the hard–soft distinction is evident from the fact that workers in the field refer to 'high'- and 'low'-level languages. Low-level languages are close to the machine code and the high-level languages are more abstract. For example the family of languages called ASSEMBLER is very low-level, whilst there are, at the other extreme, special purpose programs at a much higher level of abstraction than those normally encountered.

Representation as data structures

When a computer is given a problem it has to translate that problem into its own terms. The earliest programs represented all problems numerically but now there is some degree of choice between representation media. For non-numeric problems the division is usually made between representation as *string* or as *list* structures. String structures store linear sequences of symbols and list structures arrange symbols (which may be in the form of strings or even other lists) hierarchically. Therefore when we say that a computer has 'knowledge', this knowledge – which can be of objects, relationships, or processes – is represented in the computer as *data structures* in the string or list form. In sophisticated problem-solving systems a data structure may be a set of facts which add up to the description of a situation. Sometimes the term 'data structures' is used more loosely to describe the representation of items whose roles can be specified within the total program.

The manipulation of symbols

Computers can only 'think' in abstract symbols, and this is because the computer's knowledge base in its memory contains series upon series of electronic indicators which are identifiable by symbolic, usually numerical, means. The manipulation of symbols by the program essentially consists in identifying the contents of given memory locations by their 'addresses' and performing operations on these.[25] The essence of the symbol is that it *need* have no inherent similarity to that which it symbolises. In this way symbolic representation is *propositional* in that it represents what is the case in formal language rather than being a physical analogue of something in the world. For this reason supporters of the CTM set themselves in opposition to cognitive theorists who regard mental imagery (an analogue process) as an important or even necessary feature of thought.[26] Additionally they must convince those who regard it as highly improbable that motoric and kinaesthetic information could be represented in a symbolic code, or at least that it is implausible that it is so represented for human beings.[27]

Therefore CTM must proceed on the assumption that thought is representational, that there are representational units in the mind similar to data structures, and that the mode of representation is symbolic–propositional rather than analogical or than anything else that might be suggested.

Syntactic rather than semantic representation

This feature is implicit in what has gone before but it is worth highlighting separately because it illustrates the respect in which programs function 'mechanistically'. Under the everyday interpretation, symbols have meaning not merely because in mythical, childish and psychoanalytic contexts they resemble the things they represent but because they refer to entities and thus have intensions and extensions. Natural language is, of course, the paradigm case here where 'homme' is no more like a male person than is 'man'. Now abstract symbols such as those employed in propositional calculus – p and q – also can be made to refer, but their meaning is parasitic on ordinary language. That is, we can say that p means 'it is raining' and q means 'it is wet' but the symbols do not refer to the situations directly but refer to verbal propositions. Given this, let us imagine that somebody has put washing out to dry, that a few minutes later a neighbour telephones and tells the person that it is raining, and that the person then rushes out to the garden to fetch the washing in. We can represent the inference involved here, somewhat artificially, as: that it's raining implies that it is wet; it is raining, *therefore* it is wet. Alternatively we may express the inference in a formal manner as: $p \rightarrow q$, p, therefore q. Supporters of CTM would not, of course, have to deny that people do in fact find it easier to reason with words than with abstract symbols but they *must* assume that reasoning by semantic units of the kind achieved by the owner of the washing is not possible without access to some formal system of representation. In computer-language symbols stand for whatever objects, relations and processes we wish, but the computer manipulates the symbols, not their meaning. We may say, then, that computer logic is wholly syntactic, in the sense of being about the form not the content of data. And to say that the computer's data structures have no content means that they lack reference to the external world and therefore data-structures cannot be true or false any more than 'All F are G' is true or false when F and G do not stand for anything in particular.

To give just one example of this, the problem-solving system STRIPS[28] controls an experimental robot called Sam that is able to move around among three rooms containing items of furniture and to transfer things from room to room. Sam represents the problem situation as a data-structure which is made up of strings of predicate calculus symbols.[29] The initial data structure (the situation at the outset) is treated as analogous to the initial object in Newell and Simon's General Problem Solver, which has to be transformed in a step-by-step procedure until the goal has been achieved. What STRIPS does to achieve this goal is to perform the 'operation' on the 'object' (problem) situation as if it were a problem in predicate calculus. How we usually proceed in predicate calculus is to begin with a 'well-formed formula' (wff) and a fixed set of axioms and then see whether the formula is provable. Here, however, STRIPS does the opposite of this by erecting the goal (for example, Sam by window, table in alcove) as a *false* wff (that is, as yet to be achieved) and then attempts to make the wff true *by changing the axioms* (that is, the sequences of situations represented in data structures). The changes in the axioms (the operations) are the movements that Sam makes from start to the goal. Thus what the human being would regard as the intentional carrying out of a planned action is performed in a wholly syntactic manner by the computer:[30] strings of arbitrary symbols are manipulated so as to change the value of a formula from false to true – actions are axioms. So computer operations are nothing if not formal.

Finally, we need to re-encounter a property of computer models that, unlike the other four, they do not have in themselves but is rather attributed to them by supporters of CTM: that of possessing the logical property of intensionality. We have already discussed the intimate relation between the psychological and the logically intensional, and although the nature and extent of this relationship is a matter for philosophical debate it is fairly uncontroversial to claim that psychological sentences are those which have to be analysed in terms of intensional prefixes such as 'he believes', 'he wants' and the like. The argument for the intensionality of computer programs, which has perhaps been made most explicit by Margaret Boden[31] but which is implicit in everything that proponents of CTM say in support of their enterprise, usually runs as follows. A computer represents reality as falling under a particular characterisation; its data structures contain not 'what's there' but a selective, perspectival, even subjective, recording of reality relative to some overriding purpose – they have, in short, an inner model of reality. What is this if not intensionality?

Additionally, when a computer is solving a problem within a domain of objects (for example, Sam the robot controlled by STRIPS) it has to construct and maintain a context of what information is focal and what is irrelevant to its interests at each stage of the procedure. The difficulty inherent in achieving this is known as the *frame problem*. Thus the model of reality is rarely a static representation but may be a flexible, self-regulating frame of reference. The intensional echoes are clear.

So if behaviour is controlled by an inner model of reality rather than by reality as expressed through a stimulus then it is inevitable that behaviour will be intensional on criteria such as whether the truth-value of a description of it changes with the substitution of co-referential expressions. But does this not fit rather uncomfortably with the notion of programs being syntactic rather than semantic entities? How can something lack meaning and yet have intensionality? Strictly, as theorists such as Fodor have argued, this *is* possible. The confusion arises over the ambiguity in the terms 'meaning': the symbols which computers manipulate do not having meaning *qua* a reference to something in the external world but they do have meaning in the sense of having a formal role to play in the program – a functional meaning. The meaning of computer symbols is assessed formally and the different intensional characterisations of reality so produced differ formally not in terms of their content but in terms of what they are about. To put it another way, a computer may not strictly have knowledge about the external world because its operations are not semantic (do not involve truth and reference) but the computer can have 'beliefs' formally represented which is all that is needed for intensionality. This difficult and important claim will be thoroughly assessed in Chapter 4.

The new dualism?

We saw towards the end of Chapter 2 that Putnam's[32] expression of what is generally referred to as the 'functional' theory of the mind–body relationship resulted in something very much like dualism. Such a functional theory is essential to CTM. Putnam was arguing that because reasoning processes may be 'functionally isomorphic' as between two machines of quite different materials or between a brain and a machine, these processes are not identical to any one physical realisation. One may have, for example, short-term memories of identical functional power made of cogs, electronic circuits, or brain tissue. The accusation of dualism was levelled against this because mental functions have no foothold in the physical world if they are regarded as only contingently related to brain functions or at least the nature of their foothold is mysterious still. It is not the traditional Cartesian dualism, of course, wherein the mental is regarded as a separate 'substance', but it is certainly dualistic in its result.

How might a supporter of CTM respond to such criticism? Perhaps he would say that we have failed to understand the full implications of regarding the mind as a functional entity, and give the following kind of example. The concept of 'walking' can be realised by many different kinds of physical process or state – two legs, four legs, fingers, pictorial representation of legs with arrows – indeed we may even regard the different physical realisations as having a 'family resemblance'[33] to each other rather than having any particular physical quality in common. By our sceptical argument therefore, in regarding walking as independent of any particular physical realisation of it one is guilty of dualism and of having produced the problem of how to relate the fact of walking to its physical realisations.

If we accept the analogy between walking and mentation then this repudiation by the CTM supporter is surely correct. Walking is a means of getting from *A* to *B* using our legs, and thinking is the means of getting from premises to conclusion using our brains, or of regulating our performance in a motor task, or of expediting this that or the other process. Similarly, having a memory is the facility for storing information and retrieving it when needed, perception is the process of gathering information that we require from the world, and so on and so on. In fact once we start it soon becomes apparent that *any* sphere of activity can be given a functional gloss: painting is putting paint onto canvas in order to brighten up a room/impress friends/make money; dancing is the exercising of limbs or the breaking-in of new shoes or the release of tension through movement. It is surely true that cognition, along with many other processes, *does* have a function; but the giant step which CTM then takes from this basis is to then regard cognition as *nothing more* than a set of functions.

Once we do this, of course, it is a very easy matter to give ourselves the impression that we have solved the mind–body problem by ascribing a form of mentality to machines, because machines are nothing if not functional. Using Dennett's terminology, the functional construal of cognition and mental life in general is at the sub-personal level – not sub-personal in the sense of being mechanistic but in the sense of being wholly in terms of appropriate and efficient perform-ance. Thus, a 'sub-personal–cum–functional' account of pain would be that having pains is having the ability to withdraw your hand rapidly from flames, to say 'Ow?' when someone drops a hammer on your toe, and so forth. A machine that could do this and more would *ipso facto* have pains.

And yet the CTM protagonist may say that it is being *sceptical* about the functional view of mind that results in a kind of dualism, the dualism which keeps falling back on raw intuitions and prejudices about the essentially conscious, phenomenal, personal aspect of cognition, which appeals to the elusive, ineluctable *quality* that constitutes mental states. (Wittgenstein: 'It's not a *something*, but not a *nothing* either!')[34] Indeed, but this is a dualism between the personal and the sub-personal levels, not a dualism between two kinds of entity. Nevertheless in arguing that it is possible to simulate mental functions on a computer without thereby simulating cog-nition itself one is left with the problem of saying exactly *what* aspect of mind has been omitted. In a sense this will be my task in the remainder of this chapter and all the next; but for now I will just signpost the problem.

In viewing the mind as something more than a functional entity one is led to regard remembering, for example, as far more similar to having a pain or experiencing the aroma of pear-drops than to the workings of the storage and recall facilities of the kind built into pocket calculators. Similarly, despite the fact that coming to believe something does not necessarily 'have a phenomenology',[35] and despite the fact that there is nothing peculiar to the experience of believing in the way that there is something peculiar to the taste of coffee, we could not ascribe a belief about something to a person who was incapable of being in, let's call it, a 'state of credulousness'.[36] To take the case of memory again, it is conceivable that through brain injury a person's memory of last year's holiday is disturbed in the following way: when people ask him at which hotel he stayed, whether he went water-skiing and if he enjoyed it the answers come to him immediately, but they come in the way that they come to us when we are asked our name or the product of 2 and 8, that is, without any events or experiences actually being recalled. The sense in which this person lacks a memory of his holiday is the sense in which we are justified in saying that cognition is more than a set of functions.

The problem I have just introduced is usually referred to as that of *qualitative content*. If the problem of qualitative content could be solved, then little would stand in the way of the particular kind of dualism we are considering here – that between mental functions and their alternative means of realisation. Fodor, who is one of the most spirited advocates of ·the functional theory of the mind–body relationship, has discussed the problem of qualitative content by reference to the classic puzzle of the 'inverted spectrum'.[37] It is possible to imagine there being two people whose experiences of colour are entirely opposite but whose colour behaviours – verbal and otherwise – are identical. They both call Little Red Ridinghood, cherries and sunsets 'red' and associate 'red' with passion; they both say grass is 'green' and they both associate 'light green' with coolness and springtime and 'dark green' with envy and depression; but one of them *sees* green and *says* 'red', and vice versa. How could we ever know of this difference? The fact of our being able to make such a conjecture at all points to what qualitative content is. As Fodor says, the functionalist defines mental states in terms of their causes and effects; although this is not behaviourism because in doing so the functionalist makes reference to an internal model in the explanation of these input–output regularities. How might qualitative content enter this picture? Fodor concludes – and with refreshing honesty! – that although there have been philosophical attempts to nullify the inverted spectrum problem (for example, denials that we really are imagining an inverted spectrum or that it is only a simple case of semantic confusion):

> as matters stand, the problem of qualitative content poses a serious threat to the assertion that functionalism can provide a general theory of the mental.[38]

However, Fodor is able to be so frank because CTM to which he subscribes regards qualitative content as a side issue; it regards *intensionality* as the defining property of mentation and this is functionalism's and CTM's success story, as Fodor goes on to say.

But there is a more obvious sense in which CTM entails dualism, not as a product of functionalism but as·a property of the program–machine relationship. What could be more dualist, after all, than the distinction between hardware and software and how troublesome is the notion of a program being a kind of mind? Indeed it is so troublesome that it looks very much like classic dualism: the 'program-mind' is an abstract set of instructions that determines the operations of the 'machine-body', the machine operations are then produced as output. Quite obviously, the analogy between the program and the mind does not stand up to even the most cursory examination because accepting it means accepting a model of the mind as an instruction-giving entity distinct from *any* realisation (not just from a particular one) and as influencing the brain, if not through the pineal gland,[39] then through the interface between the brain or 'brain-code' and some kind of 'mental compiler'. It is partly to avoid this kind of embarrassment that proponents of CTM maintain a degree of ambivalence in their overall aims: an ambivalence between modelling the 'mind' and modelling the brain. Such an ambiguity is inherent in the whole enterprise. That is to say, on the one hand they point out that a program can be realised on different kinds of machine and maintain that mental functions share this property, whilst on the other hand they want their models to be *realistic* models of mental functions, not mere metaphors. They realise that if the aim of the computer model is merely to simulate processes without regard to the way in which the brain carries out these processes then they would be abandoning the claims of strong AI itself – the claim that models are not merely mimics but mimics with psychological reality, indeed mental systems. This kind of position is principally associated with the work of Pylyshyn.[40]

Pylyshyn begins from the position that the conceptual structure of AI – thought as computation, the elements of thought as formal symbols, representation as data structures, etc. – should not be regarded as a mere metaphor of mental activity but should be taken quite literally. Pylyshyn is unambiguously advocating the CTM therefore. Doing this, he says, does not give *carte blanche* but places severe constraints upon the kinds of models that may be considered. Then, in order to retain the advantages of AI as a systematic theoretical psychology whilst at the same time providing AI models with an intrinsic relevance to brain processes he posits a level of simulation that exists between the simulation of a physical system (obeying physical laws) and the simulation of an abstract representational and computational system. He calls this level that of *functional architecture*. The machine program/system does not, on this perspective, provide a model of the brain as a physiological entity, but it simulates the capacities that the biological substrate supports. This, Pylyshyn suggests, should supplant the loose application of the term *algorithm* (see Chap. 6, note 105) which in this context means any computational effective procedure that simulates a mental process without regard to whether the program functions on anything like the same principles as the mental system being simulated. Now, on this approach the computer simulation still *is* an algorithm but one which has had its inherent assumptions about functional architecture and *functional requisites* (how the functional capacities are deployed in particular tasks) independently justified: different functional architectures make possible different kinds of algorithms. Functional architecture is regarded as a fixed human endowment but the particular algorithms used in thinking may vary within these constraints from occasion to occasion.

Pylyshyn gives the following example of the way that false hopes may be raised when the functional architecture condition is flouted. Artificial vision systems based on Guzman's program SEE[41] were found to be susceptible to the Müller-Leyer illusion.[42] But the aspect of this system's functional architecture that made this possible was its having a line-recognising procedure called a 'diameter-limited scanner' which terminated earlier when it encountered 'arrow' vertices at the end of a line than when it encountered 'fork' vertices (that is, it judged the former to be shorter). But we may well ask whether the human visual system has anything remotely resembling a diameter-limited scanner! What the program does show is the result of a thought-experiment, in the weak AI sense.

This distinction between functional architecture and algorithms is based on a distinction that Pylyshyn draws between *cognitively penetrable* mental processes requiring Type I explanations and *cognitively impenetrable* processes requiring Type II explanations.[43] In Type I explanations the theorist assumes that the subject is behaving as he is by virtue of certain beliefs and goals that he possesses; and in keeping with CTM orthodoxy these beliefs and goals are construed as computations on representations. In Type II explanations he assumes that the behaviour is produced because of the mechanical principles on which the brain functions. In *both* explanations functional architecture has to be implicated, but Type I explanations are in terms of how functional architecture makes such representations possible, and Type II explanations are solely in terms of functional architecture as directly traceable to biological units. Pylyshyn has argued at length in a number of places that psychology has traditionally overestimated the degree to which Type II explanations are appropriate.[44]

But how are we to regard the relation between mental functional architecture and computer functional architecture? Here again Pylyshyn sounds some warning notes. The machine's functional architecture may be regarded as forming the programmer's *virtual machine*, that is, the constraints that are listed in the program-language-users' manual (operations, how these may be put together, which data structures are possible, how content of memory may be accessed etc.) This describes the machine as seen by the programmer, his or her view of the functional architecture that defines the range of possible algorithms. The fact is that the choice (although it is fairly limited) between computer architectures will determine to a very large extent the kind of algorithms that are produced. But on what criteria do we select between 'virtual machines' in simulating mental processes? Here Pylyshyn is not very informative. He does however suggest that meta-theories of cognition, such as that of Piaget, which assume some form of functional architecture of the mind responsible for the production of algorithms (for example, Piaget's 'concrete' and 'formal' operations) provide at once a theoretical underpinning for the concept of functional architecture and an empirical base from which to assess rival systems. When there is little experimental evidence about the input–output features of the piece of human performance to be simulated, Pylyshyn argues that the best strategy to adopt with regard to functional architecture is the 'principle of least commitment', that is, to opt for '*minimal mechanisms* wherever possible, even at the cost of a computationally awkward system, on the grounds that such mechanisms committed one to the weakest presuppositions about underlying architecture and hence ones that could easily be revised upward without the need radically to redesign the system'.[45] This was the strategy that Pylyshyn and his colleagues adopted in attempting to simulate the perceptual-motor co-ordinations involved in making visual inferences and drawing diagrams.[46]

How then should we assess Pylyshyn's programme in the context of the charge of dualism that we began with? First, there is surely nothing dualistic about the distinction between the cognitively penetrable and impenetrable levels of explanation; something like this distinction would appear to be a necessity.[47] Moreover, one may repeat that the more severely the process of simulation is disciplined by considerations of functional architecture the farther one moves away from the disastrous notion of an abstract symbol system (constrained only by the nature of the functions that it has to express) instructing a passive hardware/physiological system which may be realised in any way you please. The reason is that the functional architecture concept enables us to regard non-conscious mental processes as expressive of *what is there* in the brain, and to do this is to accept one of the central tenets of monism.

Despite Pylyshyn's approach being an excellent antidote to the evangelical, 'hey presto' view of strong AI it has inherent difficulties which may be mentioned here both in the context of dualism and as a trailer for later discussions of the topic of 'representation' in Chapter 6.

As I said, Pylyshyn is at great pains to show us that very few indeed of the psychological functions are not cognitively penetrable (that is, do not involve belief and therefore representation). This is not objectionable as it stands but it has the effect of producing a very high degree of scepticism about experimental studies which claim to be directly pinpointing features of the functional architecture. Pylyshyn claims that the near universality of the cognitively penetrable ensures that such data will be generated by algorithms which have been *made possible* by the functional architecture rather than generated by the functional architecture itself. The problem is therefore: how do we discover *anything* significant about functional architecture? The algorithm too is highly elusive: in the case of reaction-time measures, for example,[48] this can tell us nothing directly about the algorithm itself because mental processes (construed as symbolic abstractions by Pylyshyn) do not possess the quality of duration. In general, says Pylyshyn, reaction-times either tell us about essentially irrelevant features of how a particular response is physically instantiated or about the relative complexity (number of operations involved) of different processes – nothing directly about either the functional architecture or the algorithm. Much the same arguments are applied to mental imagery studies[49] to show that they tell us nothing about underlying functional architecture but much about the subject's knowledge of the object domain – what Newell and Simon call the 'task demands'. For example, if a mental image of a coin being flipped 'lasts longer' than a mental image of seeing a huge boulder being turned over this is due to our system of *beliefs* about such objects and processes.

But much hinges on how far you take this kind of scepticism, because the farther you take it the more difficult it becomes to determine what should and should not count as constraining evidence for the psychological reality of a model's functional architecture. Certainly Pylyshyn is not very forthcoming about what this evidence *is*, but very forthcoming about what it *is not*. Indeed the scepticism may run to such a point it lands us back again with functional dualism. What is responsible for this is the relatively unexamined notion (even by a theorist as exhaustive as Pylyshyn) of representation itself: that beliefs, perceptions, tacit knowledge and goals are representations. These are not semantic representations and they are not holistic analogues (as are visual images for example): they are sets of data structures whose status is wholly formal and abstract. (Hence Pylyshyn's assertion that mental processes do not have a duration). If this is the case then it may well be that, despite all intentions to the contrary, dualism may be an inevitable consequence of regarding mental processes in this way. For these representations are not hypothesised entities with any particular form of instantiation, but the result of an *a priori* assumption about the nature of thought. What could therefore count as evidence for their existence or of their nature? No physical process surely. To be radically sceptical about the power of laboratory experimentation to reveal features of thought itself or of the physiological constraints on processing – that is, beyond computational complexity, 'irrelevant' aspects of physiological instantiation and the product of task demands – is to be something very much like a dualist.

The new behaviourism?

There are a few different kinds of behaviourism but I think it fairly uncontroversial to say that they all have in common a fundamental and principled agnosticism about what goes on within the organism between input and output: behaviour–environment regularity is the sphere of interest. Obviously CTM has a very considerable commitment to what comes between input and output because it is made up of theories of it. But a considerable lack of commitment seems to be apparent in its assessment of its achievements, of the kind 'never mind the *how* feel the *what*!' What could be more behaviouristic for example, than the 'Turing test'? This is an imagined situation in which a tester sits at a teletype and interrogates two systems – one human and the other a computer. If there comes a point at which the tester cannot tell the difference between the two systems then the computer has 'passed' the test and may have 'intelligence' attributed to it in a quite non-metaphorical way. (This is science fiction at the moment, but there is at least one anecdote that pops up every so often in the literature to tell how a vice-president of a computer-services company thought that he was communicating with the program designer when in fact he was feeding the *program*.) However, I think that the correct way to regard the 'passing' of the Turing test is as a reflection of the incapacities of testers not of the computational system, that is, it is not machines that pass it but people who fail it. Whether to call a machine 'intelligent' is a boring semantic issue; as psychologists we are interested in how human beings operate – and so too should be the proponents of CTM if they are to be consistent.

Much the same kind of impulse evident in the Turing test lurks behind statements made on what I have called the 'evangelical hey presto' wing of AI. Such statements infer that because workers in the field talk about their systems 'believing', 'deciding', checking back', 'seeing', etc., which is really the most appropriate and convenient way of describing what goes on, then the onus is on the sceptic to say why they should *not*. But both this attitude and the Turing test are the expressions of mere terminological whim which tell us nothing at all about the status of AI. As John Searle[50] puts it 'no philosophical ice is cut by such examples'. Or if they do cut philosophical ice it is to reveal strong behaviourist currents. How justified is this sceptical position?

Searle describes what I am calling behaviourism in terms of a thought-experiment based on Schank's[51] influential story-understanding systems that answer questions about stories with which they have been presented and make human-like inferences from literal to assumed content by virtue of their 'script' representations. (A script is a rule-like system of event regularities by which a program – and conceivably human beings[52] – represent familiar, recurring episodes such as eating out, planning a party, asking directions.) In fact the argument has application to any of the language understanding systems that have been produced including Winograd's famous SHRDLU.[53] Here it is.

A person is locked in a room and given a batch of Chinese writing. The person has no understanding of Chinese whatsoever. Next, he is given a second batch of Chinese writing (to him: meaningless squiggles) together with rules, in English, for the correlation of the second batch with the first. Finally he is given a third batch of Chinese symbols with more instructions in English that enable him to correlate elements of the third batch with the first two. This second set of rules enables him to give back certain sets of symbols when he receives certain other sorts of symbols in this third batch. Now it so happens that the people giving him the symbols and rules call the first batch the 'script', the second batch the 'story', the third batch 'questions' and the symbols that he gives back 'answers'. The set of rules in English they call the 'program'. Let us further suppose that the captive becomes so skilled at the process of translating (to him) meaningless squiggles that he passes the Turing test – the native speakers of Chinese come to believe that this man–room system actually understands the Chinese stories so well that it answers questions about them in an intelligent, inferential manner. The system does so – as does a computer – by performing computational operations on formally specified symbols, that is, *known by their shape not by their meaning.*

Searle uses this example to show that arguments of the Turing test variety do nothing to bolster what he takes to be the two main claims that CTM would make in this context: (i) that machines really do understand stories, or at least have a primitive version of human understanding, and (ii) that the machine–program system explains something important about how human beings understand stories. As to the former, it is doubtful that workers in AI do really believe that their systems *literally* understand, but the latter is crucial. If the latter is to be sustained then it is absolutely essential to assume that when the captive in the Chinese example understands *English* he is also performing computations on formal symbols. But what is the evidence, says Searle, that people do think by manipulating formal symbols, particularly as the example shows that the efficacious manipulation of formal symbols may take place *without* understanding. He concludes:

> As long as the program is defined in terms of computational operations on purely formally defined elements, what the example suggests is that these by themselves have no interesting connection with understanding.[54]

One form of objection to Searle's argument would be that he is misconstruing CTM as seeking to explain the process of *conscious* understanding, when it is concerned with non-conscious mental process, and when it maintains a necessary degree of ambivalence between simulating actual brain-processes and the flow of information in the brain abstractly specified. In answer: AI cannot be modelling brain-processes themselves, first because the root assumption of CTM is that the mental processes with which it is concerned may be realised by a range of different physical systems. To say that Searle has failed to acknowledge that the task of AI is to simulate the brain *qua* the machine that supports understanding is radically to redraft the aims of CTM. Second, although it is indeed true that AI aims at the simulation of non-conscious, not conscious, processes these nevertheless are supposed to eventuate in and support conscious understanding – where *else* is it supposed to come from? – at least this must be the assumption if it is *human* cognition that is being simulated. Searle's argument shows that symbol manipulation may bear no relation at all to conscious understanding.

Alternatively, some would regard Searle's example as simply the other side of the same bad coin as the Turing test, in the sense that the Turing test bolsters one set of prejudices and the Chinese translator example bolsters the opposite set. For this reason Dennett calls it an 'intuition pump'.[55] But this is a little unfair because given that our interest is in psychology first and foremost should we not take the problem of how to distinguish the genuinely mental from the spuriously mental very seriously indeed? But on the other hand, is it not of enormous relevance to psychology that we can devise machines that pass the Turing test without our having to attribute to them any awareness of what they are doing; indeed this would carry the strong implication that our 'consciousness' is a mere appendage to intelligence.[56] Perhaps consciousness evolved to serve affective and volitional systems rather than intellectual;[57] or maybe consciousness has a role as a 'mental organ' similar to that which the spleen has as a bodily organ, that is, as necessary to early development (we may require consciousness to develop basic mental structures) but disposable in adulthood. Yet the trouble with this strong position is that if we jettison consciousness entirely – along with the whole baggage of truth, meaning, relevance, validity, etc. – we then find ourselves deliberately ignoring the fact that non-conscious mental processes do, as it happens, result in conscious understanding. How do they? Indeed how *could* they if they inhabit an entirely formal, asemantic computational realm? If a system like Schank's is regarded more modestly as an abstract description of the information flow within the brain rather than as a direct simulation (that is, tending more towards weak AI) then we must still, as Pylyshyn points out, justify our assumptions about functional architecture and algorithms if we are not to end up with a mere metaphor, which Schank does *not* intend his system to be.[58]

The behaviourist currents in CTM are equally apparent in the treatment of the problem of the qualitative content of mental states. Boden,[59] for example, in discussing the status of systems that simulate emotional behaviour such as Colby's neurotic program, has the following kinds of argument. First, she points out that *pure* feeling with no cognitive components is never or hardly ever experienced by us and that emotions are not individuated in terms of their essential nature but in terms of their meaning and context. (Studies by Schachter and Singer[60] can be interpreted as supporting this generalisation.) Therefore programs which display some intellectual (that is, computational) expertise in reading their own 'emotions' and drawing inferences from stories with emotional content are at least on the road to having an emotional life. But, quite simply, the purity or otherwise of emotion is neither here nor there: Othello's jealousy was in part an intellectual achievement but that does not of itself justify our ascribing a state of jealousy to a system that has been programmed to interpret hints and handkerchief-evidence sufficiently well to proceed to – the robot equivalent of – wife-smothering behaviour.

Boden's second argument relies on the publicly communicable nature of qualitative content: that we can in fact communicate our subjective states in language and particularly by metaphor (Locke's example of the blind man who thought that the colour 'red' must be like the sound of a trumpet . . . we know what he meant) and that qualitative content 'is *intelligible* in publicly communicable terms'.[61] To illustrate the latter point, it is possible to regard language not only as a formal system for communicating the structure of experience but also as the medium for expressing the content of experience – and some would claim there is no clear way of distinguishing the two.[62] 'If so,' says Boden, 'to say that a computer could have no real understanding of emotions – no matter how plausibly it used emotion *language* – on the ground that it supposedly cannot experience feelings, is to make a highly dubious claim'.[63] Should this be taken to mean that using emotion language *is* understanding emotion? If it can be then I do not know what else to call it but behaviourism. Moreover the sceptic whom Boden is addressing need not have the *a priori* assumption that a computer cannot have feelings, but may hold rather that there is more to having feelings than being able to produce emotion language or indeed emotion behaviour.

We can observe another example of what I am calling behaviourism in Dennett's later views on pain.[64] In asking whether we could build a robot that could feel pain (presumably intending a more sophisticated version of the kind of robots that are now in evidence rather than *any* man-made entity) Dennett adopts the tactic of showing how confused and contradictory is our notion of 'pain'. This he achieves by producing a catalogue of problem cases (for example, leucotomised patients who say they have intense pain which they do not mind; the possibility that hypnosis relieves pain by producing a false belief that one is not in pain) which add up to the conclusion that pain is not so much a mysterious phenomenal entity as an ir-redeemably incoherent concept. The best hope, he argues, is to produce a sub-personal theory of pain, the physiological models for which he discusses in detail. The conclusion is that certainly a robot could be constructed which instantiated a good sub-personal theory of pain – and this is probably the only kind of theory of pain we are likely to get – but certainly a robot could *not* instantiate our personal-level notions of pain because these are so confused that they cannot even be clearly stated let alone modelled. This is the excuse for the ironical title 'Why you can't make a computer that feels pain'. In fact Dennett is arguing for something very like the opposite and ends with the wry speculation that if we did build a robot that instantiated a sub-personal theory of pain our intuitions about the nature of pain (perhaps already in a state of pre-revolutionary flux) would have become altered sufficiently for us to refrain from kicking it.

Dennett is able to proceed this far because of the hard functionalist assumptions with which he began: intelligence, like respiration, he says is a purely functional concept, so artificial intelligence, like artificial respiration, is no less genuine for being obtained by artifice.'[65] This is certainly true, as I have already said, *if* you regard intelligence solely as something whose job is successfully to complete tasks and solve problems irrespective of how this is achieved. But pain is regarded by Dennett in the same light; or rather Dennett implicitly challenges us to say why it is any different from the case of intelligence. So, he says, clinging to our 'intuitions' about pain as essentially a biological phenomenon bound up with birth, death, and the 'afflictions of our soft and fragile and warm flesh'[66] is comparable to insisting stubbornly that a synthetic Château Latour is not Château Latour despite the fact that in every respect it is indistinguishable from the real thing. But it is precisely this construal of pain as a functional concept with some tangled phenomenal baggage dumped on top of it that enables such an analogy to be broached at all.

I am not denying here that non-organic yet true pain is a logical possibility; but surely much more has to be done to spell out the details of the robot instantiation (how much more will be dealt with in the next chapter). It is not enough to plump for a sub-personal theory because our personal folk-psychology of pain is somewhat anomalous; and to regard it *as* enough, to jettison the painfulness of pain because we sometimes get muddled when we talk about it, is, I think, a kind of behaviourism. Indeed it is worth bearing in mind that Skinner regards himself,[67] first and foremost, as a *functionalist*.

4

Conditions for Belief and Knowledge

In the previous chapter we were led to the paradoxical conclusion that the computational theory of mind (CTM) may result in a position that is at once dualistic and behaviourist. Whether it does so or not depends on how dogmatically its proponents interpret the strong AI program (see Chapter 3). If, as Pylyshyn counsels, they abandon their faith in the computational 'metaphor' of the mind as a kind of salvation-bringing new paradigm,[1] interpret their claims literally (for example, thought as formal symbol manipulation) and then ensure that programs are constrained by empirical validation of their choice of functional architecture and algorithms (that is, that they stay close to the evidence) such consequences may be avoided. But, as I said, it is not at all clear what form these constraints should take.

As it is usual to regard dualism and behaviourism as the polar opposites in psychological theorising this paradox deserves some immediate explanation. I will indeed give the explanation immediately, but then spend the rest of the chapter explaining and justifying it.

There are two major characteristics that dualism and behaviourism share. The first, about which I will have little to say, involves a scepticism about the relevance of biological data. This may seem strange given that the greatest dualist – Descartes – was also a brilliant researcher in anatomy, and given that many psychologisits who regard themselves as behaviourists study learning through drug-treatments and lesion-techniques. But it is well to remember that it is ingrained within the logic of dualism that mental 'rules and representations' have their own logic and internal structure whilst the body is only a more or less efficient executive. We see this in Descartes and we see it in Chomsky[2] in his use of the competence/performance distinction. As regards behaviourism, if we equate the term with Skinner's radical behaviourism then there is no doubt whatsoever that the 'organism as black box' approach can be seen as a direct rival to physiological psychology.[3] So dualism–behaviourism is an almost inevitable consequence of the base assumption of CTM that the mode of realisation (neurones, electric circuits, cogs, water-pipes) is deeply irrelevant to cognition.

The commonality between behaviourism and dualism that I want to explore in depth is their lack of interest in the *conditions* which need to be met if a mind is to be attributed to a system. For dualism 'the mind' is just there; it may develop as a kind of parallel to the body with its own system of 'mental organs', as Chomsky[4] calls them, but its very construal as distinct from the body makes a neglect of the behavioural and physiological conditions for its existence inevitable. In traditional dualism, as mind was a separate entity or substance the only condition for its existence was that which was a condition for matter as well – God. The case of behaviourism is still simpler: as the rejection of mind is the *raison d'être* of behaviourism it follows that it must also reject the notion of there being conditions for it.

There are two main ways in which the problem of conditions arises. First, if we are to say that an individual knows, believes, perceives that something is the case (to do which he must possess a set of competences gathered under the term 'mind') this carries the implication that the data he possesses about the world must have a certain kind of coherence. To illustrate: somebody views a scene in which a red cube is positioned between a green pyramid on the left and a blue sphere on the right. He says that he sees a red cube to the left of the sphere; and we provisionally ascribe to him the ability to cognise the property of 'cubeness'. But if, when asked what he can see to the right of the pyramid (assuming he understands the instructions), he says 'Something red but of unfamiliar shape' then we would have to revise our earlier ascription of the concept of a cube to him. Perhaps 'cubeness' only exists for this person in relation to sphericality? The point of this example is that the ascription of knowledge (and thus of a mind that has knowledge) to someone is carried out not only on the basis of individual successes and failures but also in terms of how the individual can bring items of data into a coherent relation. The problem comes into clearer relief when logical examples are given: the most serious defect that any knowledge system may have is the production of logically contradictory statements. I shall call this the 'coherence condition' and argue that it poses a real problem for CTM.

The second source of condition problems arises from the following assumption: no knowledge, belief or perception would appear to be possible unless the subject had some inkling of the distinction between sensory data and the source of the data in the physical world. This is related to the ability to cognise the self as a centre of knowing because it carries with it some appreciation of the self as a *possessor* of data, separate not only from the world but also from other such centres. There are a number of ways of referring to this: 'self–world dualism', 'ego–alter', 'subjective–objective', 'consciousness–datum'. I will use the term 'subject–object division' to refer to this condition.

The coherence condition

The problem raised by the coherence condition was expressed in its definitive form by David Hume, and indeed has been called 'Hume's problem'.[5] In fact it is a problem which inevitably arises with any radically associationist philosophy of mind[6] in so far as an associationist theory must regard the possession of knowledge as equivalent to the possession of atomic representations – called variously 'ideas', 'impressions', 'sensations' – and must regard the relation of these mental atoms as taking the form of associative links of one kind or another. (We dealt with one product of this tradition briefly in Chapter 1 – Hume's theory of causality.) The problem is: how could such a system ever result in understanding given that understanding requires organisation? A purely representational system of this kind only has organisation in so far as the world is organised in itself and in so far as our experience of it (for example, the order in which perceptions come to us) is organised, and that *is not* very far. (It was Kant who, after Hume, tried to describe how the mind must impose organisation on sensory data.) So we have to explain how sense/order/system/structure/organisation arise from a process which is (i) atomistic and (ii) in which the atoms are related to each other fortuitously and *ad hoc*. What is required is some supervising agency which puts the mental house in order by sifting, interpreting, categorising and making coherent this agglomeration. The obvious candidate for such an agency would appear to be some kind of inner eye or self. But this is not an option open to Hume because, as an associationist, he had to reject and did reject[7] the notion of a self in view of the fact that knowledge of such a self could only come to us as similarly atomistic impressions and ideas. It is not an option open to us either because pointing to some centre of · interpretation in such a context – an 'homunculus' as it is often called – leads to an infinite regress. This is so because if the homunculus organises and interprets the data for us, how does the *homunculus* understand it? All that has happened is that the problem has been pushed one stage further back from 'person ——➤ world' to 'homunculus ——➤ world representation data'.

Dennett[8] has an interesting argument to the effect that the conceptual structure of CTM actually helps us to solve this as a *philosophical* problem, whether or not the solution has *psychological* reality. He points out that we may regard the organisation of a program as an array of homunculi each with a specific job to perform, each relatively ignorant of the other homunculi and of its place in the total system, and each communicating with others in a predetermined manner. Indeed references to homunculi are not at all uncommon in the AI literature – sometimes facetious but usually in earnest[9] – because the concept of a data structure is somewhat homuncular. A data structure is at once a representation in symbolic form of a state of affairs and an instruction about what to do next; it is a representational atom (like an impression/idea/sensation) but one tagged with a function within the total system (the program) – with a kind of meaning relative to the task in hand. I suppose this is what justifies Dennett's calling data structures 'self-understanding representations'.

However Dennett goes on to say that AI theorists have found it necessary to distinguish between the representation and the representation user,[10] and, as he says, this would appear to be the first step in the infinite regress that CTM held promise of avoiding. But apparently 'user/representation' is not a strict duality in AI: some input-data need more interpretation than others, resulting in a trade-off between the degree of prior structure in the representation and the amount of interpretation (computation) required of the system. However one would have to be an expert in AI really to assess whether something self-like has to be posited as an interpreter of data. But certainly, to this non-expert, it is paradoxical that other proponents of CTM quote the supervisory–interpretive functions of programs such as HACKER,[11] which reflects on and assesses its own performance in order to 'learn from experience', as evidence for their psychological reality.

Although the data-structure concept may be a solution to Hume's problem in the abstract, if we are uncertain whether the solution has psychological reality it is not at all clear that either Hume as a proto-psychologist or we as students of psychology should find it satisfactory. The people who do find it satisfactory (that is, psychologically relevant) are those who have already accepted, as functionalists, that it is possible to present a wholly sub-personal account of cognition. The other kind of prejudice (a personal-level prejudice) is that, although the notion of an inner eye has no role to play here, a preferable approach is to regard the acquisition of selfhood and of representations as indissociable processes; that there cannot be a self without representations, but neither can there be representations without some degree of organisational competence that we may want to call a primitive self-concept. The mistake that associationism and perhaps CTM also makes, on this approach, is to begin with representations and then posit some process to make sense of them.

This line of thought will be extended in the discussion of the subject–object division, but since we are dealing with the problem of *organisation* we are still embedded in the coherence condition. First I need to do more to justify my hints about CTM being associationist.

Associationism establishes a 'bottom-up' framework within which to explain mental functions because it regards complex representations as having been built up from simpler elements. The history of psychology is littered with attempts to state the laws by which this process of association functions. Originally there were Aristotle's three laws of association which Hobbes restated (though association is intended in a rather different sense here).[12] It is with Hume that we see an attempt to establish psychology as a scientific (though not empirical) enterprise; as a 'mental physics' with laws of *attraction* and of *force* by which ideas and impressions were linked, on a precise analogy with the role these concepts played in physics. Hume regarded himself as 'the Newton of the mind'. Some 100 years later James Mill was still labouring in the same vineyard with his highly mechanistic associationism (for example, the complex idea of a 'tree' was cemented out of simple ideas of bark, leaves, branches, which were in turn made up of the simpler ideas of . . .). However, the 'mental chemistry' of his son J. S. Mill[13] was quite an advance on this because it assumed some activity in the mind and – as the notion of chemistry suggests – made ideas qualitatively different from the sum of their parts, just as water is more than just the sum of hydrogen and oxygen. Now let us consider the following quotation from Herbert Simon in the light of all this:

> Information processing psychology has sometimes been referred to as 'the new mental chemistry'. The atoms of this mental chemistry are symbols which are combinable into larger and more complex associative structures called lists and list structures. The fundamental 'reactions' of the mental chemistry employ elementary information processes that operate upon symbols and symbol structures: copying symbols, storing symbols, retrieving symbols, and comparing symbols. Symbol structures are stored in memories, often classified as short term and long term memories.[14]

This quotation from Simon is taken from H. Beilin's essay on the 'new functionalism' in developmental psychology.[15] Much of what I am going on to say in the next couple of pages will carry an influence from arguments presented there.

Now, 'information processing psychology' is not a neutral term: it means the psychology that carries over AI concepts wholesale into its theorising. So Simon's statement can be taken as applying to CTM in general. But the notion that symbols are the atoms of a form of AI associationism is not at all congruent with the characterisation of CTM as the 'top-down' psychology *par excellence.*[16] As we saw above, CTM certainly has a top-down methodology in that it takes cognitive phenomena at the level of strategies and algorithms and deduces the elements or data structures (Simon: 'symbol structures') from this holistic basis. But to say that the *methodology* of CTM is top-down does not preclude the possibility of its resulting in something that is remarkably 'bottom-up': symbols as the base elements of CTM's mental chemistry. What is the consequence for models of the information-processing type which utilise the assumptions and terminology of CTM? It is, as Beilin points out, that because, like all associatonist theories, the only structure they possess is given to them *ad hoc* towards the solution of particular problems, there is no essential or logical connection between the different aspects of production systems and between different production systems. Beilin quotes Newell in this context:

our task in psychology is first to discover that structure which is fixed and invariant so that we can theoretically infer the method used to perform the task . . . without such a framework within which to work, the generation of new methods, hence new explanations, for old phenomena, will go on *ad nauseam*. There will be no discipline for it, as there is none now.[17]

For example, if we employ information-processing models to explain logico-mathematical development in early childhood then these must be guided by certain *a priori* assumptions about the logical relation between items of knowledge such as the conservation of quantities, class–sub-class relationships, the number system, logical deduction, matrix systems, correlation and so forth otherwise we are likely to end up with *ad hoc* models for processes that we know to be logically related. It was exactly this 'framework within which to work' that Newell's notion of a 'process model' was supposed (in 1972) to provide. But – as Beilin says – it has not resulted in this hoped-for theoretical coherence and:

it would not be amiss to say that information-processing theory, even at this date, is a collection of models lacking a coherent theory of logical or natural process by which cognitive structures as holistic entities are formed.[18]

And why? Because if a theory's conceptual resource for explaining how our understanding is organised consists of atomistic symbols and task-relative systems of their association then it is bound to produce something that is unsatisfactory in the way Beilin describes.

Obviously the principal alternative to this is a self-consciously structuralist theory of cognition such as Piaget's[19] within which *organisation* – along with adaptation – is seen as the *sine qua non* of any system capable of intelligent behaviour. But why is organisation crucial to thought?

Our thinking takes place with a framework of rules about behavioural and conceptual appropriateness and this framework has a discoverable structure, or at least has different degrees and kinds of structure. So, for example, within the structure or rule-system there are things that can be said ('The cube is red') and things which cannot be said ('The cube is both red and green all over'). Opinions may differ as to how tight and how static this structure is, but nobody denies that intelligent thought is only possible within some kind of structure – at the very least the laws of logic and grammar have to be obeyed if nonsense is not to result. So let us take logic as the paradigm case of structure and as representing the degree of organisation in intelligent thought. How might logic originate? One form of answer derives from attention to the fact that biological systems have organisation, structure and a kind of logic.[20] This is what Piagetian theory trades on; and it enabled Piaget to argue that intellectual development is an elaboration of developmental laws that are common to phylogeny and ontogeny. Biological adaptation (morphological, sensory-motor, intellectual) succeeds by virtue of organisation and structure and fails in so far as it lacks them. Therefore structuralist theories in general and Piaget's in particular are quintessentially 'top-down'. Here are two respects in which they are so. First, whether an organism can or cannot do something is only of interest as telling us about the level of organisation that the behaviour manifests. As a cognitive psychologist Piaget was singularly unimpressed by success or failure on task items: it was how the child *justified* his behaviour – as an index of his structural level – that interested him. Second, there is no legislation in Piagetian theory about what the units or counters of thought have to be. So Piaget did not speak of thought taking place in symbols but of thought being realised through different kinds of 'symbolic function', which might include drawing, dreams, mental imagery, play-symbols and gestures as well as language. These are all modes of *analogue* representation, towards which CTM is highly sceptical, as we have discussed. Indeed an important facet of Piaget's structuralism is the view that 'operational level' (level of structure) can be expressed by many different kinds of symbolic function.

It would be well to parallel our earlier historical note about associationism with one on structuralism. The first explicit attempt to treat intellectual capacity as the product of organisation and to distinguish levels of understanding by virtue of their degree of organisation was made by Leibniz.[21] This was coupled with the view that ontogenesis is regulated by laws of differentiation and integration that impose progressively higher levels of organisation on embryonic material. But it was in the mid-nineteenth century that notions such as organisation, differentiation, integration, equilibrium and adaptation became part of psychology's conceptual baggage and they did so almost exclusively through the influence of Darwin's evolutionary theory. For Herbert Spencer, L. T. Hobhouse and many lesser writers on intelligence, 'organisation' attained almost shibboleth status. So, far from being the maverick which he may appear from the vantage point of CTM orthodoxy Piaget belonged to a 'great tradition'[22] as divergent from the associationist tradition as could be. One might say that these traditions diverged primarily over the question of whether cognition should be regarded as an *organic* or as a *mechanical* phenomenon.

In illustration of this Beilin mentions three respects in which Piaget's structuralism diverges from CTM functionalism: organisation, transformation and self-regulation. We have dealt with organisation, transformation refers to the process by which new structures emerge out of old, and self-regulation means the necessity for maintaining the stability of the system through qualitative development and the assimilation of novelties. Although this last notion involves a kind of behavioural monitoring by feedback it is quite distinct from the cybernetic concept of a feedback loop[23] which is typically employed as an *ad hoc* device in particular problem-solving tasks rather than as a regulator of development and organisation. So transformation and self-regulation play the kind of role in this structural theory that representation and computation play in mechanistic theories. And these are, of course, essentially genetic concepts – hardly surprising given that only organic entities *grow*. Earlier I said that one of the commonalities between dualism, behaviourism and CTM was their neglect of the physiological; in view of the foregoing discussion we may relate this to a more fundamental neglect of the organic features of intelligence.

I said by way of introducing the coherence condition that it was in the context of logical judgement that the condition came into clearest relief. So let us compare the structuralist and the CTM treatment of the logical properties of necessity and validity. Theories of the Piagetian type have accounts of logical necessity built into them. For example, Piaget proposed that *action* has a logic and that verbal–conceptual logic is a replication and re-organisation of this at a higher level. For example a baby's actions on objects may express a sensory-motor understanding that if A is behind B and B is behind C then A is behind C – a transitive inference of action that pre-figures (developmentally precedes) later reasoning of the kind 'John is taller than Fred and Fred is taller than George, so John must be taller than George'. Whether Piaget's theory of necessity is the best available can certainly be questioned and we may question, in particular, its comparative neglect of the normative influence of the conceptual system – but as least it *is* a theory of logical necessity. Now CTM, to the extent that it is associationist, lacks a theory of logical necessity and it lacks such a theory not so much through neglect as from principle. History again: the associationist J. S. Mill equated the laws of logic with the processes we undergo when we think and therefore regarded validity as the product of the way our minds work, to put it crudely. Indeed Mill argued that the laws of logic could be discovered by introspection[24] rather than by deductive investigation of the system of logic. CTM also assumes psychologism to the extent that it takes the logical structures of intelligence to be equivalent – even identical – to the mental computational processes: a valid inference is valid by virtue of computational processes and is distinguished from an invalid inference in terms of processes alone.

Here now is one version of an argument against this position, an argument that is present as a *motif* in Wittgenstein's writing on logic and which is a consequence of Wittgenstein's construal of thought in personal rather than sub-personal terms.[25] The argument focusses on the way errors of reasoning may be regarded. If we equate logical deduction with sub-personal events then a sequence of operations that results in an invalid conclusion is no 'worse' than one which results in a valid conclusion. For example, if a computer produces two logically incompatible conclusions from two separate sequences we may correct the program by adding another incompatibility debugging device, which is of course only *another* sequence of operations. If incompatibilities still occur then we will need still another overseeing process. But all the time the application of the norm *is* the functioning of a process. Even if we have a program with some built-in HACKER-like overseer capacity which can detect fallacies in its own reasoning this would have no more insight into the basis of validity than the system it was correcting. And what is the difference between correcting the error that $a = b$, $b = c$ therefore $c < a$ and correcting the error that the block is in the alcove when it is in the window, or that pawns can move sideways. In such a system, therefore, it would appear that logical rules lack the special *status* one would expect them to have in a system with psychological reality. Here a logical rule is *nothing more* than an instruction on a program that certain machine operations should be carried out, and they exist because the program associates certain data structures with others *ad hoc*.

The proponent of CTM might reply that this is an argument about psychophysical reductionism not about the status of logical process in AI. That is, CTM shares with the opponents of psychologism the denial that physical processes (machine hardware in this case) are responsible for logicality: is it not one of the base assumptions of CTM that mentation can in principle be realised by any kind of physical system? CTM is only psychologistic to the extent that it equates the employment of the laws of logic in thought with representation and computation through data structures – it does not equate these laws with physical processes. But, in fact, CTM must do more than this: it must make the manipulation of data structures not merely equivalent to the employment of, say, the transitive inference or the law of excluded middle[26] in reasoning but must make them carry validity. It is not merely a matter of using such laws properly, it is a matter of understanding why they are productive of validity. For the system to have psychological reality must it not understand at least something about the way in which validity works within the human conceptual system? There is, in fact, a sense in which CTM is quite correct about the irrelevancy of how thought is physically instantiated, but this is a sense which cuts against CTM itself. With regard to the laws of logic there is an irrelevancy not only of their physical realisation but of the thought-processes themselves. That is, the *anti*-psychologism[27] position trades on the fact that an inference like '$a = b, b = c, a = c$' is valid whether or not it has *ever* been made, because the validity inheres in the structure of the symbol system not in the mental process by which '$a = c$' is concluded; and this because the concept of validity is one we apply to arguments and principles not to their *employment*. The same goes for the necessary truth or falsity of some propositions.

A system's 'understanding logic' is not, then, at all the same as its being an efficient practitioner of logic. It may be a hopelessly inefficient practitioner of logic (of course computers are prodigiously efficient logical systems), but it must understand how it is that some things *have* to be true (hence the importance that Piaget placed on the subjects' justifications of their performance). Moreover, it must possess appropriately different mental orientations to valid and invalid arguments, to necessarily true and necessarily false propositions and indeed to necessary and contingent propositions. And in referring to 'mental orientation' one is raising again the issue of qualitative content, an issue which makes its appearance quite plainly in modal contexts,[28] where mental orientations of necessity versus possibility are realised in language, and where degree and kind of belief in propositions may be formalised (the so-called 'modal logics'). So one is implicating qualitative content via the concept of a mental orientation (cf. Fodor's treatment of mental orientations as 'relations' in the next section) and one must also implicate a concept of truth itself – how else could the system possess the notion of some things *having* to be true (more of the concept of truth in the next section but one).

To what extent might such orientations to validity and necessity be directly programmable? We could make certain 'intuitions' about the role of logical necessity and validity in thought part of the machine's knowledge base; but would this be the same as 'understanding logical necessity'? If, in a behaviouristic spirit, one equates understanding with giving the appropriate output then the answer must be 'yes'. But such a system would possess such an 'understanding' whilst lacking any qualitative orientation to its own propositions (that is, the problem of qualitative content does not go away). It would still lack a concept of truth because this involves more than mere efficiency and these 'intuitions about the status of validity and necessity' would still be – to return to square one – *ad hoc* operations grafted onto other operations rather than knowledge that grows out of the appreciation of the status of logic as a system for organising concepts into propositions and propositions into arguments. And to return to our starting point in the discussion of the coherence condition, such a system would still be like a Kafka-esque bureaucracy in which each functionary knows its own job but nobody else's. Such bureaucracies could function (they probably *do* function) but they would not understand their own structure: they would have an associationist rather than structural coherence.

We have seen then that the coherence condition is the condition that the elements of a system's representational apparatus should possess given kinds of relation to each other, with logical rules being the paradigm of this. To the extent that CTM is associationist the relation of elements within the system is grafted on rather than determined by the system's structure. Such systems may be efficient practitioners of logic but they must lack appreciation of validity and necessity as inherent in the conceptual system on which they are parasitic – and to lack such knowledge is to lack insight into how representational elements can and cannot be related. So in general we may conclude that systems of this kind could not know what they are doing because they cannot know how their parts relate to their whole. Moreover, such a conclusion must reprise the issue of selfhood because although Hume's problem has two faces (the problems of self-understanding and of structure) these eventuate in the same problem: how parts are related to the whole.

What CTM shares with associationism – as I said in the discussion of data structures as 'self-understanding representations' – is the assumption that we can begin with sensory data and then proceed to explain how the agent makes sense of these – the representation/computation distinction by another name. This grafting on of sense to sensibilia is like explaining graphic artistry by saying that the artist records lines on paper and then adds to them the quality of being lifelike. But what conceptual framework is available to us as an alternative to such a view, or, to continue the metaphor, how can we construe the necessity for having the goal of being lifelike determine the recording of lines on paper? To anticipate the next section, such a conceptual framework must be derivable, more or less, from the structuralist tradition in which Kant's famous dictum that 'thoughts without context are empty, intuitions [percepts] without concepts are blind' is located, and in which CTM's 'no computation without representation'[29] may be opposed by Piaget's 'no assimilation without accommodation'. (And at this point the drawing metaphor tends to merge with literal reality because it *may* be that the property of being *lifelike* – that is, *organic* – is necessary for such an achievement.)

The subject–object condition: intensionality

As I have been employing the term, to describe what somebody is doing by verbs such as 'believe', 'know', 'perceive', 'hope' and 'intend' is to ascribe intensionality to that person. The intension is equivalent to the mental state that the person is in and the physical object of the state is its extension. I have to admit that my usage of the terms 'intension' and 'intensionality' is deliberately sloppy; though I believe that, in Putnam's phrase, it is not 'fatally sloppy'. (See Chapter 2 note 22 for a discussion of the purist position on intensionality-with-an-s.)

We may also talk of an 'intensional object', existing, as it were, 'in the head': the mental objects of my beliefs are not the same as the objects, processes and relations that they concern. Moreover there may be intensional objects with no extensional counterpart as, for example, when I am thinking about Santa Claus or unicorns. So we may regard reference to intensionality as a means of expressing the fact of the duality between a mental system and the world in which it is located. It is a possible thesis, therefore, that if computational systems[30] possess intensionality then they fulfil what I called the condition of subject–object division. My thesis in this and the next section will be that intensionality is only a criterion for the possession of a mental state by an entity if we are in a position to ascribe *knowledge of the world* to that entity. What the CTM does, in effect, is to ignore the question of knowledge, and to construe intensionality purely in terms of *representation*. Thus any system which can be said to represent something has intensionality; *ergo* it is a mental system in the only sense that should be important to us.

In Chapter 3 we saw that intensionality is a property that proponents of CTM ascribe to their systems primarily because programs selectively represent reality and work through to goals. If they do this they automatically fulfil the usual logical criteria for intensionality.[31] For this reason they talk of systems seeing, knowing, believing and so forth because although such states may not be the same for the computer as they are for the human being such usage expresses the fact that computer and man are on the same side of the intensional/extensional divide. (An example of an extensional system would be a simple form of thermostat which responds to environmental events without having any model of the environment itself.) If this is really all there is to the intensionality condition then we may well wonder what all the fuss is about: having intensionality looks like a rather uninteresting consequence of being a representational system. But we will see that the kind of intensionality that computational systems possess is of a very peculiar variety; and what we will be discussing is the proposal of CTM, made explicit by Jerry Fodor, that indeed it is a peculiar kind of intensionality but that this peculiarity encompasses the true domain of cognitive psychology. What Fodor argues is that computational intensionality is a form of intensionality that exists *without* subject–object division, but that this is all that is required for a truly mental system. The argument amounts, in fact, to a repudiation of the subject–object condition.

First a caveat about making any easy equations between the

intensional and the psychological. There are problem cases. For example, being in pain is not intensional but it is surely psychological. It is not intensional because, as we discussed above and as Wittgenstein insisted, a pain (along with many other kinds of mental state) has no intensional object: having a pain is not believing something of something. We are faced with a choice here. On the one hand we say that having a pain is a *kind* of belief the extensional aspect of which is its physical or sub-personal condition, so that we can be mistaken about being in pain, and in which case having a pain *is* intensional. Alternatively we admit that intensionality is a sufficient but not a necessary condition for being psychological. But if we do accept this 'sufficient condition' option then our deeper problem reappears: a *representational* system appears automatically to fulfil the criteria for intensionality, and if intensionality *is sufficient* for being psychological then any representational system is *ipso facto* psychological. Is there not something wrong with this?

We will approach the intensionality condition by considering Fodor's argument[32] in some detail. It is an important argument but especially so for our purposes because if it is valid then much of the sceptical case that has been presented here will be shown to be invalid. The argument is an attempt to justify the theory of mind ('computational theory of the mind' is Fodor's phrase) in which mental processes are both *symbolic* and *formal* in just the way that I defined computer processes in the previous chapter. Essentially CTM regards thought as the manipulation of symbols but not symbols that mean in virtue of denoting entities: the only kind of meaning they possess comes from their arrangement as data structures – hence Fodor's initial characterisation of it as *syntactic* meaning. Fodor calls this computational property 'the formality condition' and takes it to hold for any putatively mental system whose 'counters of thought' (not Fodor's expression) only have an internal meaning in terms of their relations to each other, there being no property possessed by them through which they mean things (objects, processes, relations) in the world outside the computational system. The term 'syntactic' is somewhat misleading here, Fodor says, because there is no clear sense in which computational processes have a syntax in the way that a natural language does, so he retains the term 'formal'. Thus CTM regards thought as consisting of 'formal operations' that are 'specified without reference to such semantic properties of representations as, for example, truth, reference and meaning. Since we do not know how to complete this list (since, that is, we do not know what semantic properties there are), I see no responsible way of saying what, in general, formality amounts to. The notion of formality will thus have to remain intuitive and metaphoric, at least for present purposes: formal operations apply in terms of the, as it were, 'shapes' of the objects in their domains.'[33]

Here is the consequence of this formality condition for the intensional property of the *content* of a mental state. Content is a *semantic* notion in the sense that we can distinguish between the two thoughts (i) 'that John is tired' and (ii) 'that Sarah is elated' in terms of their content or 'aboutness' (reference, meaning, truth conditions). But there is, says Fodor, another and *non-semantic* property of mental states, which he calls *relation* – the relation that the subject having the thought bears to his or her representation of the content. For example 'Fred thinks that Sarah is elated' and 'Fred hopes/pretends/doubts/fears that Sarah is elated' all have the same content (Sarah being elated) but in each case Fred's mental orientation or relation to the content is different. (This is very similar to the notion of a 'propositional attitude' – all these verbs are called verbs of propositional attitude following Bertrand Russell's usage.) Content, as it were, points to an extension in the world; relation has nothing to do with the world at all. But the formality condition implies more, says Fodor, than the fact that it is not only in terms of semantic content that mental states are individuated but also in terms of their expressing certain relations to formal representations. The condition entails a new way of regarding content as a *replacement* for the semantic, 'aboutness' way: as fixed by the subject's relation to his formal representations of the world *alone*. Different extensions may result in different relations to representations but in individuating the content of mental states their extensions can be bracketed off.[34] As Fodor puts it:

> the computational theory of the mind requires that two thoughts can be distinct in content only if they can be identified with relations to formally distinct representations. More generally: fix the subject and the relation, and then mental states can be. . . distinct only if the representations which constitute their objects are formally distinct.[35]

Fodor goes on to argue from this that the semantic content of mental states is really none of the business of cognitive psychology, whose aim should be to examine relations (computationally construed) to representations. That is, the nature of the relation of a mental system (man or machine) to the extensions of its intensions, indeed whether there *are* extensions of the intensions, is of no consequence. So we may have a psychology of *belief* but not of *knowledge*: cognitive psychology does not explain beliefs in terms of whether or not they are true (to put it another way: in terms of the organism–environment relationship) but in terms of their formal character. (To reinforce earlier historical comments: Fodor quotes both the greatest associationist, Hume, and the greatest dualist, Descartes, in support of this.)

If Fodor is correct this would automatically render CTM immune from criticism of the kind levelled by Searle and discussed earlier. So he freely admits that a natural language system such as Winograd's SHRDLU which inhabits a block world about which it can answer questions and on which it can act in accordance with commands really does not know what it is talking about because *'about* is a semantic relation'. Indeed it is, and semantic content, as I am paraphrasing here, is the 'aboutness' concept. So on this perspective Searle's conclusion that AI systems understand nothing is beside the point: they do indeed understand nothing in the sense that they do not know what their computations are about – they have no world knowledge – but they do not require real world knowledge to simulate strongly the mental process that we undergo when we have beliefs. This conclusion flows directly from the initial assumption that mental states are individuated by the relations their subjects have to formally defined representations. Fodor calls this position 'rational' psychology and distinguishes it from what he calls 'naturalistic' psychology, which is the psychology that deals with organism–environment relationships. But why can't psychology be a bit of both? In the main body of the paper Fodor gives the arguments why this 'bland and ecumenical' conclusion will not work: psychology can *only* be 'rational'.

The argument runs thus. First, it is in intensional not extensional contexts that we are able to predict what people will do on the basis of a characterisation of their state of mind. More jargon: intensional characterisations happen in *opaque* contexts, meaning that they carry no implications about the existence or nature of an extension for the intensional object. Therefore mythological objects like unicorns or Santa Claus can occur as objects of verbs of propositional attitude in such contexts. In *transparent* contexts, on the other hand, we assume that there is an extension and then characterise it. For example 'It is true of the one-horned horse that people believe it lives in the forest' shows the use of a verb of propositional attitude in a transparent context because the existence of the animal is assumed. Fodor uses the following example to make the point about prediction: from the *opaque* context 'John wants to meet the girl next door' nothing is assumed about whether there is such a creature or whether it is female, but we can predict from this characterisation what John will do (for example, exhibit next-door-directed behaviour at the very least). But from the *transparent* context 'It is true of the girl next door that John wants to meet her' we may well be able to predict nothing about John's behaviour because, for one thing, he may not know that this girl he has been trying to meet for so long has just moved in next door.

But the conclusion that only in non-extensional, *opaque* contexts can we predict behaviour on the basis of state of mind cannot be drawn so simply because, as Fodor points out, there are some *semantic* conditions for the opaque identification of mental states. This is because of the existence of certain problem cases for which we have to differentiate between thoughts in terms of things to which they refer, not merely in terms of their computational nature. Fodor gives this example: 'Sam feels faint and Misha knows he [Sam] does. Then what's running through Misha's head may be "he feels faint". Suppose too that Misha feels faint and Alfred knows he [Misha] does. Then what's running through Alfred's head, too, may be "he feels faint".'[36] The point being that although Misha and Alfred are having the same thought in opaque, computational terms they are not having the same thought in fact because the thoughts have different referents (Sam for Misha and Misha for Alfred): that is, they are transparently non-identical. In general such problem cases exist because of the indeterminacy of reference in pronouns, in demonstratives (for example, 'this', 'that') and in identical terms with different referents (for example, 'London', England, and 'London', Ontario).

Fodor calls these cases 'semi-transparent', however, because although the mental states are individuated by the semantic property of reference the contexts are intensional on the two standard criteria of existential generalisation and the free substitution of co-referring expressions.[37] Having admitted this, however, Fodor brushes the matter to one side by referring to this semi-transparency as a 'pre-theoretical' and 'intuitive' kind of opacity (part of the 'folk psychology' which the cognitive sciences will sweep away no doubt) as compared with 'full' opacity. He then liberally allows that we should have both kinds (intuitive and full) and then ignores the difference: the fact that in some cases reference does individuate thoughts is merely a 'wrinkle'. He concludes:

> My claim is that, in doing psychology, we want to attribute mental states fully opaquely because it is the fully opaque reading that tells us what the agent has in mind and it is what the agent has in mind that causes his behaviour.[38]

This means that form not content of mental representations is what is of psychological relevance; he does not deny that representations can affect behaviour by virtue of their content but insists that content only differs when form differs. 'Pure' content does not influence behaviour, therefore there *cannot* be a transparent, naturalistic psychology. (In Pylyshyn's terms (pp. 96ff. above) this is like saying that all psychological phenomena are 'cognitively penetrable' by definition.)

How does this conclusion relate to the intensionality as a criterion for the subject–object division? What Fodor is proposing is that intensionality (or the placement of mental states in opaque contexts) is so paradigmatically psychological that the extensionality from which it has traditionally distinguished can be jettisoned. The subject–object condition for mentality should, therefore, be jettisoned also. Indeed his treatment of the intensionality condition is ingenious and very radical because he neither agonises over whether purely computational devices could or could not have intensionality, nor says 'of course they do and that makes them just like human minds in this most important respect, so therefore AI is a humanising influence upon psychology'. Rather, he proposes that what is psychologically important about intensionality is not that it is parasitic upon extensionality but that it can be characterised as a formal process which can stand *apart* from extensionality. If *people's* intensionality exists in relation to extensionality because we have a foothold in the real world (that is, we can have knowledge) then this is not really something that psychology can illuminate: what is important is that there can be intensionality *whether or not* there is this foothold.

Therefore computers need have no real world knowledge, no under-standing and no semantics for them to be mental entities in the only respect that is relevant to us. Is Fodor correct?

I believe that Fodor is incorrect both in believing that his argument results in the conclusion that a purely rational psychology obeying the formality condition is the only kind possible and in his assumption that what has resulted from the formality condition is indeed *psychology*. If Fodor *is* wrong then the defence of CTM collapses.

Where the argument appears to fall down is in its treatment of cases of the Sam−Misha−Alfred kind as wrinkles which show nothing more interesting than the inferiority of 'aboriginal, uncorrupted, pre-theoretic intuitions'[39] relative to properly worked-out bits of con-ceptual analysis. Fodor himself admits that thoughts whose inten-sions are characterised by pronouns, demonstratives and multi-referential terms have to be individuated by their real world reference. But is this not actually rather a large sub-set of our conceptual apparatus – too large to be brushed aside? The example that Fodor gives of multi-referential terms is safely fictional: he imagines that there are two 'Lakes Erie', the one we all know and another one somewhere else, and admits that two cases of the thought 'Lake Erie is wet' about the two different lakes would be two different thoughts (that is, transparently, semantically different). But if he allows this, then why not also allow 'John is hungry' about two different Johns to be two different thoughts, likewise 'the table is laid' thought separately about two different tables. Once we allow semi-transparency, we have allowed so much that the formality condition appears as an *adjunct* to a semantic content condition for the individuation of thoughts. Therefore the 'bland and ecumenical conclusion' which Fodor sought to avoid looks like being the correct conclusion.

Now to the important claim that only the fully opaque reading tells us what the agent has in mind and that this is what causes the agent's behaviour. The passage in which Fodor justifies this conclusion treats the Sam−Misha−Alfred example in a very selective way. 'We need', says Fodor, 'some taxonomy according to which Sam and Misha have the same belief in order to explain why it is that they exhibit the same behaviour.'[40] That is, Sam's belief that he feels faint and Misha's belief that *he* (Misha) feels faint. (By 'same behaviour' I assume Fodor means that they both look for chairs and ask for water.) But what has happened to the force of this problem case? The original use of the example was to show that *Alfred* and Misha both have 'he's faint' thoughts with different referents. Surely the fact that they have different referents will cause different behaviours: Misha will fetch a chair and a glass of water for *Sam* and Alfred will fetch them for *Misha*. Of course, the efficacy of the bahaviour is dependent upon the computational 'shape' of their beliefs but the behaviours are different (that is, towards different people) not only because the agents' beliefs are formally different but because their content or 'aboutness' is different.

If we brush away transparency, however 'semi', it is difficult to see how different beliefs are going to become constituted so as to effect different kinds of behaviour. In fact Fodor's acceptance of semi-transparency may be interpreted as a disguised admission that the 'bland and ecumenical conclusion' really was the correct one.

Turning now to Fodor's assessment of his conclusion as opposed to the route by which he reached it, we find the rational psychology which he believes to be the only kind possible, being regarded as a psychology of belief, not a psychology of knowledge. In saying this Fodor places himself in a long dualist tradition within which it is possible to claim that our beliefs would be the same whether or not the world actually existed – it is logically possible that the external world should be an illusion. So, belief can be hived-off from knowledge and intensionality can be hived-off from extensionality and not only leave something that is psychologically nutritious but leave that which is quintessentially psychological. But is this even intelligible? The 'beliefs' which a knowledgeless system possesses are not about anything other than the (intensional) objects that they construct for themselves. On what basis are these free-floating objects of belief ('representations' of nothing) therefore constructed? For the system must get its data by *some* process whether or not it is data of anything understood as separate from itself. The answer, of course, is that the data are given to the knowledgeless system by programmers, with the result that the system has objects of belief that have been, as it were, *put there*.

But if so then we may ask: what is the essential difference between a system of this kind and a book, or a tape recording, or a record? Books too have data and for those books that tell us how to do something (such as science and technology textbooks and cookery books) we may also have something analogous to data structures.

Clearly, though, we do not want to say that one book on our shelf believes that Barnaby Rudge was good but simple-minded and another believes that Chicken Marengo is made with black olives. But books share with computers the property of not representing a world beyond that which is put into them, like (as Fodor himself says) Winograd put a block world into SHRDLU. Now obviously the analogy does not go very far because knowledgeless devices (of the kind that computers are) perform computations on these represen-tations and therefore perform something functionally analogous to intellectual operations. But what is it about the added facility of being computational that turns representations into beliefs? In Fodor's terms, one supposes, the answer would be that computation makes possible relations to representations, thereby the analogy with propositional attitudes in human beings. But in fact the analogy between a computation and a propositional attitude is a very weak one: 'how is one computational operation like a "hope" and another like an "expectation"?' sounds very much like the opening gambit of a riddle. Moreover we do not have beliefs and other propositional attitudes about our *representations* or even about propositions, we have them about the world – the old issue is still there.

So the fact that representations can be manipulated does not make them any less things that have been put there, as words come to be in books by virtue of what authors, publishers and printers do. Indeed the computational rules are put there in the same way that the representations are put there. How do we distinguish between the belief and the representation which is its object in an AI system? As we saw in the first part of the discussion of the coherence condition it is not at all clear that the AI notion of data structures has the conceptual resources to distinguish between representation and the interpreter or believer of the representation, indeed some would claim, Dennett for example, that one of the conceptual strengths of CTM is that as the representations are 'self-understanding' the need for a separate believer is obviated. Be that as it may, there is certainly the problem of how we should conceptualise the intensional objects of the computer's beliefs if the believing and the objects of belief share the property of being data structures put there by programmers.

The conclusion is, I think, that if we can say that knowledgeless computational systems have beliefs then we should also allow that books and similar entities into which we put data have beliefs, because the mental status of computational systems essentially consists in their possession of data. But we do not want to do this because of our sound intuition (no matter how 'pre-theoretical') that believing takes place in relation to extensional objects of beliefs that are regarded, at least in some degree, as separate from the mental act of believing.

For the concept of belief is our way of characterising something which is only in the running for knowledge and which may not attain the status of knowledge. Subtracting the possibility of knowledge from the notion of belief leaves nothing very intelligible. So the significance of my derogatory use of the phrase 'put there' in the above is that for a system that is nothing more than the recipient of data plus rules there is no possibility of its taking up propositional attitudes *to* anything, because the attitude and the object will inevitably be one and the same, or rather will be nothing more than formal data. This argument – perhaps it is more of a stance than an argument – may appear somewhat facile and 'knock-down' but a proposal as radical as Fodor's will be wrong – if it *is* wrong – *radically*, and of course there is no *equation* of status here being drawn between AI systems and books: the point is that if we accept CTM's sufficiency conditions for intensionality then books too must have intensionality in that they represent reality with data. The denial is that we can *give* a system beliefs, emphatically *not* that we could ever build artefacts which could have beliefs; because there would appear to be no logical barriers to the possibility of building systems that could acquire world knowledge. What these systems would have to be like I will discuss in the next section.

Why then we should deny that Fodor's rational psychology is the only possible psychology is that this would not be a psychology at all because you cannot have a psychology of belief without a psychology of knowledge, given that belief – or intensionality in general – is only intelligible for systems which collect their knowledge from *something*. Belief is impossible for a system that has no knowledge. My final task will be to flesh out this rather slogan-like conclusion with a discussion of what it takes for a system to have knowledge.

The subject–object condition: the psychology of knowledge

Knowledge *of an object* must be held *by a subject*, and to give conditions for a system's (man or machine) possessing objectivity we are at the same time giving conditions for subjectivity. (The reason why 'condition' questions are so central in philosophical psychology is that they carry obvious ambiguity between logical conditions and psychological [genetic, mechanistic, performance] conditions.)

We may interpret much of the early part of Kant's *Critique of Pure Reason* as an attempted solution to Hume's problem; certainly it was an attempt to give conditions for objective experience and knowledge. These are of more than historical interest to the psychologist since they characterise those properties of human intelligence that I have been struggling to express here *vis-à-vis* the claims of CTM. Let us take the coherence condition, which may be split into two problems: the problem of selfhood with which we dealt first and the problem of structure. With regard to these, Kant held that the *possibility* of self-consciousness is necessary for objective knowledge (we need obviously not be self-conscious all the time but self-consciousness must necessarily be in the background); and the structuring aspect of intelligence Kant characterised by his theory of categories – a logical system that we apply in experience to produce 'the transcendental unity of apperception'. But possessing some notion of the self as the centre of awareness and some competence in the logic of classes and relations are conditions of the *subject*: there is also a condition that the *world* must fulfil. Although Kant is frequently depicted as an idealist philosopher, he claimed that the data we receive from the world should have a rule-bound connectedness independent of our ordering of the data. For example, we do in fact see a thing where we hear it, where we feel it and where we smell it – and I don't think that it does any great violence to Kant to claim that this is an argument for realism. Kant did not succeed in describing exactly how these three conditions should mesh but he went some way towards demonstrating their interdependence.

Carrying over such concerns into the psychological arena is sometimes known as 'genetic epistemology'[41] or the developmental theory of knowledge. Although the field cannot be precisely defined one may regard it as thriving on the ambiguity that I mentioned above between logical and (genetic) psychological conditions. The originator of genetic epistemology, J. Mark Baldwin (1861–1934),[42] emphasised the realism and the self-consciousness aspects; the greatest practitioner of genetic epistemology, Jean Piaget, emphasised the structuring and categorising of experience above all else. Baldwin proposed that the infant's first step in overcoming adualism (the merging of objectivity and subjectivity) is the discovery that data (though the infant does not know them as such) from the world are *refractory*; for example, that the nipple is not invariably invoked by a baby's turn of the head. So the mismatch between the child's 'conative-affective striving' and data that come to the child from *what is there* will inevitably lead to a failure, or 'embarrassment' as Baldwin called it, and this embarrassment is a necessary condition for objective knowledge. (Baldwin's treatment of the self-consciousness condition will be dealt with under 'social conditions' below.)

Piaget's interest was quite different. His epistemology was constructivist rather than realist (and paradoxically more congenial to CTM for that reason). He was therefore more concerned with how motor concepts ('schemes') can evolve from actions on the world and how they may order sensory data into a logically coherent model of reality, than with mismatches between desires and the refractory real world. Piaget's aims were explicitly Kantian, something which is most clearly seen in his treatment of sensory-motor development as the process whereby the 'categories of reason'[43] are constructed through action, and more implicitly in the importance he placed on the *reversibility* condition for objectivity. For example, action and thought, unlike perception, can be played back without altering anything; so we may turn right to change our point of fixation from table-lamp to the door then left to re-fixate the lamp and nothing has changed. But we cannot reverse the process of seeing the lamp and *un*see it; neither can an observed event (such as the lamp falling off the table) be reversed. In a similar vein Kant argued in the famous 'Second Analogy' section of the *Critique* that a condition for objective experience (more accurately: a necessary mode of application of the categories in experience) is distinguishing between those perceptual sequences that are self-caused – or 'mind-dependent' – and those that are world-caused.[44] Indeed one Kantian commentator[45] has called these self-caused perceptual sequences 'reversible' as contrasted with 'irreversible' world-caused sequences. So Piaget was arguing, after Kant, that *only through action* may we take the first step towards objectivity and that a system which did not acquire data through action ('assimilation and accommodation') could not regard its data as being data *of* anything. Indeed it is well to stress the common ground between Piaget and Baldwin on this matter: Baldwin's desire/datum mismatch may be regarded as a special case of the reversible/irreversible mismatch.

The importance of the claim that knowledge begins through action can hardly be overestimated. It implies, first of all, a *motivated* subject and it implies that innate intellectual functions have to be realised through action – they do not simply grow. Piaget has been known to quote Goethe's Faust in this context: '*Im Anfang war die Tat*' – 'in the beginning was the deed'. And it is not entirely gratuitous to mention that Faust rejected 'word', 'mind' and 'energy' ('Kraft') before deciding on 'deed';[46] for word (data), mind (a system of data structures) and energy (electrical energy) are all possessed (obviously at a *very* metaphorical level) by computational systems *at the outset*.

But is action not possessed by machines also? Yes, but the action of a computer-driven robot is governed by programs, whereas the action that exists 'in the beginning' is hardly more than reflexive – it is a biological phenomenon expressive of an appetitive system. And this action is a consequence of the machine's data base, not of its mode of *access* to data. Although there do not appear to be logical barriers to the possibility of artefacts with motivation and reactivity, organisms may be distinguished from the kind of robot-mechanisms which CTM regards as active on the grounds that organisms come to have knowledge by virtue of their motivational systems and their reactivity, not *vice versa*.

Something else that must be said about the action-bound nature of knowledge acquisition is that it carries implications in its wake about qualitative content – about consciousness and subjectivity. If we accept the Kantian condition of reflexive self-consciousness as a condition for objectivity it is difficult to see how this could ever arise in systems which are not initially conscious *qua* being subject to sensation (that is, without being *self*-conscious). Indeed the notion of action conferring objectivity itself implies that these sensory data are registered, and perhaps the only sense that can be made of 'registered' here is as 'consciously registered'. So there may indeed be systems that have a dual[47] subjectivity without a full, human objectivity – and these 'systems' are young children and animals.[48] Such primitive systems have subjective experiences or conscious mental states and they have them, as T. Nagel has expressed it, 'if and only if there is something that it is like to *be* that organism – something it is like *for* that organism'.[49] And as we have been arguing above: conscious mental states are in Nagel's words again 'not analysable in terms of any explanatory system of functional states and intensional states'.[50]

What I am leading up to is the proposition that qualitative content is not something that exists, as it were, to one side of intellectual functions, as if we were essentially rational creatures who as a consequence of also being organic systems happen to experience hunger pangs when we skip a meal and a state of sensuous tranquillity when we read a lyric poem. Qualitative content (in this context: *sensation*) may have to be present *at the outset*. Again this is not to deny that (non-organic) artefacts cannot have qualitative content as a point of logic, but it is to deny that consciousness – primitive or fully reflexive – is something which emerges simply as a consequence of a high level of computational complexity. [51]

To review: I said that a plausible way of construing the first necessary step in the objectivisation of experience is that derived from Kant wherein a division has to be forged (via three mutually-dependent conditions) between self-caused and world-caused sequences of sensory data. Piaget, and to lesser extent Baldwin, saw this as happening through action. Such action is quite non-intellectual and automatic at the outset but it is nevertheless the royal road to the collection of data which the subject can regard as *its* data of *something*. I then suggested that action may only be an objectivising agent if the data are consciously apprehended and that such relatively non-objective consciousness is quite intelligible. Therefore the possession of qualitative content – no matter how primitive – may be regarded as a condition for objective experience and later knowledge rather than as some emergent property of information-processing or purely functional systems. This is not a formal argument, but is a way of regarding the route to knowledge acquisition that can at least be justified.

Are there not, in turn, conditions for possessing qualitative content? If there are such conditions they would need to be empirical not philosophical. Some may argue that being of organic rather than inorganic material is one condition for this. This vitalist[52] proposal is clearly empirical, although it is very difficult, though not impossible, to conceive how it could be put to the test. The vitalist may also claim that only organisms have spontaneous movement and only organisms are therefore capable of truly spontaneous action. Sometimes we find associated with this the view that all organisms with nervous systems have some qualitative content and that reactivity and motivation (or entelechy)[53] are unintelligible without this. Something similar may be found in the work of Leibniz[54] who was the philosopher above all others to press the epistemological significance of being an organism (that is, an organised entity as opposed to a mere aggregate) in relation to inorganic material, and who tried to state what it is that organic life has that inorganic existence does not ('*vis viva*' or active force). In fact Leibniz failed to produce an intelligible or at least useful characterisation of *vis viva*, but that does not allow us to dismiss vitalism as some kind of mystic gesture.[55] It is indeed wrong to make *ex cathedra* statements to the effect that only brains – that is, organic machines – have the 'causal powers' necessary for thought, as does Searle[56] for example; but it is surely just as wrong to dismiss the thesis out of hand. It is, in fact, a thesis that we become more capable of assessing as our knowledge of brains and of computing machines increases.

I have said little so far about the involvement of language in knowledge. This will now be discussed under what I will call the *social condition*; although there can surely be social life without language, there cannot be human language without social life of a quite particular kind. The knowledge that animals and pre-verbal infants have of such matters as causal regularity and the properties of objects is *not* social knowledge. This is not to deny that it could be shared with others – it may well be – but it is asocial in the sense that it does not involve the making of judgements within a symbol system shared with others. A baby may know that a rattle that becomes invisible to him behind a cushion is still there, but he does not know that 'the rattle is behind the cushion' – this is the adult's gloss. And in a sense the term 'verbalised knowledge' is a solecism because it carries the implication that the knowledge expressed in language is just like the knowledge that cannot be expressed in language (by animals and pre-verbal infants), and that the two only differ in that the medium of one is *action* and the medium of the other is *words*. Language is more than a medium: the person who can make judgements is also sharing a rule-system with others and there is the possibility of both truth and falsehood. (In the non-linguistic creatures there is only the possibility of success and failure, although they may have knowledge ascribed to them by us). Given this the maker of judgements cannot be regarded as a lone centre of consciousness set off against an external world, and the child as knowledge-acquirer cannot be regarded as someone faced with the task of finding out what it all means by himself. Unless other people enter the picture at some point the individual could never come to make judgements of any kind. Despite this, epistemology has most often been conducted as if the problem were how a centre of consciousness could have knowledge of a world out there, as if acquiring knowledge *were* a solitary enterprise.[57] The British empiricist philosophers and their nineteenth century heirs certainly regarded the problem in this light.

But there is another philosophical tradition – in which the necessarily public nature of knowledge is insisted upon. Commentators on Kant differ over whether Kant regarded the categories (the formal rules of thought) as being objective *because they are true for mankind*, or whether he, like his predecessors was essentially concerned with the individual consciousness.[58] Though in *Individuals*,[59] a neo-Kantian inquiry into the conditions of selfhood, P. F. Strawson proposes that the ascription of states of mind to oneself can only take place on the condition that they can be ascribed to others. Moreover, Kant and those influenced by him such as Schopenhauer were by no means solipsists.[60]

With some justification Hegel may be considered as the philosopher of social knowledge *par excellence* because his notion of Geist (often translated as 'absolute mind') ensured that the individual consciousness was only intelligible as part of this collective mind. (However because Hegel did not make his major contribution in epistemology, it is the sociologists of 'knowledge' and those who discuss social reality[61] who have mediated this view into contemporary thought). Despite his emphasis on the individual in moral contexts Nietzsche[62] must be counted among those philosophers who rooted consciousness in social processes and opposed the idealism of the alternative tradition. The pragmatist philosopher C. S. Peirce stressed the shared nature of knowledge by way of the pragmatist's general concern for the exigencies of communication. J. Mark Baldwin's genetic epistemology had an inevitably social nature given his twin influences of pragmatism and Hegel. Baldwin proposed that after infancy knowledge-acquisition involves a dialectic between the child and others more knowledgeable and that a necessary condition of knowledge-acquisition is an initial awareness of the shared nature of meaning or 'commonness', followed by a later awareness of the necessity of this commonness. But perhaps it is the work of Wittgenstein that is most often referred to in this context, because Wittgenstein sought to demonstrate the intimate relation between knowledge and truth. In attempting to say true things we apply common criteria for truth which make items of knowledge inter-subjective – based on agreement resulting from a shared experience. Such agreement is not a sufficient condition for knowledge because individuals may agree to something that is false (for example, the fact that the whole world agrees that the earth is flat does not make it true); but it is a necessary condition because knowledge that cannot by its nature be shared is not knowledge at all.

First, let me say what the implications from this to CTM are *not*. It does not mean that computers must acquire knowledge within a community of other computers, that they must come to possess knowledge by a process of social transmission. These views do not add up to the claim that all knowledge comes to us from other people but, with special regard to Wittgenstein's position, that possession of the concept of truth must implicate some history of social initiation into a *normative* system. Wittgenstein insisted that understanding the point or force of a rule cannot be acquired in isolation from others. And to reprise an earlier discussion, if the rule system is just 'put there' what results is nothing approaching knowledge of a rule. Again, we may ask what *are* the conditions for appreciating the force of a rule? David Hamlyn[63] has suggested that some prior concept of a person must be involved, and indeed the experience of being treated as a person is necessary before any understanding of a social rule is possible. Whether or not Hamlyn is right about this, the fact remains that it is difficult to see how knowledge could be attributed to a system whose rules were just put there, which could not know when it was following a rule or what it is to follow a rule or to share an item of knowledge with another.

The implication from this leads beyond CTM to any kind of cognitive psychology that sees its task as 'finding out how the brain works' without reference to the social framework within which the possessor of the brain is functioning. It is not, as Hamlyn says,

> that cognitive functions do not have a basis in the brain, but that the individual's brain is not their only basis. That *must* be so if reference to others is required at some point if full understanding of any one individual's cognitive processes is to be attained.[64]

Moreover a neglect of the social foundations of knowledge will tend to make the problem of consciousness (that is, human, adult consciousness) still more intractable. For such a neglect points us towards the unfortunate notion of consciousness as a personal possession rather than, for want of a better way of putting it, the accessing of a public world, the world as falling under concepts. This point of view draws us outward, as it were, towards that which is known of a world. Of course, consciousness is also subjective experience, but this is a subjectivity that exists in relation to the objective, knowledge-bound, socially corrigible aspect of consciousness; and once we jettison the objective aspect – as we saw with Fodor's argument – we end up with something a-psychological. So emphasising inter-subjective processes in consciousness will tend to result in a *realist* rather than *constructivist* ontology, because any position that relies on the fact of agreement must be similarly reliant upon what there is to agree about – the physical world. It entails that consciousness is as much supported by the external world as by the brain. This question of realism versus constructivism will be discussed in the next chapter in the context of theories of perception.

The computational theory of mind – concluding remarks

There may appear to be something of a reactionary bias in my treatment of CTM, namely, the insistence that the problem of consciousness in all its various guises (qualitative content, objectivity versus subjectivity, awareness of norms, selfhood) is still very much with us, and that CTM is mistaken in assuming that a functional solution is at hand or that consciousness is an irrelevant consideration. My main defence against such a charge is best mounted by simply quoting George Miller who was among those pioneers[65] whose conception of the nature of cognitive functions helped to establish computer modelling as a central enterprise in psychology – and who is hardly likely to be dismissed as a biased witness. In discussing Pylyshyn's proposals he says that AI will remain metaphorical (*pace* Pylyshyn) so long as conscious experience eludes a computational explanation. Miller writes:

> I believe that consciousness is the constitutive problem of psychology. That is to say I am dissatisfied with a psychology that ignores consciousness as I would be with a biology that ignored life or a physics that ignored matter and energy. Since I assume that psychology is a cognitive science, I assume that cognitive science inherits the problem of consciousness.[66]

But what of the view that CTM demonstrates through the successes of AI that the intelligent performance is possible *without* consciousness? Then either we accept that consciousness in human beings can be regarded as an epiphenomenon[67] and a piece of surplus evolutionary baggage, or, as Miller writes elsewhere,

> as it seems more plausible to me – perhaps AI will prove an incomplete theory of cognition, a theory of certain lower-level processing operations that require conscious attention only when they fail.[68]

However these two chapters do tell a very negative story. In Chapter 3 I tried to show how CTM, far from solving the mind–body problem with a brave new paradigm, resurrects all the traditional difficulties of dualism and behaviourism. In Chapter 4 I have argued that CTM manages to be both dualistic and behaviourist because of its neglect of the biological context of intelligence and of the fact that conditions of coherence and subject–object division have to be met if intelligence is to be ascribed to any system; that is, intelligence in the human sense rather than in some loose, metaphorical sense.

None of this, as I said at the outset, is directed against the employment of computers in cognitive psychology to model theories in order to test whether a system of a certain kind could do the job it is claimed to be capable of doing in the way that the theory suggests. It would be foolish in the extreme to disclaim the prodigious usefulness of computers in sharpening and stimulating the theoretical psychology of information-processing and skill. Neither does it deny that artefacts *could* be produced that possess knowledge in the sense we have been discussing. But the negative thrust of these two chapters is, I think, justified in the light of what I hope to have demonstrated as CTM's sophisticated system of corner-cutting, of making psychology run before it can walk and of seeming to do psychology without actually doing it. Indeed AI's typical isolation from flesh and blood subjects (deliberate ambiguity here in the term 'subjects') results in a degree of lightheadedness sufficient for some of its practitioners to consider replacing the rather prosaic term 'artificial intelligence' with 'experimental philosophy' or 'experimental epistemology' or 'epistemics'. But even the more modest(!) term 'theoretical psychology' which has been preferred[69] still suggests a certain delusion of grandeur: AI is not theoretical psychology *itself* but a tool for the disciplining of one aspect of theory construction in cognitive psychology.

Whenever mankind has been profoundly baffled by the mind it has tended to erect analogies to the mental functions that reflect its own state of technological development – wax tablets, hydraulic devices, cameras, telephone exchanges and now computers. The instinct has been to try to make mind intelligible by showing how it is like something else. But perhaps we would do better to accept that it is not *like* anything else and the implication from this, that drawing such analogies is more likely to obscure than reveal. Each new analogy gives us the impression that 'the problem of consciousness' has changed when in fact only the context changes. And for those of you who regard this as a pessimistic and conservative conclusion I would quote again: this time the great surrealist photographer Man Ray. Ray's companion was shocked at a pronouncement from such an iconoclast that 'art never changes, thank goodness'. In reply Ray simply asked whether he thought that *sex* ought to change.

5
Perception

Many of the major problems in epistemology are rooted in our construal of perception. This is because there is a way of regarding perception that virtually guarantees scepticism. The form of the argument is usually that we believe in the existence of an external world which we come to know through sense perception, yet have no independent authority for this information. We never know things 'as they are in themselves', only the sensations to which they give rise. Certainly, we have good reason to distrust sensory information – just take the case of dreams, hallucinations, illusions, distortions brought about by drugs, the constancies (for example, things look smaller when we know they are not) . . . and so on.

But if such assumptions about perception lead to such an unpalatable conclusion should we not radically revise our concept of perception? In particular, should we not examine very carefully this assumption that sensation is a 'medium' between mind and reality and seek good reasons for abandoning some of its implications? My answer to this question is 'yes', and in justifying the answer in the main body of this chapter I will be discussing the theory of direct perception developed by the late James Gibson.[1] Gibson was a psychologist who believed that any general psychological theory of perception will be founded on a philosophical thesis, however implicit, so that bad philosophies of perception lead to bad psychologies of perception. But his work was an exemplary demonstration of the *intertwining* of psychological and philosophical concerns, not simply the dependency of the former on the latter: what we know about perception empirically will influence the concepts we deploy to describe it.

My tactic will be first to sketch briefly why such a radical revision became necessary, then to highlight the status of Gibson's theory of direct perception (TDP) as a hybrid of conceptual analysis and empirical psychology – and none the worse for being such a hybrid. Next, four major forms of objection to TDP will be examined. The first three will be rejected because they arise from various kinds of misunderstanding about the conceptual analysis offered by TDP. But the final one – about the intensionality of perception – will be treated as showing how TDP goes at once too far and not far enough. Some attempt will be made to resolve this difficulty by distinguishing between two kinds of perception, only one of which is covered by TDP. Finally the kind of perception not covered by TDP will be discussed in the context of theories of intellectual development and, more briefly, of subjectivity. In all that follows it will be *visual* perception with which we shall be concerned, whilst assuming that much the same arguments apply to auditory and haptic perception.

Theories of 'the given'

If we do not see objects directly – as the traditional approach assumes we do not – what is it that we do see? One way of regarding the divergences between the various philosophical and psychological theories of perception is as disagreements about the nature of the 'raw material' / 'input' / 'given', out of which meaningful, veridical perceptions are produced. But the fact that they all agree that there is some form of 'given' is more instructive than their differences.

Mainstream philosophical empiricism is based on the assumption that perception begins with sensory impressions or sense data – patches of colour making up a two-dimensional mosaic of sensation, on the basis of which perception of a three-dimensional, stable world perduring through time is built up by associational and inferential processes. There are three immediate problems with this.

1. Let us suppose that these sense data form a series of photographic representations of the visible world, on the retina or on the back of the brain. The mental operations of perception would then consist of giving meaning and coherence to these; of viewing and interpreting them. But how is this to be achieved unless by some kind of inner 'homunculus'? We have already discussed how homunculus theories typically lead to infinite regress.

2. The recording of sense data *as* data about something distinct from the perceiver is not a primitive and primary facility but a highly sophisticated one. To explain: in order for the subject (or indeed the subject's brain – the case is the same however we express it) to record sense data as data, he must be able to cognise something as being independent of the sensations and as giving rise to them. To treat something as a datum implies some notion of its being a datum *about* a physical world, particularly when we are supposed to be treating data as containing 'information' on the basis of which we draw inferences about reality.[2] Consider the assumption that sense data give two-dimensional information: to see the world in two-dimensional terms involves selectively screening-out and discarding cues for three-dimensionality and a construction of a two-dimensional plane or screen on the basis of these selected data.[3] The notion of sense data as being patches of colour on a flat surface probably derives from a habitual construal of perception as a kind of mental graphics. Moreover, the notion of sensation as providing a basis from which inferences about reality can be drawn probably derives from an over-assimilation of some aspects of tactile perception to vision. It makes sense to regard tactile sensations (for example of roughness or softness) as yielding clues to the nature of an object, but as Ryle pointed out, 'sensation' cannot be applied to vision in the same way:[4] we do not have visual sensations 'in' the eyes as we do in the fingers.

3. The third problem with sense-data theories is that if we receive coloured patterns which are more or less degenerate, shifting and meaningless as the 'given' and then *deduce* the character of the world from these premises, why is this deduction so accurate? And how, indeed, is it possible to make the crucial tests of data against reality? That is, if perception is a constructive process out of sensory building-blocks is it not remarkable that – apart from illusions which, after all, typically exist on the page not in the world – this construction *works*. How can we account for the fact that it works 99.99999 % of the time given only degenerate data and associative–inferential processes? We are thus faced with the following alternatives: (i) denying that there are raw data and proposing that there is sufficient structure in the light to specify the nature of the source without the need of mental inferences, or (ii) proposing enormous inferential capacities in the mind/brain to ensure that we construct the real and not something less than it.

(Neisser[5] called the latter 'processing and still more processing'.) In essence, (i) leads to TDP and (ii) to modern computational views of perception.

In the history of psychology there have been some alternatives to the 'sensationist' or 'associationist' viewpoint: principally the close relatives 'phenomenology' and '*Gestalt* theory'. But, as was implied before, these three meta-theories differ among themselves only over how one should regard the given, about what constitutes the sensory raw material. In his monograph *The Psychology of Perception* (see note 2) D. W. Hamlyn argued that *Gestalt* theory shared with sensationism the assumption that there is a level of raw sensory data on the basis of which perceptions were later produced. One theory said it was 'wholes' or *Gestalten* and the other said it was the atoms of conscious sensation – which somehow had to be 'glued' together. Similarly, phenomenologists such as Husserl proposed that the 'given' was a kind of a-semantic field of experience. Such theorising about perception, Hamlyn argued, implied a misunderstanding of the nature of the distinction between sensation and perception. (Although Hamlyn no longer holds such a view on the relation between sensation and perception [personal communication] I am quoting it as a possible thesis.) Sensation is a necessary condition for perception, *not a stage in the process of perception nor a part of it.* This is to say, for perception to take place our sense organs have to be stimulated and this stimulation transduced into neural information. If this did not happen there would be no perception. But perception is not 'having sensations' plus something else – inference, association, judgement or whatever. 'Having sensations' for such theories was something like the most primitive level of consciousness.

There is in this area what may be called a 'linguistic' problem. We want to say that sensation is necessary for perception whilst denying that sensation is an element in the process of perception; and yet not end up with something deeply paradoxical. This is not helped by the fact that the terms 'sense-experience' and 'sensation' are sometimes used interchangeably; when the former suggests some subjective state and the latter suggests a physiological process as sketched above. One can appreciate why Gibson came to use the term 'sensation' less and less frequently as he developed the theory.

The obvious question to ask at this point is: how did we ever get into such a tangle in the first place? One answer, though surely not the only one, might be that it was the doctrine of the soul which, by encouraging the construal of the senses as windows behind which the mind lurked, allowed us to believe that the act of perception and the object of perception were ineluctably separate, though bridgeable by the medium of sensation. On such a view, ontogeny was the opening of the windows and the cleaning of the glass. In this way the mind was not only set apart from nature but was conceived as existing, as it were, logically prior to natural processes.[6] This picture was only seriously questioned when the possibility presented itself that mind could be the product of nature, of physical and social processes. It presented itself by way of evolutionary theory. That is, we came to replace the assumption that reality could more or less correspond to our mental pictures of it, with the view that evolution has produced minds that have access to reality – otherwise what use would a mind be? So if we accept the fact of evolution we accept the fact that the world produced our awareness of it, and, given the assumption necessary to evolutionary theory that what develops is adaptation to the actual physical and social world (not a mental picture), a kind of realism is guaranteed. Therefore, the empiricist idealism that allows the kind of sceptical position with which I opened the chapter is incompatible with evolutionary theory.[7] To return to the doctrine of the soul; accepting evolutionary theory therefore means not only denying a role to God but also means accepting a kind of realism. After all, the greatest exponent of empiricist idealism, George Berkeley, regarded realism as equivalent to blasphemy.

Following from such evolutionary premises then, we have been furnished with a system – a perceptual system – by means of which we have direct access to a material environment that is not dependent upon our awareness of it.

The theory of direct perception (TDP)

It is this picture of the organism evolving a perceptual system through adaptation to its environment – or ecological niche – that Gibson uses to replace what one may call perception as contemplative and passive. In the latter perception is regarded as a process by which a brain receives input resulting in 'an appearance in the theatre of consciousness'[8] of an object and a background. However a TDP perception is an achievement made possible by the continuous adaptation of a perceptual system to an environment in which the organism is active. There may indeed be appearances in the theatre of consciousness but attending to them will tell us little of interest about how perception works.

Gibson contrasts a perceptual system which will 'orient, explore, investigate, adjust, optimise, resonate [that is, respond to light input to which it is 'tuned'] extract, and come to an equilibrium'[9] with what he calls a 'special sense'. 'Special sense' represents the view of sensory reception within a modality that one finds in psychophysics, where input is passively received by the projection area of the brain. A perceptual system, on the other hand, is an integrated hierarchy of organs which are constantly adapting to information in the world: (i) lens, pupil, chamber, retina – one organ, (ii) eye with accommodatory musculature, (iii) two eyes within the head, (iv) eyes in a mobile head, (v) head on a body. These do not record snapshots of reality, but extract persistence by picking up *invariants* in the flux of energy coming from the world. In vision, invariants are properties of the optic array (the structure of the light at the eyes) which do not change when there are changes in point of view and illumination, movement and local deformations. Evolution has designed perceptual systems to record these directly, and if this were not so we would never have achieved perception of an objective world. We will discuss examples of invariants later, but for now we may regard them in the following manner. The perceptual system is constantly moving relative to the environment (even when we try to attain perfect stillness our eyes are making tiny saccades that cannot be voluntarily controlled) and more often than not something is moving and changing in the environment as well. However there are some properties of the 'energy flux', as Gibson calls it, that do not change within a time-span relative to the subject's interest (for example, finding a place to sit down, watching a bird fly), and these are the invariants.

In his book *The Senses Considered as Perceptual Systems*, Gibson characterised this as 'information-pickup' – which led to some misunderstandings because 'information' as in 'information theory' and 'information processing' is normally regarded as a transmission from one point to another. But information in Gibson's sense is not that which is transmitted. It is that which is *available* in the world to be collected by the organism's perceptual system. Therefore the world (including light rays in this), unlike words and pictures for example, does not *convey* information: it *is* information. But in what form does this information exist for us? Surely, like the traditional theories of perception, Gibson must allow that information is present in light rays, and that light rays are nothing if not indirect media. Gibson's answer would be that we must change the way in which impinging light is regarded. For the psychologist of vision, unlike the physicist, light should be regarded as *ambient*, as that which is reflected from the terrestrial world towards a point of sight ('station point') which is ever-changing. Intensity of light is of little interest to the psychologist, only the changing perspectives which present 'structured light'. In other words we should not construe light as carrying stimulus energy for our receptors, but as carrying stimulus information that is already structured by virtue of having been reflected from surfaces in the environment. The optic array has this structure because the environment has this structure.

Much of Gibson's work has been concerned with specifying the nature of optical structure. In his work on the direct perception of what he called 'surface layout' Gibson contrasts his own approach with that which sets itself the problem of specifying how the third dimension (which is 'lost' by the two-dimensional retinal image) is inferred by way of certain 'cues' for depth (linear perspective, apparent size, superimposition, relative motion, accommodation, binocular disparity, etc.). Gibson challenges this assumption by presenting cases in which the optic array directly carries depth information. One of the most celebrated demonstrations that depth is not an abstract inference utilised the notion of *gradients of texture*.[10] The microstructure of the ground specifies distance directly because observers can regard the elements of the texture (for example, tufts of grass, clods of earth) as evenly spaced. (They usually are in the artificial environment as well, for example, the tiles on tiled floors are most often of the same size as one another.) Therefore size variance can be perceived because two objects of the same real size resting on the ground will cover equal amounts of texture despite their different distances from the observer and therefore different 'virtual' sizes. Also, people find it quite easy to bisect stretches of distance (for example, between two receding markers) and far stretches can be matched to near ones despite the fact that the visual angles did not match at all.[11]

Another way in which Gibson studied depth was by artificially 'purifying' the information for depth in the optic array in order to produce a kind of illusion that went 'beyond' reality, rather than 'past' it as do the more frequently studied illusions. In the 'pseudo-tunnel',[12] for example, an array of 36 plastic sheets with centre holes of decreasing size, alternating black and white, are hung one behind another before the observer. When the observer has one eye covered and keeps his head immobile he sees something like an archery target, but when the head is allowed to move and the other eye uncovered the observer sees a cylinder, a solid tunnel along which a ball could be rolled. (Note how different this is from the more standard cases of illusion where the illusion only appears when vision is *restricted* in some way.) No edges are reported. What the observer is doing in this situation, according to Gibson, is not making inferences from a two-dimensional image but directly picking up information specifying a tunnel.

One of the main sources of information that we have about the three-dimensionality and solidity of objects is provided by the fact of their mutual occlusion and disocclusion. Gibson insisted that the facts of occlusion and disocclusion are specified in the light rather than inferred on the basis of 'object concepts' or 'cues for three-dimensionality'. Work by Kaplan[13] is often quoted as evidence for this assertion. Kaplan took a series of movie shots of randomly textured paper, modifying each frame by cutting away thin strips from one of the sheets of paper. The result was then shown as a movie. Although each frame looked like *one* sheet of paper with no visible contours within it, what was visible on the film was one surface moving behind another or, if the film was reversed, out from behind another – a clear edge was visible. Thus progressive deletion of microtexture yields a perception of occlusion and disocclusion.

I hope it is apparent that the active nature of perception is all-important for Gibson; not as being the *result* of action (as for Piaget, see below) but as taking place in the context of action. The perceptual system is part of an 'input–output loop': the observer makes information available by action rather than just receiving it. Many of Gibson's observations specify how this can happen. For example, movement creates a 'flow field' or 'streaming perspective' – the point to which we are headed or from which we are retreating is still, whilst 'outflow' specifies approach and 'inflow' specifies retreat. By this process of 'visual proprioception' (which babies appear to utilise to monitor their own posture)[14] we literally see that and how we are moving. Another example: if one object enlarges relative to others that are still, we see it as 'looming up' towards us. (This is very primitive phylogenetically, for if the magnification of a shadow – virtually 'looming' – is skewed a crab will jump to one side or the other depending on whether the virtual object moved to left or right.)[15] If the whole array expands focally then we see ourselves moving even when we are not.

Now, none of these kinds of stimulus information would be informative if they did not contain invariants because there must be persistence through change. In the previous example, as the observer moves forward the point to which he is moving must be still. The evenness of gradient texture ('equal amounts of texture for equal amounts of terrain') is one of the invariants that enables us to judge size as distance varies in our first example. In shadow-projection experiments,[16] to take another example, the observer sees the projection of a rotating wire Necker cube as a *solid* cube rotating or he may see something that looks like a swing window opening towards him when the slant of a shadow-caster is changed behind the object. It is no easy matter to say what are the invariants here.

The notion of an invariant is Gibson's re-drawing of the notion of constancy – as a property of the environment as opposed to a mental construct: but it is rather like an article of faith within the theory that invariants are necessarily *there* to be picked up. For example, Gibson writes:

> There must be invariants for perceiving the surfaces, their relative layout, and their relative reflectances. They are not yet known, but they almost certainly involve ratios of intensity and colour among parts of the array.[17]

And as Neisser comments 'The claim that they [invariants] exist is the largest promissory note in ecological optics'.[18] It may be seen as an example of Gibson moving from a piece of conceptual analysis about the necessary properties of perception to an empirical hypothesis. But as Neisser goes on to say: 'we can adopt a good many of Gibson's ideas without accepting his claim that *all* visible permanent aspects of the environment are specified by simple invariants'.

A further feature of Gibson's theory (only made explicit in his last book) demands mention – the notion of affordances. An organism would soon succumb if it did not have behavioural knowledge of what its environment allowed it to do, that is, what it *afforded*. Water affords swimming, grass affords walking, openings afford entry, a brink will afford falling off if we are not careful. Gibson was arguing that perceptual systems do not become adapted to such things as lines, angles, planes, and all the other features of geometrical optics and that we must acknowledge this by regarding items in the organism's environment from the organism's point of view. The notion of affordances cannot, however, be divorced from that of the invariant. For to perceive that something affords stepping upon or throwing, Gibson would have to claim, one must be perceiving the invariant specifying the affordance. Therefore the notion of an invariant is itself not strictly a geometrical notion that controlled experimentation of the shadow-projection kind may lay bare, and this does not make it any less 'promissory'.

Although Gibson did not see himself as doing philosophy he saw TDP as bolstering epistemological realism, and indeed made this explicit in an article in a philosophical journal.[19] But those philosophers[20] and psychologists[21] who have discussed these philosophical tendenceis have been pretty unanimous in judging Gibson to have confused conceptual and empirical issues here. And this is indeed so if we regard the arguments for and against realism as dealing exclusively with the nature and function of certain concepts, and TDP as essentially a marshalled set of empirical findings. I believe, however, that TDP's true worth emerges most clearly when we regard it as a piece of conceptual revision backed up by empirical 'considerations'. In addition to this it allows the generation of hard empirical claims about the mechanics of perception.[22]

In regarding TDP in this light one is not thereby denying that it is *possible* for the conceptual/empirical confusion to come about in general theories of perception. Indeed Hamlyn's *Psychology of Perception* clearly demonstrates how such a confusion arose in the case of *Gestalt* theory, as well as with some other theories of perception. The *Gestalt* theorists made claims that were often a mixture of speculative neuro-physiology, philosophy, and genuine psychology (for example, about relational learning and the onto-genetic primitiveness of certain competences). What Wertheimer's 'Laws of *Gestalt* Forms' amounted to was not a set of empirical claims and discoveries about the process of perception but statements of the necessary conditions for *any* veridical perception, for example, that there should be a distinction made between figure and ground. Although, as I hinted above, there is *something* of this way of proceeding in the notion of an invariant (see immediately below) this kind of confusion is not typically found in Gibson's writing. The approach was first to set out general proposals about the nature of perception: what it is we perceive; the way in which sensation should be regarded; the concepts of information, invariance, affordance, along with certain important distinctions such as that between radiant and ambient light. Some of this could be regarded as conceptual analysis or philosophy and some could be regarded as what I called in the first chapter 'competence–characterising' psychology. The evidence for TDP was treated quite separately. And this was not evidence for a series of hypotheses derived tightly from the above generalities; they are better regarded as considerations that make the TDP empirically plausible. Sometimes as in the cases of the pseudo-tunnel, the demonstration of competence in bisecting distances and the Kaplan experiment, the considerations were novel empirical data and sometimes they meant pointing to familiar though unacknowledged facts in order to highlight their significance, such as the still points and streaming perspective in self-movement.[23] In essence, Gibson was saying:

> This is how the process of perception should be regarded, and when it is regarded in this way look at the good sense we can make of these (either familiar or novel) facts about perception.

So there was both conceptual re-analysis and empirical psychology. A theory as ambitious as Gibson's was bound to point in two directions at once.

We can, in fact, be too purist about the conceptual–empirical division. As I said in Chapter 1 all philosophers employ considerations that are more or less empirical; it is only when such 'data' become contentious[24] that they begin to do science. What about Descartes's deployment of empirical considerations *against* realism – some of which are presented at the end of the first paragraph of this chapter?

Objections to TDP

Problem 1: *Inferential processes in perception cannot be disposed of because pickup of information cannot be direct in the way TDP assumes it to be.*

This objection rests on the assumption that we cannot but regard perception as based on certain *correlations* between features of what

Gibson would call the ambient light and features of the distal environmental *layout*. In their detailed critique of TDP Fodor and Pylyshyn[25] call these $S1$ and $S2$ respectively. They interpret Gibson as claiming that $S1$ contains information about $S2$ and conclude:

> To summarise: Gibson has no notion of information over and above the notion of correlation. You can, no doubt, pick up properties of $S1$ and no doubt, some of the properties of $S1$ that you pick up may be correlated with properties of $S2$. But you cannot pick up the property of *being correlated with* $S2$, and it is hard to see how the mere existence of such a correlation could have epistemic consequences unless the correlation is mentally represented, for example, as a premiss in a perceptual inference. We can put it in a nutshell: sensible constraints on visual direct detection make properties of light its natural object. And then the question 'How do you get from an epistemic relation to properties of the light (*viz.* pickup) to an epistemic relation to properties of the layout (*viz.* perception)?' seems to have only one conceivable answer: by inferential mediation, like the Establishment says.[26]

A difficulty with this conclusion hinges on the meaning of 'correlation'. This term only carries sense if it is possible to conceive of the terms of the correlation varying independently, if in fact the variables mean anything taken separately. But how might the structure of the optic array vary without this being related in *principle* to variability in the layout? Similarly, given a light source, what sense can be given to the notion of a layout varying *without* optic array varying in an associated manner? $S1$ and $S2$ are related in principle not correlated empirically; which is rather like saying that one of them cannot be *thought* without thinking the other. To modify an analogy from Hebb: it is like saying that length of a rectangle is 'correlated' with its area when one of the terms in which area is defined is, of course, length.

One obvious objection here is that we can surely talk of empirical correlation between $S1$ and $S2$ here because in illusions and other cases we do not see the world as it really is. If the correlation is not 100 % therefore how can it be called one 'of principle'? True, the case is not as strong as the length/area case because the optic array/layout relationship is not logico-mathematical; nevertheless their relationship is *conceptual*. Other analogies: the concept of a motor car necessarily includes drivability over the face of the earth and the concept of a plant necessarily involves that of growth from seed. The fact that cars sometimes fail to function and that seeds fail to germinate does not affect these conceptual truths. That is to say, it is not our 'good luck' that cars are drivable and that plants grow rather than not. It is not our 'good luck' that we typically see what is real.

It would of course be going too far to claim that the layout/optic array relationship was *wholly* conceptual because if light did not travel in straight lines then the relationship would not exist as it now does. But if that were the case, our notion of veridical vision would have changed so fundamentally that a conceptual shift would have taken place. This is one of my reasons for denying that the $S1/S2$ relationship is an empirical one.

The point I am trying to make here is a relative of one made above about sense data. There we considered the fact that sense data can only be conceived as such if we can also conceive (i) that which they are data *about*, and (ii) they carry information about that for which they are data about. Similarly, for the observer to have some notion (expressed computationally for Fodor and Pylyshyn) of $S1$ – an optic array carrying information about $S2$ which is the layout – he must *already* possess the notion of the layout as it really is, and the notion that the information may be more or less accurate. But how does the observer ever acquire this distinction?

It may be thought that this is a too 'intellectualised' way of regarding the observer's relation to $S1$ and $S2$. But this is the way it has to be, given an inferential model. Indeed Fodor and Pylyshyn do themselves talk, in the above quotation, of an observer's 'epistemic relation to' pickup and the layout, and of the correlation as being represented as a premiss in an inference. But an observer could only have an epistemic relation to pickup *as* pickup and could only mentally represent a correlation between pickup and layout if he could regard pickup as providing information about something real. So to regard $S1$ in the light that Fodor and Pylyshyn wish to do on behalf of what they call the 'establishment theory' is to re-commit establishment theory to something with the status of sense data. Of course, on TDP, pickup is not represented as anything because TDP is an emphatically non-representational theory.

However, it must be admitted that much of the trouble here is caused by the deep ambiguity in Gibson's notion of information. As Gibson says the usual meaning of information is that of knowledge communicated to a receiver, but information for TDP means that which exists in the layout to be picked up. Evolution has tuned perceptual systems to pick up this information, but that which they possess in doing so is not information, not knowledge gained from a source. (We will later discuss how the term may be supplanted by that of 'property'.) But why invite paradoxes in this way? Matters are aggravated through Gibson's tendency to use 'information' in something like the traditional sense (for which Fodor and Pylyshyn quote chapter and verse). In short the term 'information' invites the misconception that TDP can be characterised as a theory of how correlations between $S1$ and $S2$ are picked up – as if $S1$ could give 'information' about $S2$.

However, the matter cannot be left here because the positive face of the theory (the negative face being the opposition to sensory data) has yet to be considered: the claim that invariants must be picked up as a condition for veridical perception. With great thoroughness Fodor and Pylyshyn try to show how unsatisfactory this notion is. The main problem, they claim, is that to say that a condition for veridical perception is that something must remain unchanged in a changing array is tautologous. It is a defining feature of perception that it involves invariance, so this is a logical not an empirical condition for perception. The authors show that defining invariants as (i) ecological properties, (ii) as those properties which lead to lawlike generalisations from instance to instance, (iii) as phenomenological properties, (iv) as 'that to which perceptual systems respond' all fail to establish invariants as having some existence outside a tautology.

How damaging is this? For TDP invariants are posited on the basis of a conceptual analysis of perceptual acts rather than induced from empirical evidence. Given that what arrives at the sense organs is a constantly changing tide of energy, that this does not form a medium of sense data, that no inferential system could construct stability on the basis of indirect sensory data, there must be something in the energy flux that is invariant. Implicitly, an invariant is defined as that which could never be inferred – hence the charge of emptiness. But empty statements do have the advantage of guaranteed truth and empty statements made in a context which has traditionally fostered conceptual confusion and prejudice may serve as important correctives. (For example, the empty statement 'blacks and whites are both human beings' may serve a similar function in the context of another kind of prejudice.)

Let us remember that the notion of an invariant is supposed to be replacing that of 'constancy', which had previously led to theories of how the observer utilises cues to deduce true size, shape, colour, motion etc. from degenerate, ambiguous, fluctuating data constituting the 'virtual'. So in a similar way the positing of these mental constructs (the constancies) was empty: of course there are such things, otherwise we would never see anything. But neither constancy nor invariance theory moves from saying that such entities have to exist because of the nature of perception to the experimental demonstration of their *existence*: they are *a priori* assumptions which direct empirical research. Let me give the following quotation from Gibson in support of this:

> If *invariants* of the energy flux at the receptors of an organism exist, and if these invariants correspond to the permanent properties of the environment, and if they are the basis of the organism's perception of the environment instead of the sensory data on which we have thought it based, then I think there is new support for realism in epistemology as well as for a new theory of perception in psychology.[27]

Such a fundamental assumption, Gibson is saying, has strong implications for epistemology. But this does not make the assumption a point of *logic*.

TDP must allow, I think, that the invariance notion is over-inclusive and elastic[28] in a way that the constancy notion is not. But one wonders how well the computational theory's pivotal concept of 'inference' would stand up to the kind of rigorous analysis that Fodor and Pylyshyn give to 'invariant'. Would it not emerge with a similar kind of 'emptiness' – like many fundamental assumptions?

PROBLEM 2: *Because TDP refuses to posit processes of representation and computation mediating input and brain function (because concepts such as pickup are treated as primitives) it has no resources for explaining how perception actually works, rather than just saying what it is like.*

Many critics[29] have made the point that whatever conceptual advantages TDP may or may not have over the establishment theory it does involve quite a principled agnosticism about what the brain *does* with the structured input – reference to Gibson's behaviourist roots sometimes being made at this point. Gibson does not, after all, include the *brain* as part of the visual system! Presumably this was because he would have regarded a study of the workings of, say, the ocular-motor system as telling him what he already knew in physiological language, and because TDP does not regard brain-processes as determining what is perceived. The brain is treated as a necessary condition for a perceptual system to function; but this mode of functioning can only be revealed by evidence about what perceptions arise out of what observer–environment relationships. This hard stance will not be defended here. But what I will try to do is show how TDP could abandon this purism without abandoning its substantial case against representational accounts of perception.

What Gibson meant by the immediacy of perception was that what mediation there is (light transduced into electrical signals at the sense organs) is of no *psychological* relevance. He said that psychology proceeds at the molar not molecular level,[30] a claim with a similar status to one discussed in Chapter 1 regarding the impossibility of explaining actions by reference to muscle contractions and nerve impulses. And what Gibson tended to do in his last book was to dub questions about neural transduction and the like as matters of 'vision physiology'. However, as Ullman puts it, 'if the extraction of visual information *can* be expounded in terms of psychologically meaningful processes and structures, then it cannot be considered immediate'.[31] To what extent, if any, was Gibson correct in assuming that between direct information pickup and neural processes there was nothing psychologically meaningful?

Gibson writes:

> Direct perception is what one gets from seeing Niagara Falls, say, as distinguished from seeing a picture of it. The latter kind of perception is *mediated*. So when I assert that perception of the environment is direct, I mean that it is not mediated by retinal pictures, *neural* pictures, or *mental* pictures![32]

But the fact that perception is not mediated does not deny the possibility that the competence that produces direct perception may be 'decomposed', that is, investigated by examining the set of conditions for it. What Gibson insisted is that this decomposition should not be into non-conscious mental performances coming between pickup and the neural level. So in terms of the division of types of psychological explanation given in the first chapter Gibson is denying the relevance of performance hypotheses to his empirical characterisations of competence. He is denying that we should say 'perception of *X* is possible because we do *a, b, c* . . . non-consciously'. But the possibility of constructing *genetic* and *mechanistic* models still remains: we may test TDP's characterisations by decomposing its implications into developmental, comparative and physiological models.

As for genetic decomposition, if veridical perception is not a cognitively mediated achievement, then the pickup of information from invariant properties of the array should be present in children young enough to lack anything but the most primitive cognitive capacities. (This will be discussed later.) Moreover Gibson's characterisations of competence provide us with a theory of what develops; specifically, the ability to extract invariance though transformation develops. The work of Eleanor Gibson[33] is, of course, well known in this connection. In the case of mechanistic decomposition, although Gibson excluded the brain from his definition of the perceptual system, the account of the nature of the 'input–output' that TDP offers has strong implications for the kind of neural processing that must be carried out (of course TDP does not deny the necessity of such processing), as well as telling us of what the mechanistic explanation has to be an explanation. Gibson's denial of the performance road need not, therefore, kill curiosity about the determinants of perceptual competence; need not mean that the only data on visual perception that we may discuss must come from studies of intact adults of the kind reviewed in Gibson's books. This is *not*, however to say that TDP is testable in any straightforward manner. Developmentally there is the problem of specifying when a perceptual competence is not being serviced by cognitive (memorial,[34] attentional, learning) competences. In brain research there is the problem of specifying the invariants that the perceptual system is supposed to be picking up. If, as Ullman has persuasively argued, these cannot be clearly delineated the implications for the nature of the neural processing are very uncertain.

On the other hand the kind of decomposition favoured by the computational theory of mind involves the theoretical decomposition of visual input into algorithms[35] or coded procedures – which may in turn be theoretically decomposed into neural processes 'Algorithms' are defined by Ullman, in his presentation of the case against TDP, as including 'processes, representation, and the integration of information'.[36] As we have seen in previous chapters, the algorithm concept is tied to computation, so the example that Ullman gives to justify the necessity of the algorithm level is that of trying to unravel the internal workings of an electronic calculator. Restricting ourselves to studying (i) the rules of arithmetic (supposedly the structure of the optic array) and (ii) the currents and voltages of the components (neural level) will not get us very far without some theory of representation – an account of how arithmetical operations are mapped onto the electronic mechanisms. This representation may, for example, be binary, decimal or in some other code. So even if we want to explain how a person sees Niagara Falls when he is standing before it we require an account of the terms in which the visual input is coded. Ullman gives two further general considerations in favour of the algorithm level:

1. the algorithm level is not immaterial and mentalistic because it is a necessary *language* not a set of intervening mental acts
2. dispensing with the algorithm level means an inevitable underestimation of the complexity of nonconscious processes in perception.

All this hinges on the *analogy* between how a person sees what is in front of him when he is standing with his eyes open and explaining how a calculating machine works, an analogy made possible by the assumption that the former involves representation. But what sense can be given to the claim that perception *must* involve a nonconscious level of representation 'between' the conscious and the neural? It is almost impossible to conceive of thought that is nonrepresentational – but *perception*? We have already discussed the problems with sense data and to an extent sense data theories are the paradigms of representational theories of perception. Additionally, much work needs to be done to distinguish perceptual representation from non-perceptual representation. Then what about point 2 which implies that the intuitive appeal of TDP may do more harm than good by making us underestimate the complexity of perception? But we may ask: What is the nature of this 'complexity'? A supporter of TDP would not deny that perception involves complex processes that are profoundly unamenable to revelation in consciousness, but he would insist that if these processes are not within the perceptual system as defined by Gibson then they are neural processes. In which case, theories couched in algorithm terms must either be theoretical models of the fine-grain deployment of the perceptual system, or they must be theoretical neuro-psychology. In the latter, a particular algorithm would be seen as a piece of shorthand for a set of neural processes. But the great danger inherent in the algorithm approach is the reification of such theoretical models, so that representation of processes within a *theory* becomes representation of visual input within an *organism*.

If the algorithm were reified in this way then not the least of the problems would be that of saying how these abstract codes result in visual experience (a familiar problem with computational theories). How are code and experience related? Certainly the code is not the experience. Another way of putting the same kind of point is by saying that when we see, we do more than succeed in gaining knowledge of what is in front of us: we gain this knowledge by the process of seeing (rather than some other way), that is, by having visual experience. But algorithm theory (in its reified form) deals with coding knowledge into abstract symbols irrespective of how the organism comes to have visual experiences. Now it may be said that Gibson *also* encounters this problem – indeed Hamlyn[37] has said just this – but, as we shall discuss under problem 4, this may be solvable by the placement of TDP within a larger explanatory framework for perception. Unfortunately I am having rather a short way with representation, but as the next chapter is devoted to this issue the matter can be left here.

PROBLEM 3: *Perceptions are hypotheses so they cannot result from the direct pickup of information.*

This position, as developed by Richard Gregory,[38] is that in perception we do not pick up information in Gibson's sense but information in the sense of *evidence* for one percept rather than alternatives. Thus perceptual input does not provide data as in 'sense-data' but as the term 'data' is used in science. Here are some[39] of Gregory's reasons for holding that perception is hypothetical:

1. Perception goes 'beyond' the evidence (for example, I assume the

table on which I am writing has four legs although I cannot at present see any of them. I see a table, not a rectangle of wood.)

2. Perception is *predictive* rather than reactive in so far as it involves skilled performance. It is controlled by an 'internal running model' as experimentation is carried forward on the basis of working models.

3. Perception is often ambiguous, in that the perceptual evidence can be accommodated by more than one percept (for example, the Necker cube, figure/ground alternations, the duck/rabbit figure) just as a set of data may support more than one hypothesis.

4. Perception often involves the extraction of familiar patterns (such as speech) from a mess of background irrelevance; just as (one assumes) the collection of evidence for an hypothesis is guided and focussed by expectations about the nature of possible data.

5. The system is sometimes tricked into mistaking an unfamiliar array for a familiar one (for example, the classic illusions, but also examples like Gibson's pseudo-tunnel). I assume the analogy here is that government by an hypothesis creates, in science, a kind of empirical tunnel vision (no pun intended).

6. Perception is paradoxical as in the case of impossible objects such as the Penrose[40] triangle. That is, we see objects that just *cannot* exist in the way we see them. Gregory regards this as 'Perhaps the most striking evidence for regarding perceptions as hypotheses (rather than selections from the world, as held for example by J. J. and E. J. Gibson) is the case of the impossible object which exists. To give a formal argument: (i) This perception is paradoxical; (ii) No parts of the world can be paradoxical; hence (iii) This perception is not part of the world'.[41] Elsewhere[42] he has criticised TDP mainly on the grounds of developmental implausibility and because of Gibson's description of retinal images as 'fictions'.

In some respects this account of perception has more in common with TDP than with computational theories, despite the fact that the perceptions–as–hypotheses account and the computational account both regard perception as inferential. This is because Gregory does not base his proposal on a metatheory of the nature of *mental processes* but, like Gibson bases much of the argument on what I called above empirical considerations. Also like Gibson, Gregory emphatically rejects sense–data theories in the way that representation theories do not wish to do. But unlike Gibson, Gregory offers no radically new conceptual analysis of the nature of perception over and above his deployment of these empirical considerations. Because of this – as we shall shortly discuss – Gregory must still posit something like sense data to make his account hang together. But before we deal directly with the proposal that perceptions are hypotheses, let us ask whether the six considerations that I have just listed really do argue against TDP:

1. The fact that perception goes beyond the evidence is only another way of saying that the information specifying an object *can* only be partial. It is not merely that to perceive a table I do not *need* to perceive the legs because the flat surface suitable for writing on provides sufficient information: we *never* see an object from all angles. So Gibson would agree with Gregory that perception is a selection: the optical structure is not the structure of the object as we know it to be. But this is a conceptual truth about the relation between perception and knowledge, not a consideration relevant to our choosing one metatheory of perception rather than another.

2. Again Gibson would agree with Gregory that perception is active rather than reactive. Perception is a continuous process in which output from the observer and input from the layout form a loop. However, for TDP, it is only 'predictive' from the perspective of a psychologist watching the perceiver: the perceiver is acting on the world and the fact that action 'runs ahead of' input makes this look like 'prediction' (an inferential process). But it only has the character of prediction if we assume a set of data at time t_1 on which basis we predict new data at time t_2 – something that TDP rejects. It is not prediction from the perspective of the actor–perceiver; this is an intellectual gloss put there by psychologists of perception.

3. Objects and arrays may indeed contain information specifying more than one percept (for example, the pseudo-tunnel), so that in some circumstances we (that is, highly sophisticated visual beings) are able playfully to contemplate the presented alternatives. But it is a long way from accepting this to the position that perception *normally* involves the inferential preference of one percept over others. Gibson's theory of affordance allows for ambiguity and for the possibility of misperceiving affordances (for example the well-known 'visual cliff' experiments of E. J. Gibson) and if there can

be ambiguity, then in creatures with highly developed reflective capacities there can be the deliberate manipulation of this ambiguity. By and large the possibility of ambiguity leaves the proposal that perception is the direct pickup of optical structure untouched.

4. Indeed we *are* highly efficient at sorting the perceptual wheat from the background chaff, but might this not just as well serve as an illustration of direct information pickup? The perceptual system is able, partly by reason of innate priming and partly through learning, to achieve this. If it is relevant to a particular metatheory of perception at all such a capacity would tend to make *less* plausible those accounts that regard perception as the inferential construction of percepts out of degenerate data, because such a view makes the capacity all the more surprising. TDP would say that the structure of the relevant information is different from that of the irrelevant information and that our perceptual systems are tuned to this difference.

5. As I have already said, illusions are either of the type that by-pass reality (such as the Müller–Leyer) or that go beyond reality (the pseudo-tunnel). In the former case all a supporter of TDP needs to say is that the information is insufficient (in the Müller–Leyer the two lines do not actually *end*); in the latter case the information is too pure (that is, the display is arranged so that certain affordances are artificially isolated and highlighted), and in all this it must be remembered that objects and displays that cause illusion are typically things made up by people. Illusions in the natural world that do not result from the nature of the light (for example, oasis illusions are caused by the effect of rising heat on light rays) are very rare indeed.[43]

6. I must confess to being puzzled as to why Gregory takes 'impossible' objects like the Penrose triangle (similarly one may in principle make a model of an Esher drawing) as such strong evidence for his hypothesis theory; and likewise the 'formal argument'. The second premise of the latter (that no part of the world can be paradoxical) is empty because no part of the world can be unparadoxical either, given that being or not being a paradox can only occur as the object of a judgement. Things are not paradoxes in themselves. Similarly who would ever claim (premiss iii) that perceptions (as opposed to information) *were* part of the world? Certainly not Gibson. From the perspective of

TDP items like the Penrose triangle possess what may be called 'anomalous affordances'. But why should we not say that such affordances can be picked up directly like any others? Gibson's supporters have sometimes been accused of protecting their theory from incompatible instances by the habitual glib counter that the example is not 'ecologically valid'. ('If someone now says that [the example] is not "ecologically valid", I think I shall scream' wrote Fodor in one such debate.)[44] That said, a wooden model of an impossible figure is nothing if not ecologically *in*valid!

Let us now turn to the positive face of Gregory's thesis, as distinct from this construed as arguments against TDP. An hypothesis is a supposition or conjecture answerable to evidence, evidence that is either confirming or disconfirming. But what is to count as evidence for a perceptual hypothesis? In some cases we may simply answer 'more perception', as in 'Is it a bird? Is it a plane? No . . . it's Superman'. That is to say, we are sometimes uncertain about what it is we are seeing, and may take steps to enrich the information. Nobody would quarrel with the use of the term 'hypothesis' here. But this is not how Gregory is using the term. Perceptions are hypotheses for Gregory because the perception always goes beyond the data in the way that a scientist deliberately goes beyond his data via an hypothesis to make predictions of the outcome of fresh experiments. But here the evidence cannot be more perception because perceptions are *hypotheses* . . . and so on. This point, along with many other problems for the thesis, has been made by Elizabeth Anscombe.[45] If the evidence cannot be more perception (such as looking under the table to see the legs and meanwhile having the hypothesis that the table has a flat top) then there are two alternative ways of construing 'evidence': (i) as sensory input – light rays to be transduced at the receptors; and (ii) as sense data. The former cannot be evidence because they constitute physical processes, not data about anything. As for the latter, Gregory rightly wants to avoid commitment to sense data, with all the problems they entail.

Three more sceptical points are deserving of mention. First, the other main empirical consideration that Gregory fields is the poss- ibility of ambiguity. In all cases of ambiguity he mentions this is not ambiguity about what the observer believes really to be there (for example, 'Is it *really* a duck or a rabbit?') but, what I called above, a playful, contemplative ambiguity. On the other hand an hypothesis is about what is really the case, and hypotheses necessarily *compete*. That is, although data from one study can be covered by, say, two hypotheses, further experimentation is supposed to decide between them because, if they are genuine hypotheses, reality should not be able to accommodate both. Hypotheses are not, George Kelly and his followers notwithstanding, merely 'construals' which we apply to reality. Second, hypotheses are abstract generalisations about functions and structures, not statements about particulars. Scientists make predictions about empirical events, but these are *in the service of* hypotheses not the hypotheses themselves. Perceptions are invariably concrete however.[46] Third, there are ways of doing justice to the many insights that Gregory's account of perception contains without recourse to the hypothesis model. For example (see point (ii) above) in emphasising that perceptions involve anticipation Gregory is in fact joining forces with Gibson in rejection of the traditional passive–contemplative view of perception. Indeed Neisser has taken the position that Gibson's TDP does not account for how such anticipations can occur (this is one aspect of Gibson's rejection of the cognitive with which we will be dealing next) and has suggested that the well-worn[47] notion of a 'schema' may do the job here. The anticipatory schema at once determines what information will be accepted and directs the pickup of information.

PROBLEM 4: *Perception is intensional, whereas TDP treats it as extensional.*

A well-known example from Anscombe[48] serves to introduce the distinction between perception as an intensional activity and perception as the establishment of an extensional relation between a perceiver and an object. A man goes hunting with his father. During the course of the day he aims his rifle at a dark patch behind some foliage that he assumes to be a stag and fires. The result is tragic because the dark patch was his father. What the hunter perceived intensionally (perceived$_i$) was not what he perceived extensionally (perceived$_e$).[49] Seeing is typically believing and beliefs can be wrong. Now, to the extent that TDP deliberately eschews the cognitive it *cannot* be a complete theory of perception. This lies at the heart of many of the criticisms which have been directed against Gibson's position.

So Gibson has little, if anything, to tell us about perception as believing. For essentially the same reasons his theory is uninformative about perception as having visual experience, and in this respect it shares the difficulties of algorithm theories sketched above. This is because the beliefs involved in perception are infused with experience: the hunter has a visual experience of a deer despite the fact that the experience is extensionally of his father. If, as has been argued along the way in the previous two chapters, we may say that non-perceptual beliefs have a phenomenology then surely we must say that perceptual beliefs have a different, perceptual phenomenology.[50]

In fact, perhaps one reason why sense-data theories of perception have proved so seductive is that they capture the important intuition that perception involves belief and experience. Indeed they do some justice to the difference between perception$_i$ and perception$_e$. This point has been well made by Hintikka,[51] who gives the example of somebody seeing a piece of chalk on a table that also contains a number of other items. There are at least two things one can say about chalk: (i) it is white, (ii) it is the smallest thing on the table. The person sees$_i$ the chalk as white but does not see$_i$ it as the smallest thing on the table. However he sees$_e$ it as both. To talk of the observer's sense-data having the property whiteness but not that of being the smallest captures a valuable intuition about perception. (Though, as Hintikka argues, this 'element of truth' in sense-data theories is not sufficient to justify their reinstatement.)

However it is possible to argue that these objections to TDP can be sustained without necessitating its abandonment. Indeed they show us how to 'purify' the theory in such a way that its novelty and worth emerge in stronger outline. We need theories of perception$_e$ as well as of perception$_i$. Let us begin this purification process by considering three cases of how an individual may relate to an object.

1. 'He must have walked past the tape-recorder because there are his footprints'.
2. 'He must have seen the tape-recorder because he stepped over it'.
3. 'He must have seen the tape-recorder because he started to look for a hidden microphone'.

The context of 1 is clearly extensional. We can substitute any description for 'tape-recorder' (for example, 'John's present') and the sentence's truth value is unchanged. The case of 3 is quite different. The person must have seen the object *as* a tape recorder for his behaviour to make sense, so there is some restriction on what can be substituted. 'John's present' would not do unless we have already established that the subject *believed* the present was a tape-recorder. Case 2 is something of a hybrid. The person must have gained some visual knowledge of the object, at least as three-dimensional and of roughly such-and-such a depth; but he need not have seen it for what it was.

Now let us remove the second clause from the three sentences, putting the full-stop after 'recorder', and take the 'he' in question to refer to a cat. Suppose that we watch the cat approach the tape-recorder, sniff it and then jump over it because it was blocking its path. Later the cat may come and curl up on the object for a nap. Obviously the cat does not perceive the object as a tape-recorder, but the context is not purely extensional either. The case is similar to 2 above. The cat sees the object to be three-dimensional, solid, of sufficient size and strength to support its weight. In what sense then is the cat seeing the object? Some of the properties of the object that the cat sees, such as its three-dimensionality, are not properties which the object has by virtue of its relation to the animal. We may contrast this with properties such as being edible, an escape route, footwear, all of which are defined *vis-à-vis* what the organism requires of the environment.

I will now give a short list of what may be called extensional properties (properties$_e$): fluidity/solidity, touching/not touching, masking/being masked, two-dimensional/three-dimensional, moving in relation to a fixed point/not, supporting X/not. (Note that I am including under properties$_e$ properties in relation to a point of vision, but not to characteristics of the observer's body. Therefore 'providing concealment/shelter' would not be properties$_e$.) Here are some intensional properties (properties$_i$): being throwable, being usable as a weapon, being coins/tables/walls. Properties$_i$ are defined in relation to the interests of the organism and in relation to the conceptual system within which the organism is operating. Now, for properties$_e$ it is a solecism to say that we see them *as being X*: we see them *to be X*. Thus we do not see water *as* fluid, we see it *to be* fluid because that is what it is. Similarly we see the water at Niagara Falls *to be* falling not *as* falling. So in describing the cat example we may say that the cat perceives$_e$ the property$_e$ of being solid and three-dimensional and perceives$_i$ that the top of the tape recorder has the property$_i$ of being a suitable place for sleeping. But though we may distinguish perceiving$_i$ from perceiving$_e$ the former is dependent upon the latter.

I cannot, however, pass on without acknowledging a similar distinction that has been drawn by V. C. Aldrich[52] because Aldrich's distinction is not *quite* the same and because I will want to refer to other aspects of Aldrich's taxonomy of types of perception later on. Aldrich writes:

> To make this point clear, I need to introduce a new term to make a new distinction between what I shall call a thing 'in extention' and the thing 'in intention'. 'Extention' here is exclusively a space-term, unlike 'extension' which also has a purely logical use applying to linguistic expressions. A picture, for example, is something in extention and in intention. That is, it is rectangular, framed, too heavy for hanging by a thread. One finds this out by simply perceiving and practically dealing with it. This is the thing in *first order* extention.[53]

Being rectangular is certainly a property$_e$ on the present account (the shape will determine how the cat jumps over it) and so is being framed if this simply means having a material border. But being too heavy to hang by a thread is a property$_i$, because this is relative to the interests of the organism and to its conceptual system. May one perceive$_e$ the property$_e$ of being 'heavier than'? My very tentative answer would be 'yes', – 'tentative' because this may involve *estimation* – but more of such problems later.

To return to Gibson: as we discussed, much trouble has been caused by Gibson's use of the term 'information' because it is very difficult to conceive of information which is *not* relative to the requirements and cognitive state of the individual. (As Hamlyn put it, 'information is only information to or for somebody or something'.)[54] That is, Gibson wrote as if his topic was perceiving$_i$ properties$_i$. But why we need a theory of direct perception is that perceiving$_e$ and perceiving$_i$ are not *contingently* related: perception must be based on an act that is *not* an intellectual construction. That is to say, it was indeed the hunter's father's bad luck that the relation between perception$_e$ and perception$_i$ is not perfect; but it is not our good luck that perception$_e$ and perception$_i$ typically *do* share the same object. This is essentially the same point that I was trying to make above in the context of Fodor and Pylyshyn's argument from 'correlation'.

However, it seems quite clear that Gibson would not have accepted this limitation of TDP to perception$_e$. Indeed, what is the theory of *affordances* other than an attempt to stake a strong territorial claim on perception$_i$ whose principle cases are those involving 'seeing as'? The theory of affordances quite deliberately runs together perception$_e$ and perception$_i$. Again, Gibson writes:

> The important fact about affordances of the environment is that they are in a sense objective, real, physical, unlike values and meanings, which are often supposed to be subjective, phenomenal and mental. But, actually, an affordance is neither an objective property nor a subjective property; it is both if you like.[55]

Gibson was assuming that the conceptual apparatus he had developed to explain the former would explain the latter as well. Fodor and Pylyshyn provide an exhaustive set of arguments as to why it will not.[56]

Before considering theories of perception$_i$ in the next section it would be well to say a little more about perception$_e$, particularly its implications for realism. First the question of self/world dualism. In the previous chapter it was the conceptual or perhaps perceptual$_i$ aspects of this that were examined; indeed it is customary (Kant–Piaget) to treat this as essentially an intellectual construction. But although the *conception* of ourselves as being separate from the world is an intellectual feat one may reasonably say that it is based on the perception$_e$ of the *fact* of division. We do not, after all, perceive ourselves *as* bodies in a three-dimensional space containing objects, we see ourselves *to be* such. Gibson believed (whether rightly or wrongly is an empirical question) that we certainly perceive$_e$ the distinction between the self-caused and world-caused sequences:

> The uncontrollable variation, the one that cannot be reversed by reversing an exploratory movement, is information for an extended event [e.g. a ship sailing downstream][57] just as the invariant that remains after a controllable variation is information for an extended object [e.g. the front of a house][58] (bracketted additions my own).

Gibson goes on to claim that this process of extracting invariants over time may occur at 'higher levels, including those called intellectual' – a claim similar to the Piagetian one – to be discussed later – that perceptual activity 'pre-figures' conception.

In order to understand perception$_e$ a little better let us move 'behind' it (rather than 'beyond' it to perception$_i$) to consider ways of having relations to objects in the environment that are *more* extensional than perception$_e$. In a metaphorical sense one might regard these as modes of perception$_e$. For example: breathing is the perception of oxygen; being knocked down by a cyclist is a way of perceiving her approach; drowning is a way of perceiving an aquatic environment; the evolution of a fur body-covering is the species' perception of a sub-zero milieu. The metaphor at least has a foothold. Perhaps this clarifies my earlier remarks about the way evolutionary theory bolsters realism: perception is not only the contemplation of the 'out-there', it is a way of being affected by the world. Evolution is the history of these effects. So one way of describing the message of TDP is that we should not be over-impressed by the analogy between a perceptual system and a cognitive system, but should bear in mind that in the other direction there is an analogy with a respiratory system.

Perception$_i$ and intelligence

There are at least two ways in which perception$_i$ involves intelligence: (i) because 'perceiving as' involves concepts, and (ii) because perceiving$_i$ things veridically can involve judgements, criteria for accuracy and estimation (as opposed to the appropriateness relevant to perceiving *as*). Only a couple of remarks need to be made about (i). Usually, seeing something as falling under a concept is a quite conservative affair such as seeing the thing off which I eat my meals as a table. But sometimes not: Marcel Duchamp was able to make (some) people see a urinal as a work of art,[59] thus perceptually assimilating it to sculpture. Perhaps the danger with 'perception as' is that of *over-*assimilating it to intelligence. When we see an X as an X (including *some* knowledge of X's structure, functions, potentialities, even history) we do not merely have perception$_e$ of something to which we add what may be called 'cognitive content'. (One difficulty with this kind of bifurcation is that it sets the problem of accounting for the foothold that cognitive content gets on perception$_e$.) Perhaps we can put the point by saying that perception$_i$ is a way of *being aware* of what is presented to us, as opposed to intellectually assessing a representation of reality. This is the 'infusion of belief by experience' which I mentioned earlier. For instance, there is all the difference in the world between intellectually framing the possibility that if certain kinds of modern sculpture may be called works of art what is to prevent the assimilation of this urinal to the category (all this being thought whilst viewing the object) and becoming aware of the urnial as an aesthetic object. I am afraid that the matter of 'qualitative content' rears its rather woolly head whenever this kind of perception$_i$ is discussed.

Now let us turn to the question of perception$_i$ as judgement and return to our cat. As regards perception$_e$, a particular object is no *less* three-dimensional, solid and on the floor for the cat as it is for us. Similarly, if a cat succeeds in perceiving the darker area in the centre of a piece of wood as a hole then its success in doing this is not *inferior* to our own. But this does not imply that the cat's perception of objects as physical entities is the same as our own. The difference may be captured by saying that because the cat's 'object concept' is less developed than our own then its perception$_i$ of objects is inferior. We know that cats have less understanding of such things as the casual relations objects can enter into and of the continuing existence of unperceived objects than does the pre-verbal human infant: roughly, cats reach something like Piaget's sensory-motor stage 4 very quickly in their development and *stay there*. Additionally, just as self-world dualism may be perceived$_e$ (see end of previous section) it also has to be perceived$_i$ That is, perceiving$_i$ the divergence between ourselves and the world must have *some* relation to our conception of our place in the world. One may safely assume that a cat's 'being-in-the-world'[60] is quite different from our own. Considerations such as these force us to approach the question of how perception$_i$ and intelligence are related, as modes of judgement.

I think the best way of getting a handle on the difference between levels of perception$_i$ (as between the cat and the human infant, and the infant and the adult) is by way of the efficiency with which perception$_i$ enables the organism to make judgements about properties$_e$. That properties$_e$ are the objective, physical attributes of objects and layouts does not entail that the only level on which they may be perceived is that of perception$_e$. Recall the problem case of 'being heavier than' and Aldrich's example of 'being too heavy for hanging by a string'. The weight referred to in both cases is a property$_e$ but it has to be assessed by a judgemental act that should be placed under perception$_i$. There are, in short, some properties$_e$ that *can* be perceived$_e$ and some that *must* be perceived$_i$.

Earlier I referred to Aldrich's notion of seeing 'in extention' whilst comparing and contrasting it with our own 'perception$_e$'. This was however, as the quotation showed, a 'first order' extention. By the term 'second order extention' Aldrich intended the cases where we clearly make what I called perceptual$_i$ judgements of properties$_e$. For example if we determine that the picture weighs about such-and-such and is about a foot square then we are seeing the object in second order extention. Aldrich calls this 'observation' and although Aldrich's taxonomy is different from the present one in certain crucial respects[61] this term 'observation'[62] does indeed capture the kind of perception$_i$ that I am trying to sketch out at the moment. In observation we make judgements about properties$_e$ of objects and arrays *other* than by the kind of direct process described by Gibson.

I now wish to illustrate how observation forms a hinge between intelligence and perception by reference to Piaget's theory of the developmental relation between perception and intelligence.[63] We may best appreciate the status of the theory by seeing it as a theory of *observation*, and therefore as not directly contradicting the claims of TDP.

For Piaget, perception and intelligence are both forms of action, and just as actions must be organised within a system to be successful so too must perceptions. Unorganised actions are clumsy or inappropriate; unorganised perceptions are distorting. They are distorting because the longer we fixate on a point in an array the more likely we are to overestimate its size. To counteract this tendency the child must develop a system of perceptual 'auto-regulation' which involves a constant changing of the point of fixation, balancing each fixation against others by decentration, recentration, comparison, transportation, and anticipation (usually referred to collectively as 'decentration'). This kind of auto-regulation is seen as strongly analogous to intellectual auto-regulation as represented by Piaget's model of concrete and formal operational thinking. Yet at the same time Piaget stressed certain basic differences between perception and intelligence; indeed he listed fourteen differences such as the fact that the latter is reversible[64] and the former is always perspectival.[65] So cognition that is perception-like (that is, like unregulated, centrated perception) is invalid cognition; as seen in the young child's cognitive centration on uni-dimensional attributes of displays in conservation experiments. However Piaget was adamant that intelligence does not grow out of the mechanical principles of perceptual auto-regulation. Rather, perception and intelligence share a dependency upon auto-regulation because they are both determined by *sensory-motor* processes. So when we see perceptual auto-regulation developmentally preceding ('pre-figuring' in Piagetian terminology) intellectual auto-regulation this should not lead us to assume that there is some direct lineage ('filiation' in Piaget's terminology) from the former to the latter. They are products of a third factor — action.

Piaget employed the classic illusions and constancies in order to show how decentration leads to increasingly accurate *quantitative estimations*: children decentrate little and therefore make poor constancy estimations and are highly susceptible to the classic illusions. Thus what the theory purports to describe is how regulative activity during perceptions *tunes* our observations towards veridicality and away from distortion.

But in perception$_e$ the situation is quite different. We do not have to *estimate* whether a body is three-dimensional or two-dimensional, rotating or still, changing size or remaining the same size, triangular or square, standing erect or lying flat. (I am deliberately presenting absolute, either/or cases because these are the clearest examples of properties$_e$ that can be perceived$_e$.) In the study of perception$_e$ we always ask whether X is seen *at all*, not how well it is seen. On the other hand the size relation between two lines presented in an illusion-inducing context or that between a near, variable stick and a far, standard stick in a size constancy set-up are also properties$_e$ but they cannot be picked up directly because they are relative and quantitative rather than absolute and qualitative. If, therefore perception$_e$ and perceptual$_i$ judgement, or 'observation', are modes of accessing different kinds of property then Gibson and Piaget by-pass each other in essentials. Or, more crucially for our present purposes, we have an illustration of how the latter is 'intelligent' in a way that the former is not.

In addition to allowing some accommodation to TDP this construal of Piaget's perceptual theory as a theory of observation may also protect it from an objection raised by D. W. Hamlyn.[66] Hamlyn asks how it is that a perception can be corrective on Piaget's theory unless it has access to norms in terms of which it may assess *how something should look*. The correction that Piaget describes is a mechanical process in the sense of not being conceptually mediated;

but the notion of correct ways of seeing things brings with it the notion of standards and rules for the application of concepts. Therefore the system that Piaget describes cannot be corrective but may only make correction possible, and, one assumes, Hamlyn is implying that if perceptual correction does take place this *would* be mediated by concepts.

How might Piaget answer the point that correction must be relative to a standard? I do not think he would have answered it by saying that decentration is simply automatic and that it just 'happens to' the child (indeed there is nothing automatic about children's developing ability to explore figures visually – it becomes *less* automatic with age)[67] because decentration is determined by the sensory-motor system and therefore to that extent primitively intelligent. But how might the process get underway at all unless some – for want of a better word – 'need' for corrective activity were recorded by the auto-regulative system? In the case of action on objects there is no such problem because the actor typically receives immediate feedback as to the success or failure of the action. If, as Hamlyn interprets Piaget as claiming, the perceptual auto-regulative system is that which makes perception possible *at all* then it is difficult to see how Piaget might answer this point.

But perhaps there is another way of regarding Piaget's proposals. Let us suppose that by a process not unlike that which Gibson describes the child begins by picking up the properties$_e$ of objects and arrays, that is, he perceives them without the need for any auto-regulative process. Let us suppose that at the age of, say, three years, the child is superbly skilled at perceiving$_e$ what is there but a very poor observer (perceiver$_i$) of properties$_e$. Let us further suppose that the child's perceptual–cognitive system records mismatches between perception$_e$ and observation in the sense of 'how the array looks'. To illustrate: the child plays with lego bricks and perceives$_e$ that when the bricks are slotted together edge-to-edge they are the same size. However he observes that they often do not *look* the same size. They look different sizes where one moves away from the child. Moreover because we tend to fixate more to the left than the right-hand visual field the child in our example may find himself observing bricks on his left looking a little larger than bricks on his right.[68] Thus the child – or the child's perceptual auto-regulative system – sets about correcting this with the processes described by Piaget. Thus the normative input into the auto-regulative system may not necessarily come from

socially determined concepts but from the world as directly perceived. So in this sense – as I expressed it previously – the process of
decentration is one for *tuning out distortions* in observation, not for
making veridical perception possible at all.

Certainly such a construal of Piaget's model would find no favour
with Piagetians because they *would* wish to maintain that *all* early
perception is distorting in order to allow their assumption that the
child 'constructs' reality through action. But Piagetians are very
unlikely to find data to support such a fundamental thesis from
studies of the relative susceptibility to illusions of children and adults
and of estimation. Such data are relevant to the tuning of a perceptual
system not to its basic access to reality.

We have just been discussing how Piaget's theory of perceptual
development may be restricted to a theory of observation in order to
save it from certain *logical* embarrassments. In a similar way some of
the phenomena which Piaget treats under cognitive development may
be assimilated to perception$_e$ in order for the theory to accommodate
to certain uncomfortable empirical findings. Over the past few years
researchers on the infant's perceptual capacities have unearthed more
and more evidence for the human perceptual system's extensive pre-
adaptation. To refer merely to the principal British work:
T. G. R. Bower's evidence[69] for the perception of constancies by six-
week-old infants is well-known and more recently, studies by
Butterworth,[70] Lee[71] and others have suggested that infants may be
able to perceive self-world relationships directly, and may even
directly perceive the mother's line of visual regard.[72]

For Piaget these are intellectual constructions; for Gibson they are
modes of direct perception. But there need be no conflict between
these two positions so long as Piagetian theory is taken as an account
of the child as knower not as perceiver$_e$. To illustrate how such a
division might operate let us take Bower's equally familiar data on
the development of the object concept in infancy.[73] Bower gives
evidence that very young infants' anticipations of object reappear-
ance are consistent with them having some appreciation of that
object's continuing to exist when unperceived. But this is long before
the infant *acts* in accordance with knowledge of unperceived
existence, before he carries out the appropriate retrievals of objects
that are completely occluded. The account of this phenomenon that
Bower offers is in terms of the younger infant possessing knowledge
of objects on an 'eye-object' level and the older infant having such

knowledge on a 'hand-object' level. But may it not be possible to regard the eye-object level as a manifestation of the competence of a perceptual system in the Gibsonian sense – as perception$_e$ in the present terms – whilst allowing that Piaget's equilibration theory may account for the infant's sensory-motor knowledge? (The term knowledge, I would suggest,[74] is only appropriate in the latter case.) Of course what Piagetians wish to do is give a sensory-motor account of the former as well as the latter.

Up to now we have been principally concerned with the difference between perception$_e$ and perception$_i$ *qua* observation. But what of the more general question of how any kind of perception$_i$ ('perception as' or observation or some other type we may not have considered) can arise? How is it possible that a perceiver should be able to have a mental orientation to objects of perception. Well, given the way that perception$_e$ has been defined this question almost answers itself: if perception$_e$ is direct and immediate then perception$_i$ must be indirect and mediate. In perception$_i$ a psychological distance is established between the world and the perceiver. But what is the nature of this mediation? The following possibilities present themselves. J. Mark Baldwin[75] proposed that the original agent of mediation is memory: once[76] we can 'lift' perceptual content away from the here-and-now we are thereby making it the 'object' of a mental attitude and thus establishing the possibility of perceiving with a mental attitude. In fact there is something of this view in Neisser's proposal, mentioned previously, that successful perception is dependent upon the establishment of anticipatory schemata: anticipation is only the other side of the memory coin. The most explicit statement of a distancing-by-mediation view was made in Werner and Kaplan's thesis[77] that mediation is achieved via the symbol – originally the gesture and later the word. Piaget's notion of the symbolic functions – play symbols, dreaming, drawing, imitation, language – could be adapted to do similar theoretical work. Indeed Piaget's action 'scheme' or sensory-motor concept can itself be construed as an agency for the divorcing of mental orientation and perceptual object that is the hallmark of intensionality.[78] Therefore action may be treated as mediation. Now of course neither Baldwin, Neisser, Werner, Kaplan, nor Piaget were making such proposals in the service of a theory of perception$_i$; my aim has merely been to suggest that we do not lack the conceptual tools for such theorising.

But if a theory of the 'mental' side of perception$_i$ is at least conceivable, what about the 'object' side? We need an account, that is, of what perception$_i$ is directed towards? What is wrong with the answer 'reality', especially in view of our support for TDP? What is wrong is that reality is the object$_e$ not the object$_i$ of perception$_i$. The object$_i$ of perception$_i$ is mental.[79] But just because of this we should not return full circle to the 'establishment' view that this mental object is a *representation* because this would mean brushing aside all the arguments for TDP and also those presented in the previous chapter against Fodor's conception of an intensionality without an extension. A preferable term is one employed by Searle who calls the object$_i$ of perception a *presentation*. The presentation is not something that we construct but it is a referential core towards which we have a propositional attitude or mental orientation just as in standing before an object we have a spatial orientation towards it.

But some would bridle at this comfortable and commonsensical conclusion. Those who would quarrel with a strict division of the kind made here between the perceptual object and the perceptual mental act would tend to belong to the existentialist tradition within which Kierkegaard argued that the object of perception is deeply subjective. Recently A. Hannay has written in support of a more subjective construal of, in his terminology, the 'what' (as opposed to the 'how') of perception. What he is keen to deny is that the perceptual object$_i$ cannot be infused by the viewer's mental orientation. Or in Hannay's terms: 'the visual "what" can be corrupted by the visual "how" '.[80] He presents the following example of how this can be so. A scholar of austerely restricted academic and social habits who spends his time in close intellectual work comes, through the offices of a rich and worldly friend, to experience a wealth of new sights, interests and ways of life. On returning, the scholar finds that his study looks to him a spartan and grey place, a place restricting the development of understanding rather than affording it. It may even appear tawdry. But after a few weeks the study regains its old familiarity. Hannay's conclusion is that the range of properties mentioned (spartan, grey, tawdry, familiar) are not inherent properties of the things and place, but are properties given to them by an individual's mode of perception.

The reference to an 'individual' is important here for this reason. I defined perception$_i$ (*qua* 'perception as')[81] as opposed to perception$_e$ as having to involve a relation between the subject and his/her environment. Thus the perceiving of something as a 'hiding place' is perception$_i$. But – and this is the existentialist theme – in Hannay's example it is the relation between an *individual* and the place that is relevant: a hiding place on the other hand can be perceived as such by *any* member of the same species. Being 'familiar' could mean 'familiar to only one person'. It suggests a *history of experience* which 'hiding place' does not. Being familiar is not an ecological property and it does not rely on the application of criteria: something *feels* familiar. What Hannay is saying therefore is that perception can also be a mode of feeling and feeling dissolves the subject–object dualism of intensionality. He applies the term 'situational' as well as Aldrich's term 'aesthetic' to this. [82]

6
Representation

The problem of representation is: what do we think in? If this question were given to a cross-section of the population I suspect many would say 'words', many 'words and images', some 'images only' and a few 'neither'. Some sensible souls would reject the question as meaningless. Some well-informed souls would refer to the controversy which raged some eighty years ago around the Würzburg functionalists' claim that there are 'imageless thoughts'. In fact, asking people does not get us very far at all.

Let us accept that people's reports of how they think will be very various and inevitably dependent upon how they interpret the question. Nevertheless I think we can consider – if it's not too early in the day – three alternative views of the status of words and images as modes of representation. First, one may see words and images as *media*. That is, they are the means by which the deep, non-conscious, abstract process that is thought itself is relayed to us – they carry the content without being the content and enable conscious monitoring (sometimes called metacognition) of mental processes. But they are emphatically not what we think *in*. A second view is that modes of representation – particularly mental images in this case – are the *objects* of thought. In memory for example we literally re-present an event, person or landscape and make it the object of thought before our mind's eye in lieu of the real thing before the body's eye.

Third, we have the position that words and images *constitute* thought: the medium *is* the message. On this view there is a kind of nonsense that results from taking thought to be something over and above (or 'below' and 'beneath' on the first view) that which we know ourselves to be thinking in. But should we not be very uncomfortable with this? Does it not amount to a refusal of the question? Certainly it is reminiscent of those mock-profound answers that Zen masters give to puzzles:

> Question: 'How do you get a goose out of a bottle without breaking the bottle or killing the goose?'
> Answer: 'There! It's out.'

How can we accept a view like this whilst believing – as psychologists must – that there is something to be *explained* about thought and that there can be empirical theories of representation. In general I will argue that indeed this third position is the most defensible, and that a version of it can be held that is psychologically nutritious.

In this chapter we will begin by dealing with conceptual arguments about what representation is *not*. This will lead to some positive conclusion in line with position three above. In the light of these conclusions two questions will be discussed of immediate concern to cognitive psychologists: (i) what is the status of theories that explain mental processes in terms of subjects' utilisation of mental images? and (ii) is it possible in principle to determine empirically what mode of representation experimental subjects are using?

The case against representational theories of memory

Many would take the view that it is almost a logical truth that in remembering something we represent it. But should this be taken to mean that memory *has* to function by way of the construction of representations *qua* mental pictures of the past which we consult, or representations *qua* physiological traces isomorphic to the event which cause us to have knowledge of the past? Such views have been vigorously criticised by Norman Malcolm in his book *Memory and Mind*.[1]

The arguments Malcolm deploys against these positions are supposed to be those of the later Wittgenstein. Whether or not they are Wittgenstein's arguments is of no concern to us here. There is, in Fodor's phrase, a 'miasma of exegetical dispute' over such questions; and this is best avoided by psychologists.

Let us begin with the view that memory involves knowing about the past by way of mental pictures, a view which we find in various forms throughout the British empiricist tradition from Locke to Russell. In fact it is Russell's version given in *Analysis of Mind* that Malcolm discusses. A memory is an image-copy of a past event; so the content of our memory of where we put the car-keys is our mental image of putting them beside the telephone. But this is obviously not all we need because how do we know that the image which pops into our head is past and is indeed the information about the relevant event? Russell's answer was that the image is the object of a 'propositional attitude' which lends a 'belief-feeling' about the pastness and relevance of the image (that is, that it is not pure imagination).[2] The image itself, however, is tenseless. Other theorists within this tradition such as C. D. Broad said that the image felt 'familiar'.

But how, we may ask, is that an *account* of memory? It stops short just at the point at which something substantial might be said. For what we want to know is: If we are guided by an image that feels familiar, past, fitting, why does it feel so, on what information is the feeling based and how does this enable us to make accurate and confident reports? Russell and Broad would answer: 'Well, it just does. That's a fact about people', but, as Malcolm says, if we are going to be satisfied with stopping the explanation here by a brute appeal to human nature why then were we not satisfied earlier? That is, we say that it is a natural human power to judge the pastness of our images and place them in time; but might we not equally well say that it is a natural human power to give accurate reports about the past more often than not. If we are going to appeal to natural human powers let us do it as soon as the appeal is needed.

The image-copy theorist would reply that the appeal cannot be stopped as soon because without the postulation of an image there is nothing *mentally* present to stand for the past. We might answer the copy theorists in the following way. First we give some examples, as does Malcolm, of memory without the evocation of a mental picture. For example, my wife asks me where the car-keys are and I just say 'by the phone' without needing to call up a mental picture of keys by a telephone. If the copy theorist denies the introspective plausibility of recall without *some* mental picture – no matter how brief and sketchy – then we must say that whether or not the image happens the image is insufficient to carry the memory content in the way the theory demands. Indeed a picture in the head may be of no use to us at all. Why?

As Wittgenstein argued an image, picture, rule, schema 'in the head' has in some way to be *interpreted* if it is going to be of any use to us.[3] Moreover no sensory copy can carry with it the rules for its interpretation, and there can be an infinitude of interpretations of any picture or rule. Even if they arrive with a set of interpretive principles *these* would have to be interpreted and so on. In general the meaning of a mental representation can never be intrinsic to it – a point closely related to the private language argument (see sections 2 and 3). So even if an image of keys lying next to a telephone *did* pop into my head at my wife's question why do I not interpret this as what the telephone table looked like just after I phoned the garage yesterday, or as an image reminding me to pay the telephone bill. Postulating memory images as the raw sensory analogue does not get us very far because we have to explain the nature of the connection that we make between present mental contents and the past: the connection does not lie in the mental content itself.

Malcolm wants the point to be more radical than this. If memory is dependent upon representation in the way that copy theorists have it then it is not even a *true* memory. To give one of Malcolm's illustrations: a man had witnessed a naval engagement during the last war and claimed a memory of it. But when he was asked specific questions about it, such as how many vessels were involved, he referred to a volume of naval history, to a representation. So really we would say that the man had no memory of the battle at all: he was either a fraud or self-deluded. 'But' says Malcolm, 'the point that is so obvious in regard to the physical representation applies with equal force to the mental representation.'[4] We would have to deny the memory was genuine 'if he derived his information entirely from an image together with some peculiar feelings such as "familiarity" or "pastness"'. In the following chapter Malcolm links this kind of mistake to the still more fundamental one of which the later Wittgenstein found his earlier self guilty in *Tractatus*: the view that thought must somehow be *isomorphic* to reality to be true of it. Wittgenstein showed this to be unintelligible, and Malcolm reviews these arguments.

But there is a somewhat different version of the copy-theory of memory which proposes that, rather than remembering through *consulting* images of past events, we remember because images cause remembering; for example when in calling up an image of where the keys are I also remember where I left my pen – next to the telephone. But this is imagery-aided reminding, not memory itself. Memory images do not cause the memory of what they represent. This is because in cases where we do have mental imagery in remembering, the mental image and the memory are one: the former does not cause the latter. This can be most clearly illustrated in the case of mental maps. Some philosophers[5] and psychologists[6] would take the view that we evoke mental images of (say) a terrain in order to answer questions of the kind 'Where is the village of X?' This implies that the information is present *in* the image and that we get it *from* the image. But if we have the information in the image what need is there to obtain it from the image; it is there and we put it there in constructing the image in the first place. The construction of a mental map of the landscape did not cause our ability to recall the location: it was the *embodiment* (Malcolm's word) of the ability. However if we called up a mental image of the landscape in order to plan our route we might thereby be reminded of the existence of the village Y that we had forgotten to visit. In this sense only does imagery cause remembering.

Although we might agree with Malcolm here, it is possible to dispute the nature of the thesis he is showing up as false. As I take it, the view which reveals itself as untenable on Malcolm's analysis is that mental images are the necessary *objects* of memory activity to which we adopt a propositional attitude of an appropriate kind. His arguments seem to have no force against the position that mental images may *embody the act of remembrance*, without being mental objects, in some cases at least. Yet Malcolm feels that he has shown that any view of memory is absurd which explains a memory 'solely in terms of present mental contents',[7] that is, even if the mental content is *not* regarded as the object of some propositional attitude. What such theories all neglect, he says, is the influence of the past. For this reason he rejects Russell's famous proposal that, logically, all our memories could have been caused five minutes ago. This is unintelligible, argues Malcolm, because attributing memories to people requires that we assume many of the claims to be true. But because this objection concerns the criteria on which we attribute mental states to other people all it can tell us is that we should call these 'memory-beliefs' or 'memory' rather than memories. The nature of these criteria do not make it impossible that all memory-beliefs at 4.40 on 22nd July, 1982, could have been produced by some malevolent demon five minutes previously. The fact that in our *concept* of memory there is a non-contingent relationship between memory-claims and the past does not speak against the role of present mental contents in the act of remembering.

What I am saying is that we may still have a theory in which memory is regarded as ultimately dependent upon present mental activity but which denies that this is the dualistic 'image-object plus belief feeling' process of the kind suggested by Russell. What positive thesis does Malcolm himself offer? Essentially Malcolm's position is that we remember things (for example, remember to do things) because of '*past* experience, perception, or training'.[8] Thus the fact that he had been asked to do so and did not have to be reminded by the present mental event of seeing bread before his mind's eye, is a sufficient account of John's remembering to buy a loaf. But *is* it?

Malcolm has a number of examples, dotted throughout the book, of which the following is one. Smith's dinner-date says she can't make it so Smith decides to phone round a number of other friends to see if they will stand-in. Each time he picks up the receiver to call another number he does not recall the event of his original date-cancelling. We might call this a 'dispositional' view of memory on analogy with the dispositional account of mental terms such as 'belief' offered by Ryle.[9] Such an account sees the past as determining present behaviour without the need for any present awareness of the determining event by the agent.

This is certainly a true generalisation about what happens in the stream of everyday behaviour: the past *does* affect present behaviour without such interpositions, but what if events press on the agent in such a way that he finds that he has to recall an event from the past in the sense of bringing it into consciousness? This may happen in the case of a challenge. The telephoner is asked by a friend why he needs another dinner date. He answers. The friend says 'That can't be. She told me she was coming just ten minutes ago – you must be mistaken.' The telephoner says 'I can clearly recall her saying . . .'. Similarly, my wife says that the car-keys are not by the telephone so I think back through my actions after parking the car . . . More will be said in defence of this provisional conclusion later on, but I think we can say that 'in the background' of all memories of the kind that Malcolm discusses there is the *possibility* of present mental occurrences that we may call 'thinking about the past' which are embodied in mental imagery. If the agent could not think about the past in this way then we would say that he was acting under a compulsion, not because of something remembered.

The other use of the representation concept to which Malcolm objects is psychologists' explanation of memory in terms of traces stored in the brain. According to Malcolm such theorists are confused in just the same way as those who explain memory by mental images: 'The physiological theories have merely *transferred* the propositions, which are assumed to constitute the core of memory, *from a mental medium to a neural medium.*'[10] For this reason he deploys much the same arguments and examples in the service of the negative thesis. Should he? I think not, principally because his arguments only work against a very literal construal of the term 'trace'. If 'trace' refers to something like a neurally-coded version of a particular event, more or less isomorphic to the original experience and with a definable brain-locus, then indeed this inherits all the conceptual difficulties of the *mental* picture account. Malcolm is right if we regard the trace as a kind of neural 'picture'. But it is possible to employ the trace concept in a quite non-literal manner in order to capture a conceptual necessity of memory. All we need to agree here is that *some* change must take place within the central nervous system after the event if recall is to be possible (or recall-behaviour in the case of thoughtless conformity with an instruction). We do not have to say what is the *nature* of the change, but we cannot get by without such an assumption and avoid classical dualism.

Moreover if we use 'trace' in this liberal way as meaning something like 'brain-change necessary for memory-performance' then many of the conceptual points that Malcolm makes regarding the inappropriateness of the term 'storage' lose their force. For example, he says that we do not have to assume that something that endures through time is stored any more than we need to say that a woman who 'retains her good looks' has 'stored them'. True, but it is only on the crude 'picture-code' interpretation of 'trace' that we *need* to talk about storage. On the non-literal usage it is the physical basis of retention to which we are referring. Analogously, for the woman in the example to have retained her looks there must be *some* physical indices of remaining beauty.

Given this, the analogy between the mental-picture view of memory and trace-theory breaks down. As Malcolm shows, for a given piece of memory-behaviour it is not necessary that the person should currently be recalling the event at the time of performance (telephone example), although I argued that the possibility of such a mental event should be present in the background. So conscious activity may not occur in the act of remembering. But – again, if we are not classical dualists – it *is* necessary that some brain-process supports recall or recall-behaviour.

It need not be a brain-process of a particular kind but some physiological process *is* necessary where a mental event (that is, conscious act of recall) *is not* necessary.

Some of the arguments that Malcolm deploys against theories of how the brain 'codes' information also trade on a somewhat over-literal construal of the object of criticism. For instance he attacks some well-known proposals of Sutherland,[11] derived from his work on form discrimination in the octopus, regarding the rules and symbols 'used by the brain' in retaining an abstract description of a shape. Such a theory, he says, could not be true because of the kind of entity that the brain is. Brains do not belong to a 'community of speakers' and cannot therefore possess any kind of abstract representational system. In illustration he describes the case of a child who holds out his left hand when told to hold out his right:

> Did the child's brain make a mistake too? Presumably when the child heard the sound 'right', something happened in its brain, and then the child held out its left hand. Was this event in its brain 'correct', or was it 'incorrect'? What nonsense![12]

Either we interpret this broadly Wittgensteinian thought as paralleling the kind of position that was adopted in Chapter 4 regarding the necessary role of social factors and norms in the explanation of cognitive functions or we take it as a fundamentalist view that explanations in terms of brain-function are not merely partial but confused and worthless. It is clear that Malcolm favours the latter.

Malcolm is surely right to point out the dangers of loose metaphorical talk about the brain's 'handling symbols'. But he is surely wrong to dismiss any kind of theorising in which what the brain does with information is described in logico-mathematical language. Here, in fact, we have an exact parallel with the distinction between strong and weak AI and also a comparable degree of ambiguity between theorising about 'the mind' and about the brain. If such a theory is claiming that the brain employs symbols in its operations, that given neural processes are directly translatable as symbols, that there is a *symbolic level of representation*, then Malcolm's objections have some force. But if what is intended is an abstract description of what the brain achieves – as a kind of theoretical neurophysiology – then the objection has no force. A theory of what the brain achieves in a task such as discrimination learning (for example, detection of horizontal and vertical bars as units) will have a bearing on general theories of brain function. That is, if we can show that an animal does *x*, *y*, and *z* in performing task *A* then this will determine how we try to explain the brain-functions that support this: a set of performance 'whats' will have implications for the physiological 'how'. Malcolm claims that no physiological evidence could support or disprove hypotheses of the kind put forward by Sutherland. Again, construed literally, he is correct because a symbol or rule cannot *be* a neural process or set of processes: symbols and rules are in a sense in the researcher's head not that of the octopus. But on a more liberal interpretation all Sutherland is doing is framing, on the basis of behavioural evidence, an abstract description of the job the brain does for the octopus.

The case against natural language representation

It is possible to take the view that the medium of much of our thought is verbal, that such thought is an inner version of public speech. And this seems a trite, even banal, claim: 'that's the problem of thought solved, next problem please.' But what exactly are the *arguments* against such a view? If it could be shown that these arguments are bad ones, although we would not be left with a substantial theory of thought we would have a signpost to the right road.

In his book *The Language of Thought*[13] Fodor develops the position that indeed there is a medium in which we think that may be called a language, but strongly denies that this medium is a *natural* language such as English, German or Swahili. Indeed he dismisses the natural language view of thought out of hand as something that just cannot be taken seriously. Why? For the simple reason that it automatically denies that animals and pre-verbal children think. But, what is wrong with holding a version of the natural language view of thought which states that those creatures who have a natural language think, at least some of the time, *in* this language? This view would be agnostic about how animals and pre-verbal children think. Moreover, the mere fact that we must justifiably attribute 'thought' to verbal and non-verbal creature alike does not argue for the view that there is some medium *common* to both that may be called a 'language of thought'. In Fodor's example the fact that both animals and humans find disjunctive concepts 'harder to master' does not of itself suggest that there must be some common denominator in our representational media. 'We can account for this fact if we assume that the representation system that *they* employ is like the one *we* exploy'.[14] Yes, we can, but *must* we? Disjunctive tasks (for example, to respond to either a square or a triangle but not to both together) may be more difficult than conjunctive tasks (for example, to respond only to both square and triangle together), but this may be because the former task is 'inherently' more difficult in the way that 'find the square root of X' is almost certainly (though not necessarily) more difficult than 'find the square of X' *in systems using totally different representational media.* This is because of the relative computational complexity of the tasks. The fact is, psychologists may hold (i) that tasks are differentially amenable to solution in different representational media such as words or pictures as well as (ii) that just because certain tasks are of similarly relative difficulty in different organisms we do not have to conclude that these organisms are representing the tasks in the same way. As we shall see in the final section of this chapter, some would take an even stronger view, that behavioural data alone can tell us nothing about the representational media employed by organisms.

The main argument that Fodor presents for a language of thought that determines and supports thinking is a developmental one. Its aim is to show that children could not acquire language unless they already possessed a language of thought. However I want only to *mention* this argument now because much of Chapter 7 will be taken up with it. Our present purpose concerns 'what we think in', which *can* be treated as a separate topic from 'what we need to acquire language'.

So let us move on to Fodor's positive characterisation of the language of thought and to his defence of this view against the Wittgensteinian thesis that a 'private language' is inconceivable. As we have already discussed, Fodor's view of thought is computational, so it is not surprising that he parallels natural language (*qua* any language in which an organism communicates with its environment) with a program language and the language of thought with a machine language. Like computers, people need compilers to translate their program language into their language of thought. No compilers are of course needed for the machine language itself because

the machine is *built* to use the machine language . . . its formulae correspond directly to computationally relevant physical states and operations of the machine. The physics of the machine thus guarantees that the sequence of states that it runs through in the course of its computations respect the semantic constraints of formulae in the internal language.[15]

Therefore what it means for us to understand a statement like 'snow is white' is (i) that we have a representation of the English language sufficient to understand the conventions being employed (that is, we must be English speakers) but *additionally* (ii) that we should be so constructed that the sentence is translated into a particular kind of brain-code or formula. (This is of course the exact opposite of the Malcolm view which has just been discussed.) The language of thought is indeed directly translatable into neurological processes as is a computer's machine code into mechanics, with the regularity of both being 'guaranteed' by the physics of the systems.

The language of thought is then a private language in so far as its rules are not fixed by public convention; unless we include the social factors in brain evolution under 'public conventions'. But is this the kind of private language to which Whittgenstein was objecting? Wittgenstein[16] argued that there could not be a sensation-language with terms such as pain which an individual had acquired purely from observation of his own sensations. He might invent a word for a recurring sensation and re-apply it to what he took to be re-occurrences of the sensation but the result would not be a language. The reason is that without some public – broadly behavioural – criteria in terms of which the application of words would be *corrigible* the individual could have no concept of 'following a rule'. Following a rule is something quintessentially public and social. And it cannot be overstressed that Wittgenstein was not talking here about an *empirical* impossibility – some psychological version of a perpetual motion machine – because he meant that without public corrigibility the individual *could* not be following a rule. If there are no rules there can be no language. (It should be evident that the final Malcolm argument we considered is an echo of this.)

Again, Fodor is quite dismissive. He interprets the private language argument as meaning that without public corrigibility the individual 'user' will never *know* whether the terms have been 'coherently applied'. But, he says:

there still may *be* a difference between applying the term coherently and applying it at random. *A fortiori*, it doesn't follow that there isn't any *sense* to claiming that there is a difference between applying the term coherently and applying it at random.[17]

That is to say, the lack of public corrigibility may keep the person in ignorance about his success of application, but nevertheless we can still conceive of him doing more or less well in the private application of his terms to his sensations. Now, as I said above, it is well to avoid the 'miasma of exegetical dispute' about what Wittgenstein really meant; but is this not to misconstrue the argument? Wittgenstein is saying not that the individual has no way of *knowing* if his application is coherent. Rather, the point is that without public criteria there is *nothing to know*, no object of knowledge. 'Coherence' and 'randomness' are terms that simply have no application to criterion-free procedures. The insistent question is 'What would it mean for the person to be correct in his application if he is the only one deciding on the correctness?'

Nevertheless, Fodor may be correct that the private language argument does not nullify the kind of proposals he is making. (In fact he alternates between saying this and saying that the private language argument is just a bad argument). Fodor might say, as I hinted above, that the language of thought *is* public from an evolutionary perspective. For presumably the language of thought was evolved by organism–environment interactions mediated through public conventions, despite the fact that for each individual member of the race it is private *qua* that person's relation to the world. Alternatively, he might say that in terms of his interests the private language argument hinges on a merely terminological issue about the use of the terms 'rule' and 'language'.[18] I do not actually believe that these answer Wittgenstein's point, but for the sake of argument let us say they do.

Fodor now proceeds as follows. He says that for Wittgenstein the matter of coherence in a public language such as English or German is that of maintaining an appropriate relationship between utterances and 'paradigm public situations (which are) facts about the world'.[19] But the successful carrying out of this 'intention' to make one's utterances cohere with the 'facts about the world' is not just a matter of intention alone but also of *beliefs* about the world.[20] Hence, I may have the correct linguistic intention to use term X only in P-situations but have the *wrong beliefs* about what P-situations actually are, in which case there would be little or no coherence between my utterances and the world. However there would be correspondence between my linguistic policies and my beliefs, the point being that even in a *public* language the stable relation is between the usage and the speaker's beliefs about the way the world is, not between the usage and the way the world *actually* is. (In fact we have discussed a version of this 'solipsistic' kind of argument in the second section of Chapter 4 and suggested there that this cannot be so because there must be *some* relation between belief and reality, otherwise there would not be beliefs. But we will assume for now that it *is* acceptable to make this move.)

The notion of belief that Fodor has is quite a standard one: people have propositional attitudes of belief (but also of hope, fear, etc.) towards *propositions*. Propositions are not sentences but that which sentences express and in virtue of which they are true or false. Thus, 'John saw Jane', 'Jane was seen by John', 'Jane was the object of the visual act which John instigated', 'John *sah* Jane' all express the same proposition.

If we express this in the computational theory of mind (CTM), language-of-thought terminology we may say that for any public-language propositional attitude towards proposition *P* 'there will be a corresponding computational relation between the organism and some formula(e) of the internal code such that "*the organism has the propositional attitude iff*[21] *the organism is in that relation*" is nomologically necessary'.[22] Thus what makes a belief possible is a computational process of a *particular* kind: there is a *lawful* relationship between brain computations and beliefs. However Fodor is not saying that the organism's computational relation to formulae of the internal code *causes* the organism's relation to propositions (that is, its belief of them), that one *event* causes another. Rather, these are, what he calls 'contingent event *identities*' (my emphasis) such that: '*having the attitude R to proposition P is contingently identical to being in computational relation C to the formula (or sequence of formulae) F*'.[23]

Although it is already implicit in what has gone before Fodor makes explicit the lawlike nature of these contingent identities. He does this by drawing an analogy between public conventions and private lawlike regularities. We can say that in a public language *S* uses '*a* is *F*' (for example, 'Snow is white') to represent the fact of *a*'s being *F* only when it is the case that the following holds conventionally: *S* believes that *a* is *F* when he assents to '*a* is *F*'. In the private language of thought on the other hand we may say that *S* uses '*a* is *F*' to represent *a*'s being *F* only when the following is nomologically necessary: *S* believes that *a* is *F* when *S* is in computational relation *C* to formula *F*. There is a lawful relationship between believing *X* and being in a certain computational state analogous to the lawful relationship between remembering something and one's brain storing (Malcolm notwithstanding!) information of a certain kind. Fodor regards this as meeting the challenge of the private language argument by showing that the relation between propositional attitudes and linguistic forms *need not be conventional*.

Of course the proposal that beliefs are computational states lies at the heart of CTM; and as I spent all Chapter 4 disputing this claim I will now only mention that such a view neglects the conditions which must be met if we are to say that a system has a propositional attitude to any truth. But there are other problems with Fodor's proposal. These concern the purported 'nomological necessity' of the relation between propositional attitudes and computational states.

Fodor claims that the internal code is 'presumably determined by the innate structure of the nervous system'.[24] How are we to interpret this? In view of the fact that Fodor spends much of the early part of the book arguing against reductionism we must assume that he does not believe that the lawful regularities of thought are guaranteed by causally lawful neurological processes. Presumably Fodor would argue that their neurological instantiation may be highly disjunctive (that is, formula *G* may be represented by structures *a* or *b* or *c* . . .). But, as we have just seen (quote on pp. 185–6 above) he also says that for computing machines the 'formulae correspond directly to computationally relevant physical states and operations of the machine: The physics of the machine thus guarantees that the sequence of states . . . respect the semantic constraints of the formulae in the internal language'. Should he not hold this to be true of the *human* machine as well? If so, this seems to be suggesting something very similar to 'psycho-physical laws' in Davidson's terminology. Indeed, on Fodor's analysis, what else but brain-structures *could* guarantee the regularities of thought, if 'conventions' are not being allowed to do so? So is it the case that if we adopt anomalous monism then we must reject the machine code analogy out of hand? I do not know the answer to this because I am not sufficiently confident about the correct interpretation of Fodor's position on the physical instantiation of human machine codes.

We can leave the question of reductionism to one side here because what is at issue is the relation between such supposed entities as human-machine codes or brain-codes and the possession of propositional attitudes to representations. Fodor makes the assumption that the brain *is* a system of this kind: that it has something strongly analogous to the machine-code of a computer. In fact this is an assumption whose truth Fodor never once calls into question. He merely says that the computer–brain analogy is illuminating when the occasion arises.

A supporter of Fodor might say that indeed the assumption that the brain has such a 'machine-code' may be false but if we abandon it then we abandon the possibility of a cognitive science. But we do not, and to believe that we do is paradoxically to share a mistake with Davidson's 'psychology as philosophy' thesis which we discussed in Chapter 1, because, in order to explain cognitive performances we need *not* start from the premiss that there is a lawful relation between brain states and mental states. Rather, we try to understand the general principles on which the brain functions such that it can support these competences. But at this point Fodor might deploy the arguments regarding the necessity for a language of thought in language acquisition, so we will leave this issue until the next chapter.

Much of the motivation behind the language-of-thought thesis stems from the belief that *sentences* – or more primitive natural language units – cannot be the objects of mental attitudes, and that therefore propositions (that is, abstract, truth-carrying entities) must be. Before passing on to consider what it means for propositions to be the objects of mental attitudes I want to mention one attempt, by H. H. Field,[25] to put natural language sentences where Fodor would put propositions. I do not know whether Field's thesis is philosophically correct, but I think it is well to show that such an analysis is possible.

Field analyses a belief-relation as a composite of two sub-relations: a relation between the individual and a sentence and a relation between the sentence and what it takes for the sentence to be true.[26] Thus he begins with: '*X* believes that *p* iff there is a sentence *S* such that *X* believes *S* and *S* means *p*'. In order for this to encompass the beliefs of non-verbal creatures one can say instead 'sentence or *sentence analogue*' where a sentence analogue is 'some psychological entity which . . . has the kind of meaning or content which sentences have'.[27] Field sees the sentence analogue as possessing a syntax, but a far simpler one than that of the sentence. To place such a program in context, this desire to dispense with such troublesome intensional entities as propositions (principally in the analysis of meaning rather than in that of mental representation) and to translate them away via extensional terms (for example, 'designates' or 'is true') is one shared with a number of other materialist philosophers such as Quine[28] and Davidson.[29]

Such an analysis, Field argues, allows the position that mental representation might be in natural language. The sentences of inner representation are inner tokens[30] of the types of sentences that we normally speak or write. The physical difference from the public tokens is hardly relevant, he says,[31] because if a spoken token of a sentence can be judged to be type-identical to a written token why not the inner and the outer tokens? Interestingly, he suggests that the issue of whether these internal tokens *can* be said to be type-identical to the spoken or written tokens is essentially an empirical matter that concerns the extent to which linguistic development involves conceptual development. That is to ask: is it possible that 'learning a first language involves *extending* an initial representational system to include an isomorphic copy of the language being learned'?[32] If so then the acquisition of new concepts is required and type-identity between internal and external tokens of sentences is possible.[33] As we shall see in Chapter 7, Fodor, on the other hand, would reject the notion that genuine, qualitative, *learning-governed* development takes place at all: linguistic development becomes possible because of a prior 'conceptual system' or language of thought which is no more type-identical to sentences in a natural language than are machine-code rules with programming language rules. Fodor *has* to argue this if he is to sustain the view that beliefs are constituted by relations to brain formulae; because if so these formulae must be independent of, and thus *genetically* independent of natural language development. The way that Fodor would put the matter is: natural language is dependent on the formulae, and these formulae are dependent on nothing in the world, thus they are innate.

Of course, my aim here is not to pit Field against Fodor. My point is that Field's analysis at least shows that the natural language view of mental representation is far from being the patent non-starter that it is under Fodor's treatment. But, what needs to be done to cast doubt upon the position that it is *propositions* that we believe?

Let us take a fairly standard analysis of the concept of belief of the kind offered by Armstrong.[34] First, the Humean theory of belief as conscious occurrence is rejected on the grounds that we believe lots of things that we have never had occasion to think about (for example, that paint is not a refreshing drink). Similarly, it makes sense to say that John believes that his wife is being unfaithful to him despite the fact that John is currently fast asleep. Considerations such as these lead us to be more sympathetic towards a 'dispositional' analysis of belief of the kind offered by Ryle, in which saying that A believes that X is equivalent to saying that A is disposed to assent to X, act in accordance with X, etc., in much the same way that saying glass is brittle implies its disposition to break when struck. But the problem here is that we do *in fact* manifest beliefs consciously, in Hume's sense, without ever speaking or acting in accordance with them. So as the manifestation of belief must be behavioural on the dispositional account this is a problem. Therefore we end up with the position that beliefs are *states* of the individual because in this way we can allow both that people may have beliefs of which they are never, or not currently, aware, and that beliefs may be manifested mentally but not behaviourally.

Can we analyse belief-states as propositions? The first clear problem is that, as Armstrong puts it, 'propositions themselves are nothing'.[35] Although the term 'proposition' originally meant a definitely linguistic entity it is now used to indicate something wholly abstract: 'proposition' is a concept indicating the *absence* of something particular. Well, it may be said, a programme of the Fodor types allows us to reify these concepts as formulae in the brain's machine code – and what is wrong with this? As this brings us back to square one, we must try another approach.

A major difficulty with the belief-states-as-propositions view was indicated by Dennett in an extended review of Fodor's book.[36] The difficulty is that if we reject the dispositional analysis of belief entirely (which Fodor does with a one-sentence joke)[37] then we are led to multiply believed propositions to infinity. To illustrate this problem, it is merely a matter of communicative context and a desire not to be silly which makes it acceptable to say, about a sleeping John, that 'John believes his wife is being unfaithful' but not acceptable to say of him that he believes that the Statue of Liberty is larger than his cat or that a pocket calculator can be damaged through using it as a hammer. But the fact is, despite their silliness as attributions, John *will* assent to these propositions if asked to do so (in a psychology experiment, say), so surely it is an implausible claim that he has to represent as propositions all that can be manifested as conscious occurrences, sentences, or behaviours. Indeed considerations such as these make the 'state' theory of belief itself implausible: *it is not possible for a person to be in an infinity of states anymore than to believe an infinity of propositions.*

A possible way out might be simply to conjoin the Humean and the Rylean analyses and say that beliefs are not states but 'they are dispositions to be subject to certain kinds of conscious occurrence, or to assent to certain questions, or to behave in certain ways'. A 'disposition' is a concept too of course, no less than propositions; but in this case it does not matter. This is because 'disposition' is being used negatively here to exclude the view that beliefs are representations. Perhaps there is something to be said for this; although, because it is only a negative thesis, it has no implications at all for what might be the nature of the cognitive competences that produce these dispositions.

Perhaps one reason why the dispositional analysis is so unpalatable to many is that it fails to give a special status to the mental act of believing X in contrast to merely acting in accordance with a *characterisation* of our behaviour as 'believing X'. It is one thing for our behaviour to fulfil another person's description of it and quite another for us to be in a mental state that *we* characterise in a certain way. Our initial question was, after all, 'What do we think in?' rather than 'How should the competence that underlies belief dispositions be characterised?' So let us return to the analysis of Humean conscious-occurrence type belief as 'having a mental attitude towards a proposition'.

The view we are now discussing was called by J. M. Baldwin[38] in 1902 the 'dyadic relation' theory of propositions: one half of the dyad being the mental attitude and the other half the abstract proposition. Elsewhere[39] I have suggested that extending this to cover modal differences between propositional attitudes (for example, believing something as a necessary truth versus believing something as a contingent fact) may capture important differences between the thinking of young children and that of ourselves. But it is one thing to have an heuristically fertile way of characterising different ways of believing and quite another to use this as a theory of mental *representation*. Describing people as having attitudes to propositions may be a psychological fiction, albeit a useful one in some contexts.

The central problem with the dyadic relation account is how we characterise the attitude as distinct from the proposition. Consider the following dyadic characterisation of a belief: 'War is inevitable' plus belief. What is the mental status of the belief? What possible sense can be made of a belief directed at some linguistically expressible entity when the act of direction has itself no linguistic clothing? Is it like a feeling? But how can we feel in this context independently from the object of the feeling? How could we, for example, distinguish our belief in the proposition that it is going to rain from the thinkable proposition that it is going to rain?

The 'public' face of this problem is that of meaning in speech, and it arises mainly from the fact that one sentence can express many different speech acts.[40] For example 'John will get the job' may be an expression of incredulity, a bald statement of fact, a decision or a joke, and it is tempting to say that a different 'thought' or 'mental attitude' underlies or is being directed at one proposition here. It is tempting to say that the thought is separate from the linguistic expression. But the crucial questions are: 'What would remain if we subtracted the linguistic expression? Would qualitatively different mental attitudes remain?'

In both the mental and the public cases the following point is being made here. Although a sentence does not 'exhaust' a thought, although the thought is always 'richer' than the sentence, a thought cannot be something that can stand on its own without the language in the cases we have been considering; it is not something added to the sentence.[41]

But some would say that Wittgenstein's picture does no justice to our experience of thinking. Do we not often struggle to find the right expression for our thoughts and feel as if the thought is already there and has a shadowy existence which we 'know' when we have translated or failed to translate it into words? But, as Wittgenstein put it, if we insist that we have the thought before finding its expression what could we say to the question 'What did the thought consist in, as it existed before the expression?'[42] This question is unanswerable, implies Wittgenstein, because it can only be seriously posed by someone in the grip of the material metaphor for mental processes that he was opposing.

Wittgenstein's typical approach was not to argue people out of their misleading metaphors but to present them with appropriate metaphors:

If the technique of the game of chess did not exist, I could not intend to play a game of chess. In so far as I do intend the construction of a sentence in advance, that is made possible by the fact that I can speak the language in question.[43]

Indeed maybe an *im*material metaphor is illuminating: the thought that we are trying to express in words cannot exist without the words any more than a hole can exist without its surrounding.

The case against images as mental objects

Obviously, only some of our thought is verbal. We recall melodies and sounds, think about people, things, places and events in such a way that whatever characterisation we wish to give of the experience it is definitely not wholly verbal. (The case of pre-verbal children and animals I shall mention briefly at the end of this section.) Now it hardly seems sensible for psychologists to spend time trying to question people about the nature of these experiences: some people will always swear that they never have 'mental images' and some that they are constantly swamped with them. It all depends on what you mean by a 'mental image'. Of course the private language argument can be applied to attempts at taking introspective data as objective reports about 'how it is with me'. Nevertheless mental imagery is a quintessentially psychological topic,[44] and so the status of the mental image must be a major issue in philosophical psychology.

Much of the philosophical scepticism about mental images is directed against their description as inner pictures which we 'see', and much of it is motivated by the fear that accepting mental images is tantamount to accepting sense data. Perhaps the most discussed sceptical case is that of Ryle[45] which was presented as part of an anti-dualist denial of the separate reality of inner mental occurrences. Essentially Ryle's aims were twofold; (i) to give a 'behavioural' analysis of imagery in such terms as 'erroneously expecting', thereby providing a bridge to overt happenings; and (ii) to show that cases of imaging which did not fit into (i) are misdescriptions of other kinds of performance such as using one's knowledge of how things sound, look, smell or of seeming to see something when one is not seeing it. In the present context it is well to regard the behavioural analysis of imagery in (i) as quite different from Wittgenstein's demand, in the private language argument, for public criteria. The former, which employed by G. H. Mead became known as social behaviourism,[46] is the treatment of the inner as a part of or herald to the outer, rather than being an event 'in its own right'. Thus its placement in a correlative behavioural world supposedly eliminated the need for a dualist analysis of mental life. Wittgenstein, on the other hand, despite also being an opponent of dualism, was concerned primarily with the philosophical 'grammar' of talk about mental images. He was less committed than was Ryle to any thesis of imaging and his analyses lacked the kind of negative implications about the autonomy of the mental that Ryle's possessed.

Much of Ryle's analysis is taken up with showing how the mental image is not a picture. This is also the approach adopted by Dennett[47] in his case against images. Unlike a picture, the argument runs, a 'mental image' has *indeterminate* features. Thus, if we have a mental image of a tiger, there is no sense in asking how many stripes the animal has – unlike the picture case. Both Hannay[48] and Fodor[49] have described the weaknesses of this argument. Its principal weakness is that pictures too can be indeterminate: you can have a blurred photograph of a recognisable tiger whose stripes certainly cannot be counted and you can certainly have an impressionistic or schematic drawing of a tiger of which the same is true. However, Dennett's argument does imply an important generalisation about mental imagery: the image must always be determinate in *some* respect. For example a mental image of a man must be of him standing up or sitting down, running or walking, facing you or turned away, engaged or not engaged in some activity, etc.

It is the very specificity of mental images that, some have argued, makes them hopeless candidates for cognitive media. (It is a specificity which springs from the image's more or less sensory nature.) For how could that which is concrete express an abstract idea? This is the objection made by Berkeley to the Lockeian doctrine that abstract ideas have the form of mental images which resemble that to which they refer. For example we have the abstract idea of 'triangle' because we have stored something that is triangular. But how could one have an *abstract* idea of a triangle, argued Berkeley in his case against all abstract ideas, because such an image must be neither equilateral, nor right-angled, nor isosceles, etc.? However, as Hume later suggested, having an abstract idea could still be the having of a particular image, so that the abstract idea may be analysed as the ability to evoke *an* image. In short, there is no reason why the specific should not express the general. Indeed, as I will argue below in the context of theories of 'propositional' representation, the notion of abstract representation is very difficult to maintain.

When we consider Wittgenstein's[50] scepticism about mental imagery we find some of the points that we encountered in Malcolm's objections to mental 'representation' in general. In discussing Malcolm I suggested that we accept his arguments against the necessity of imaging in memory behaviour and against the view that we 'read off' what we want from an evoked image, whilst insisting that memory of the kind discussed by Malcolm necessarily implies a kind of back-up ability to have a present experience of a past occurrence with a particular qualitative content. Without this the person would be judged to be acting under a compulsion in Malcolm's examples, rather than because of what he had re-membered. Probably Wittgenstein would deny the necessity for such a back-up, but in any case his principal denial was of the possibility of a language derived exclusively from sensation not a denial of representation in memory; and the relation between the two is not at all clear. He did not seem to be denying the fact of imagery experience any more than he was denying that pains are painful. But pains and mental images were not, on Wittgenstein's analysis, mental objects about which a particular description could be either appropriately or inappropriately directed. Introspection fails in this context not because different people describe their mental contents in different ways but because the descriptions and the objects of description are not separate. The case is similar for meaning and intention. The image should not be regarded as something over and above the characterisation of it as we discussed in Chapter 2.[51] So, if one person says that she thinks in images and another says that he does not, what are they disagreeing about? According to Wittgenstein they are not disagreeing about the applications of words to mental content: one is saying in effect 'I think I see pictures when I think' and the other 'I think I do not see pictures when I think'. This tells us something about the deeply problematic nature of the concept of 'thinking' and something about what happens when we stretch it beyond its everyday application (for example, 'think of a number'), but nothing about mental life.

There is no denial here that imaging is a case of mental performance; but there is a denial that this performance involves the having of private mental pictures. 'The mental picture is the picture which is described when someone describes what he imagines':[52] that is, the picture only has a meaning within the context of public intercourse and no private picture exists *at the outset* to be described. Thus if two people compare their images of the same object, for example, San Francisco Bay Bridge seen at night from the south, or by day from the east,[53] then it only makes sense to say that their *descriptions* differ.

So in his scattered comments on mental imagery Wittgenstein was employing philosophers' mental-image talk to highlight the muddles that result from treating the mental (meaning, intention, proposition, understanding, sensation, indefinable or ineffable feelings, images) as something to which we 'point inwards'. This is a Cartesian habit, and it is not how we come to understand the mental. If Wittgenstein is correct then the clear implication for psychology is that representation in mental imagery is essentially parasitic upon public performance, because it cannot be talked about apart from public performance.

But we may question whether Wittgenstein was justified in assimilating images to these other mental phenomena. In the passages in *Philosophical Investigations* in which imagery is mainly discussed Wittgenstein alternated imagery examples with the more familiar pain and intention examples as if they all inspired the same kind of muddle. But do they? In his book *Mental Imagery: A Defence*[54] Hannay suggests that they do not and draws a distinction between what he calls 'mental *process* language' (about what happens in thought, therefore including imaging) and 'mental *activity* language' (where intelligibility is dependent upon behaviour – emotion, sensation, desire). Attention to this distinction may enable us to liberalise the private language argument in its application to mental imagery. (In fact my use of the distinction will be somewhat different from that of Hannay, not radically so but sufficient to make our final conclusions differ).

We can appreciate the distinction between mental process and mental activity language by noting that we may talk of an 'essentially inner process' but not of an 'essentially inner pain or anger, or intention'. In the latter there is no outer version with which to contrast the inner case. The standard form of the private language argument applies in the latter case; and the criteria that we require are behavioural of course (for example, pain behaviour, anger behaviour, action taken). But in the former case we know what an outer version is quite apart from any inner manifestations: the *process* of getting washed, mending a puncture, peeling a banana. Therefore, descriptions of our mental *processes* have a *prima facie* intelligibility that the 'inward pointing to' mental *activities* (as defined above) lacks.

On this basis then we may liberalise the notion of an outer criterion. Only in the case of mental *activities* do we need public *manifestations*; in the mental *process* case it is sufficient that there be public phenomena of the *kind* we mean. This entails, as Hannay puts it, that in imaging, but not in cases such as that of pain, the privacy is 'contingent': the mental image is a species of the genus image, and we know about public images – hence the power of the picture metaphor. But mental activities are not mental species of the genus activity – they are *sui generis*. Hannay takes this to be the 'salvaging' of the mental image;[55] but what has been salvaged? The answer that Hannay appears to give is 'their pictorial property'. That is to say, although Wittgenstein is correct that the describer of his mental images does not read-off characteristics of an inner picture (but that the characterising is at once indissociable from the mental process and constitutive of it) 'if they were not the properties they are [the individual] would not be giving the description he does give of what he imagines'.[56] Imaging is a mental process which has a pictorial property that is not parasitic upon public performance in the way that having pains and intentions and being angry are parasitic.

Another term that ranges over inner and outer – in addition to 'process' – is 'object'. For there is a *prima facie* intelligibility to the claim that my San Francisco Bay Bridge is a mental object that is absent from the claim that this pain in my arm is a mental object. Has the status of the mental image as being a mental object been salvaged from the private language argument? I think not; and the objections already made to the dyadic relation theory of verbal thinking are again relevant. However, rather than reprise these objections I will turn to a radical thesis directed against the view that images are mental objects which, paradoxically, arises within the philosophical tradition against which Ryle's and Wittgenstein's arguments were directed – that of Cartesian dualism. Within this tradition Sartre arrived at much the same point as these theorists, as it were, from the opposite direction. But my main reason for referring to Sartre's *The Psychology of Imagination*[57] at this point is that Sartre offers a good description of what can be salvaged of mental imagery after it has been exposed to the private language argument.

One may regard Sartre's task as that of relating two views of thought within a theory of imagination.[58] There is Brentano's thesis that all thought is 'intentional' – directed to an object (Chapter 2, note 22). There is also the broadly Cartesian view, elaborated mainly by Heidegger, that there is a necessary gap between the conscious being and the material world.[59] Given these, the status of imagination is somewhat paradoxical: *qua* thought it must take an object, but *qua* an imaginative act of consciousness it must be autonomously subjective.[60] Sartre's way of retaining both views whilst accounting for imaging was to deny that imaging is the having of *mental* objects, that rather the object of imagining is the material object imagined – for instance, the object of my imaging Peter (Sartre's example) is *Peter* not my image of him. Sartre also denied that the mental aspect of imaging takes objects because mental images lack just those properties which objects must possess. For an essential feature of our relation to objects, not found in our relation to images, is that we take perspectives on them and characterise them (especially verbally) in a potentially infinite number of ways. This feature of the relation between conscious beings and the world is captured in the 'intensionality' concept.

One may also say that our relation to objects is potentially imaginative in that we can always deny that things are true of them and denial involves the cognitive construction of something unreal (= imagination).[61] This denial works both ways: the very fact of having a mental image of Peter denies that Peter is present; and (another example of Sartre's) the fact of appreciating the music hall artiste's impersonation of Maurice Chevalier means a denial of her female body.

But are there not serious obstacles in the way of holding that the object of imaging is the absent material object? For obviously in some cases there *is* no such object. If we form a mental image of a golden mountain, for example, what is the object of the thought here? No clear answer is forthcoming; although one suggestion open to Sartre is that we must assume that imagining *realities* is at the heart of imagination in a similar way to that in which, some philosophers have claimed, we must assume in developing a theory of meaning that truth-telling rather than lie-telling is the norm. Additionally we may say (as I did in the discussion of Fodor's methodological solipsism in the second section of Chapter 4) that a psychology of belief is impossible without a psychology of knowledge . Be that as it may, the negative part of Sartre's thesis is very clear: there is no mental image in consciousness as a mental object, but this image is a manner of relating to real objects (perception being another manner).

Much of this negative case consists of descriptions of criteria for object-hood that images fail to fulfil. The most important of these is the fact that real objects 'overflow' our perception of them. For as we see something of an object there is always more to see, something unattended to in the act of attention, and something more to be known in the act of knowing.[62] This is not the case in imagining, where having the image both constitutes and exhausts the nature of the image due to the fact that it is we who give what the image contains. (A similar point has already been encountered in Malcolm's comments on mental maps.)[63] Sartre calls this the 'transcendence' of the image, meaning 'the material of the mental image to be already *constituted* as an object for consciousness'[64] (my italics) and it is equivalent to saying that because what we know of our images is all they are, our knowledge of them is in a *transparent* rather than an *opaque* context so we do not have any intensional relation *to them*. The fact of this 'pure' intensionality entails the impossibility of a dyadic mental relation.

But is this phenomenologically true, that is, true of our actual experience of imaging? M. Warnock believes not. Sometimes, she says, we '*treat* the image as a given object of attention', in cases, for example where we 'conjure up an image in order to find out more about the object under consideration (for example, I may deliberately envisage someone in order to find out whether or not he has a moustache)'.[65] But what we are actually doing here is thinking harder, not employing some pictorial aid. Indeed if it were a case of employing a pictorial aid, Malcolm would say, it would not be analysed as a genuine case of remembering. Conjuring up an image is part of the process of remembering, not something separate from it. In fact I think that if we carried out a phenomenological analysis of cases like this we would discover that what we do here is envisage *situations* in which the aspect we are interested in (for instance, moustaches) becomes focal (as in drinking a cup of tea). An initial effort has to be made towards the right kind of image; the image does not merely pop into our heads with the answer. True enough, we are still *treating* the image as an object of attention but the image's transparent nature still prevents it from *being* an object in Sartre's sense.

What then *is* the mental image? Sartre's answer is that it is an *act not* an object. It is, in fact, a form of thought not a mental content: 'The image serves neither as illustration nor support for thought. It is in no way different from thought.'[66] Hannay sees a 'grammatical justification' of the image-as-act thesis in the fact that images 'are indeed qualify*ings* of the world in imagination'.[67] Another way of putting it would be to say that the image is an intension 'caught on the wing'.

Now this radical thesis is intimately associated with the equally radical proposal that thought is defined in terms of its awareness of itself. For Sartre uses the word 'consciousness' as equivalent to 'self-consciousness'.[68] Such a view makes it easier to hold that the image is the act of thinking because it denies that the act of thinking could be the product of some hidden inner process: 'A mental image occurs immediately as an image, because the existence of a psychic phenomenon and the meaning it has for consciousness are identical'.[69] He admits that this commits him to the position that there can be no such entity as 'an unconscious', and later illustrates the point with reference to claims made by analysts of introspection about the symbols or 'schemas' produced in studies of free association. He discusses A. Flach's[70] data: one subject images the word 'compromise' as two men merging into each other, another the word 'Baudelaire' as a patch of blue-green colour like vitriol, another 'proletariat' as a dark, rolling sea . . . 'What we must *not* do here', says Sartre, 'is to say that each schema is a symbol of the subject's unconscious associations, of thoughts unconsciously generated, nor is it the expression of or the support for a thought that further analysis can reveal.' It *is* the thought, or in Sartre's jargon a 'presentifier'.[71]

We need not necessarily follow Sartre in regarding consciousness in this way to agree that the image-as-act thesis does serve as a very thorough denial of the dyadic relation theory of imaging. It also has the advantage of making it possible to conceive how non-verbal creatures (and also young children who may have some verbal communicative competence but are unable to think in natural language)[72] might think 'in images'. If the mental image is the object of a dyadic relation – a picture rather than an 'intension caught on the wing' – then it is impossible that any creature should think in images. This is because pictures – like words – are radically in-determinate in the sense of being open to infinite interpretation, as we discussed above. One of Wittgenstein's examples is that a picture of a man walking uphill may just as well be taken as a picture of a man sliding downhill backwards.[73] Similarly, is our image of Peter an image of the fact that he is cleanshaven, short in stature, caucasian, or what? Pictures do not bring their meaning with them. And if this meaning has to be supplied through the other term of the dyad (the intension *to* the picture) then the image is not that *in* which we think. Paradoxically, because Fodor[74] assumes that the only construal of the mental image that there could be is as a mental picture/object, he uses a version of this very argument to suggest that non-verbal creatures could *not* think in images.

What positive thesis remains?

I will simply list here some of the conclusions towards which these discussions have travelled:

1. Although memory is not achieved via a mental picture, 'back-up' phenomenal access to the original experience is associated with genuine memories.
2. Arguments against the memorial trace only have force when the trace is construed as an isomorphic record of the event. We must assume that the brain is affected in *some* way.
3. Arguments against brain 'coding' only have force against theories which reify the coding as a *level* of representation. Construed as theoretical neurophysiology, reference to coding is unexceptional.
4. Even if we do not allow that the private language argument can be applied against the theory that a brain language or 'language of thought' underlies natural language (and other) thinking, it is not possible to put forward a language of thought theory without making unwarranted and philosophically problematic assumptions about the *lawfulness* of the psycho-physical relation.
5. There are two kinds of problem with the view that thinking is being in computational relations to propositions. It is difficult (i) to regard propositions as being the objects of beliefs, and (ii) to maintain the 'dyadic relation' view of thought that this entails.
6. A dyadic relation theory that takes sentences as the objects of mental attitudes is similarly problematic. Therefore:

7. Some thinking is a natural language process of a non-dyadic kind.
8. A liberalisation of the private language argument enables us to regard imaging as a mental process not parasitic upon social and material manifestation.
9. The non-dyadic view of imaging as an *act* is appropriate. This makes intelligible the view that thinking can take place partially or solely in images.

Where does this land us? I believe it suggests that there are no conceptual barriers against the view that thinking is constituted by natural language and imaging processes. (The possibility of motoric representation has not been considered.)[75] In psychology this would suggest some kind of dual-code theory of representation.[76] So, thus armed, let us turn to two of the most troublesome conceptual problems in the experimental psychology of representation.

Two issues in the psychology of representation

The cognitive penetrability of the mental image

Although cognitive psychologists do not divide themselves neatly into two camps, some of them are definitely, to use Dennett's phrase, 'iconophiles' and some 'iconophobes'.[77] S. M. Kosslyn is clearly in the former category and Z. W. Pylyshyn clearly in the latter, and their disputation in the journals about the functional necessity for image representation has taken on the character of a classic debate. Like all such classic debates however it is really about deep preferences for one mode of explanation over another far more than it is about the interpretation of data within rival empirical theories. But for such a debate to be so intense and, admittedly, so intellectually nutritious it is clear that each protagonist must be right about something and each must be wrong about something. What might these 'things' be? Here, first of all, are the bare bones of the controversy.

The argument is not over the existence of mental phenomena such as we might describe as 'having a mental image of X'. Indeed Pylyshyn has himself researched extensively in the area of 'mental imagery' and gives his subjects instructions of the kind 'form an image of X, rotate the image, change your point of fixation on the image from a to b, etc.' Rather, the debate concerns the question of whether subjects require such images to perform given cognitive operations (are they *functional*?) or are they products, accompaniments, or epiphenomena of some 'deeper' non-analogue, propositional, mode of representation. Four main kinds of data speak for the functional necessity of images.[78]

1. *Image transformation.* The most discussed example here is the work of R. N. Shepard and his colleagues on the 'rotation' of mental images. For example[79] when subjects are shown a pair of drawings of three-dimensional figures and asked to say whether the pair are different perspectives on the *same* figure, they typically report that they judge congruence/disparity by rotating the figure 'in their heads'. Crucially, when the angular disparity is varied (that is, the amount of rotation required) there is a direct linear relationship between the time subjects report the rotation to have taken and the amount of disparity (that is, for every equal increment in disparity an equal increment in reaction time).

2. *Visual image scanning.* Studies by Kosslyn and others[80] have shown that when subjects are asked to construct an image of a presented scene (such as, a map of a desert island) and then instructed to scan from one location to another (perhaps from the trees to the beach) there is a correlation between the actual item–item distance and the reported scanning time. This holds irrespective of the number of items scanned through.[81]

3. *The overflowing of images.* Sartre, as we saw, said that the perception of real objects overflows whereas 'inspection' of images cannot do so. Kosslyn, however, tells us that in a sense images do overflow our inspection of them: when, for example, we imagine ourselves walking towards an object and at some point the object first fills our visual field and then flows 'behind' or 'beyond' us. This mental experience has a perceptual character, argues Kosslyn, because subjects report that imaging movement to smaller objects overflows later than to larger objects (linear relationship again).[82]

4. *Relation between subjective image size and the speed of search for properties.* If subjects are told to form an image of something (for instance, an animal) and then say whether it has a certain property such as a tail, and they are also told to make some images big and some small (for example, a small image of an elephant, a big one of a mouse) then there is a direct relationship between search time

and *subjective* size. Later studies showed that the *actual* size of the property determined search time, not its semantic association with the animal. For example, cat's 'claws' took longer to find than cat's 'head' because claws are smaller. The opposite was true for subjects given no imagery instructions.[83]

Kosslyn deploys this and other evidence to argue that mental images are quasi-pictorial media which we utilise in an analoguous way to that in which we utilise genuinely pictorial media such as maps, photographs, and filmed records. These quasi-pictorial entities have spatial extension and our experience of their inspection has important parallels to the inspection of real objects. In this lies Kosslyn's main argument for the functional role of images in thinking: as in perception we obtain *information* from an entity extended in mental rather than physical space.

The principal argument that Pylyshyn[84] employs against this position, as we have already briefly mentioned (Chapter 3, first section), is that because mental images are cognitively penetrable[85] (that is, determined by our beliefs and goals) then such data reflect our beliefs not features of a representational medium. Broadly, any image that we form must be formed on the basis of our tacit knowledge of the domain. Thus, the reason we 'see' a green filter when told to imagine a transparent yellow filter being placed over a blue one is that we know something about colour mixing: the image does not go beyond this knowledge. Any image that we have is a product of pre-existing *tacit knowledge* (see Chapter 3, first section) and of the knowledge that experimenters feed to their subjects via the instructions. But if appeals to image inspection, transformation etc. are to succeed then the images must be autonomous and genuinely informative. That is, they must be relatively independent of the knowledge that could generate a non-imageable solution.

Moreover, as part of a critique of iconophile experimental studies, Pylyshyn says that although they purport to be asking their subjects (i) to solve a particular problem by a particular kind of representation they are in fact asking them to (ii) 're-create as accurately as possible the sequence of perceptual events that would occur if you were actually observing a certain real event happening'.[86] In (ii) the duplication of the perceptual features, that Kosslyn quotes as evidence for the function role of imaging, is a direct result, therefore, of the *task demands* (see previous references to Pylyshyn in

Chapter 3), not evidence for real cognitive processes. In illustration of the distinction he mentions the case of Mozart[87] who said that he 'heard' a whole symphony in his imagination but heard each part of it simultaneously and apprehended its structure and quality as a whole. This is a case of (i) says Pylyshyn, but not a case of (ii). Mozart's experience is auditory imaging with practically no similarities to real audition; whereas (ii) would have been his imaging a performance of a symphony 'in real time and in complete detail'. Obviously if it is (ii) for which you ask your subjects then your data will 'confirm' the 'quasi-pictorial' nature of imaging, when imaging *may* typically be of the Mozartian variety.

In meeting the challenge of cognitive penetrability Kosslyn[88] accepts that he must indeed claim that the properties of the image analogue are innately determined and cognitively impenetrable. But, he argues, the existence of cognitive penetrability as a variable in image production and utilisation does not show that the properties of the analogue medium play no role in processing. The fact that non-analogue processes play a role in performance 'in no way bears on the truth or falsity of the claim that one component is an analogue spatial medium which supports mental images that depict an object or a scene'.[89] The divergence between the tacit knowledge and the imagery accounts should be dealt with empirically not by trading knock-down conceptual arguments. If we do treat the accounts empirically we will see that the tacit knowledge position is less precise, general and falsifiable than the imagery position. Moreover the evidence clearly favours the imagery position, says Kosslyn. For example, he quotes evidence[90] to show that subjects' judgements of when black and white grating lines blur at a distance is influenced by the 'oblique effect' found in recent studies in perception. In the oblique effect subjects in perception experiments judge vertical lines to blur into a grey field at greater distances than oblique lines. None of the subjects in the imagery studies knew of the oblique effect so the genuinely perceptual nature of imagery was causing these results not the subjects' knowledge of the domain. He also answers Pylyshyn's failure to find the 'image distance scanned – reaction time' correlation (ii above) by proposing that for certain distances and circumstances, when subjects have to locate another part of the image (when, for example, it is beyond the boundaries of their mental visual field) they will allow the first image to fade and construct a new image at the required location. He calls this the 'blinking transformation'.

Pylyshyn rejects this move as special pleading and suggests that the reaction time data cannot accommodate such a transformation.[91]

How should we regard this debate? First, Kosslyn clearly has a dyadic relation view of subjects' utilisation of images. Indeed in their computational model Kosslyn and his associates regard the 'image buffer' as a cathode ray tube;[92] the image being analogous to the visual display of a computer. This is, of course, nothing if not a mental object; and therefore the arguments of the first and second sections of this Chapter may be deployed against it. But on the other hand Pylyshyn is denying that having mental images is a form of visual experience necessary to certain kinds of cognition. Certainly this denies the broadly Sartrean position we were led to endorse, that the imagery *is* the thought. Indeed such a view is diametrically opposed to the beliefs of computational theorists such as Pylyshyn, and indeed Kosslyn.

What of cognitive penetrability? Given the intensionality of the image it is difficult to see how Kosslyn can deny that image production is constituted out of beliefs and goals. In a sense he does not deny this because in his computational model of imaging he includes conceptual information for image production stored in long-term memory and admits that some forms of access to images is cognitively penetrable. But any dyadic relation theory must give *some* constitutive autonomy to the image as a mental object, otherwise it will be *transparent*, that is, incapable of yielding more than its inspector knows of it. So despite Kosslyn's detailed attempts to specify the computational nature of the processes underlying image generation and utilisation (which Pylyshyn[93] holds up as a good example of 'unconstrained'[94] modelling) the deep mystery remains of how image generation could be independent of what is believed.

Therefore the 'oblique effect' data mentioned above (and there is more of the same)[95] which shows that imaging subjects are susceptible to perceptual phenomena of which they could have no knowledge acquires major relevance. How might we accommodate it within our account that regards imaging as an intensional act without a mental object? There seem to be two principal alternatives to Kosslyn's interpretation of the data: (i) the *perceptual* demonstration of the effect is not dependent upon the structure of the light at all, because in the imaged case there is no light; and (ii) the imaged version of the effect is a product of past experiences with such lines on which the subject cannot reflect but which influences judgements unconsciously. If (i), then the perceptual effect may be determined by task demands. For example, subjects may have a lower threshold for *judging* blurring in oblique lines irrespective of what they *see*. If (ii), then the effect is the product of wholly tacit knowledge. But unfortunately neither of the alternatives is very attractive: for (i), because such claims are very difficult to test, and for (ii) because it is empirically very implausible. Nevertheless these alternatives are more attractive than Kosslyn's proposal that the image is *so* perceptual that it is duplicating the effect of light-rays on the brain! More needs to be said on this issue than I have space for.

This brings us to a consideration of the highly literal manner in which Kosslyn interprets the case for the quasi-pictorial nature of imaging. Quite apart from the logical objections to the dyadic relation account of imaging that this entails, why is it necessary to show that imaging is of an entity with precise metric characteristics and which can 'move through' a kind of mental space in real time? As long as the case for imagery is made in this way it will be vulnerable to the tacit knowledge objection, and then failure to answer such objections will inspire the false conclusion that imaging is not functional. The case for imagery must be differently based, given the arguments in the first and third sections of this chapter. The perceptual nature of imaging consists in its sensory quality – it is sensory mental activity. The fact that it is not at all like real-time perception in many cases is no reason at all for scepticism. In fact the Mozart example which Pylyshyn gave is particularly instructive here because it provides an excellent illustration of how thinking can be sensory whilst lacking almost every physical resemblance to perception except a sensory qualitative content. I am sure such thinking was functional for Mozart despite this.

Risking the glibness, which any brief treatment of the debate must invite, one may therefore offer the following 'resolution': Pylyshyn's arguments from tacit knowledge trade on the intensionality of the image and therefore have force against the essentially dyadic relation view of imaging that Kosslyn offers. But Pylyshyn is wrong to take this argument as showing the psychological redundancy of imaging. For the positive evidence must convince us of one thing if nothing else: that is, of *people's firm beliefs about the sensory nature of some of their thinking*. The experiments seem to cure them of agnosticism about imagery! Are we to say that these beliefs are illusory? And what sense could be made of their being illusory? Perhaps 'knowledge' is a better description of what people have about their experience of imaging (Sartre would take this position given his assumption about the necessary self-conscious nature of thought). But perhaps something between belief and knowledge is what we require. There is no object so neither is really appropriate; and yet (cf. Hannay's liberalisation of the private language argument) the subjects know what they are describing, given the analogy with the outer version of such processes.

Could this sensory mental action be epiphenomenal? There are, I suspect, never any decisive arguments against the epiphenomenalism view, given that it is really a kind of blanket scepticism. But we may ask nevertheless: is it likely that evolution has arranged for us to have the illusion that we are thinking when the thoughts have already taken place or are taking place beneath the level of consciousness?

Can we decide between dual-code and propositional theories of representation?

The principal alternatives to imagery theories of representation are the propositional theories. Although there are different kinds of propositional theory[96] they all share the assumption that representation is a rule-bound system for coding information strongly analogous to the kind of system used by computers.[97] In addition to being rule-bound (that is, with their own particular 'grammar') and yielding truth-values (they state facts in a way that pictures cannot, as we have seen) propositional representations are *abstract*. Indeed it is in being abstract that they most decisively diverge from natural language representation because although words *carry* abstract concepts they have sound or shape; whereas the sensory nature of the units is irrelevant in propositional representation. A proposition is 'supermodal'. As we saw in the discussion of Fodor's position, propositional representation involves a form of private language intimately linked to a theory of how the brain codes information.

The prime advantage of propositional theories lies in their promise of explaining how it is that we can remember and know facts without having the exact words and of explaining how we can move between mental 'pictures' and words: propositions are a kind of '*interlingua*'[98] between different sentences with the same meaning and between different modes of conscious representation. Despite this, as some writers have commented,[99] one is still left with the uncomfortable problem of how, if we move from one (verbal or image) representation to a semantically equivalent one via this *interlingua* how do we move from the initial representation to the *interlingua*? Do we need another *interlingua*? However such an argument only speaks against the *necessity for*, not the *possibility of*, propositional representation. Needless to say, such representation is not amenable to conscious reflection.

J. R. Anderson[100] presents an argument to the effect that, radically divergent as propositional and non-propositional theories of representation are, it is not possible in principle for behavioural data to decide between them. We do not think, the argument runs, simply by having representations; we think by performing operations (transformation and decoding, as well as encoding) on these. What theories should specify therefore is not only the mode of representation but also the nature of the processes that *operate* on the representations. But once we include process assumptions (for example, how the individual manipulates visual or abstractly-coded units of representation in thinking) rival theories become *indeterminate* about the representation, or encoding methods, they are proposing. By having different process-assumptions, theories which postulate different representational media can cover just the same data. So Anderson concludes that we should be agnostic about representation and concentrate on developing theories that just cover the data, which, as he says, is quite challenging enough.

The argument has the following stages:

1. A review shows that although the *a priori* arguments against image representation do not work; any data that imagery studies produce can be covered by a propositional theory.
2. With the possible exception of the data on inference-making, there are no compelling data in favour of propositional theories.
3. A formal argument is presented to prove that any theory of representation can be mimicked by an entirely different theory through compensating for differences in encoding by different assumptions about transformation and decoding processes. The mimicking theory is able to preserve all the internal distinctions in the mimicked theory.
4. An illustration of the formal argument with mental rotation data is given.
5. Consideration of non-behavioural criteria for discriminating

between representation theories (physiological, parsimony, efficiency) shows that physiological criteria hold out some hope although such discrimination is really in the realm of science fiction at present.

The principal criticisms of Anderson's agnosticism can be classified under three headings as follows:

1. Problems with the formal argument.
2. The possibility of there being empirical criteria for discriminating between theories which Anderson undervalues.
3. Propositional theories are not empirical theories in the way that image theories are.

(Note that although Anderson's agnosticism is between *dual-code* versus propositional theories, the debate is principally over *image* versus propositional theories.)

The first involves a dispute over whether there could be a function, called by Anderson f, that maps the encoding of stimuli from the model to-be-mimicked on to the mimicking model one-to-one by having an *inverse* that also ensures that the transformation and the decoding in the mimicking model are computable.[101] Hayes-Roth[102] claims that (i) given the huge variety of perceptual encoding f would have to be infinite, and (ii) that the assumption that f has an inverse is *ad hoc* and runs against some available data. Pylyshyn[103] argues that it is in principle impossible that the encoding of an image in propositional form, or vice versa, could preserve stimulus distinctions. The second essentially involves the sub-debate over the assumptions that different representation theories make about computational complexity, and about whether and how reaction-time data might discriminate between the theories in these terms.

The third criticism is fundamental. We shall approach it by way of the 'propositioning' of mental rotation data that Anderson offers. Let us assume that Anderson has succeeded in showing that there might be a propositional theory that accounts for the linear increase in rotation time with the angle of rotation. What has this theory actually succeeded in doing? It has in fact *post*dicted rather than *pre*dicted the data, because the structural elements of the propositional account are essentially determined by the observed finding. In another context Kosslyn[104] has made the same point but adds that what he regards as a 'typical' propositional theory is incapable of accounting for his finding that subjectively larger images 'rotate' more slowly. But what is a 'typical propositional theory'? It is in the nature of them – specifically in their abstract nature – that there is in principle no form of data to which they cannot accommodate. Propositional theories are potentially *universal*.

I said in defining propositional theories that they are heavily influenced by computational concepts, and this influence comes into clearer focus when we consider the potential universality of propositional explanation. This is, in fact, a *consequence* of such theories' computational nature, and it relies specifically on the claim[105] that any behaviour that can be clearly described can be computed (or be specified) by a machine with *recursive* functions, with rules that can be re-applied indefinitely and reflexively. Being computable entails being capable of realisation in a proposition-based language such as the predicate calculus. In fact it is around the nature of the recursion of computational rules that Anderson and his critics differ in their discussion of his formal argument. Very roughly, Anderson takes the position that the encoding procedures of the model to be mimicked can have a form of recursion[106] that enables their inverses to be computed and the function f to operate; and the critics deny this. What Anderson is doing, therefore, is extending necessary computability from that of encoding representations (which all accept) to the necessary computability of the *processes* operating on representations (transformation, decoding) – which is highly controversial. If this *is* allowed then it is possible to show that any representation theory can mimic another: the computability of *any* kind of operating process makes their flexibility *and thus their capacity to mimic* unlimited.

One way of interpreting Anderson's 'success' is to say that it demonstrates that propositional theories are too powerful.[107] A more radical way of putting the matter is to say that really propositional theories of representation are not theories at all. They are formal descriptions, as Hayes-Roth put it: 'propositional descriptions *per se* do not constitute models, they simply re-express observations in formal syntax'.[108] In reply Anderson[109] said that this was, in fact, his point, and that he was employing just this feature to show that only representation–process *pairs* can be tested. But if Anderson is going to extend the universal computability of representations to that of the processes that operate on them then the critical point has not been answered, but actually reinforced. In this case the modes of encoding, transformation and decoding which he considers are themselves not theories of processes, but are, in Hayes-Roth's terms, re-expressions in formal syntax. Therefore the reason that Anderson 'succeeds' in showing the indeterminacy of dual-code versus propositional theories is that it is in the nature of propositional theories to be indeterminate in this way relative to any other kind of theory. The argument is not therefore one for agnosticism. Rather, it is a kind of *reductio ad absurdum* of propositional theories – showing them to lack empirical status. It is also a *reductio* of the unconstrained application (cf. Pylyshyn) of computational procedures to psychological processes.

I should emphasise that this conclusion does not speak against theories of brain-function expressed in the form of codes and rules, that are, in a sense, propositional. As I said earlier in discussing Malcolm's dismissal of Sutherland's shape-abstraction model, such accounts only become problematic when they are reified as levels of representation rather than treated as formalised theoretical neurophysiology. The important difference is that although such coding sequences have abstract symbols and rules of formation they do not have *truth-values*. They do not encode facts about the world, but hypotheses about brain-function. The above conclusions only have force against propositional theories in the full truth-carrying sense.

But cannot propositional theorists – like proponents of CTM in general – just straddle the two theoretical domains, being happily ambiguous about whether their coded sequences have truth-value or not? (After all, Anderson does propose that only physiological evidence could really decide between rival theories of representation.) No; to do so would be to run together an intensional domain and physical processes; and if there is anything in the arguments for anomalous monism, this must be unacceptable. But even if there is not, it is surely wrong to treat statements about the world and statements about brain-function as equivalent in this way. And so we find ourselves in rather the same spot at which we arrived in our discussion of Fodor's language-of-thought proposals.

As I said earlier in passing, although Anderson's arguments were directed towards the indeterminacy of propositional versus dual code (that is, image plus *natural language*) theories the critics focussed on the *image* versus propositional division. This is because the implicit assumption within contemporary cognitive psychology (made explicit of course by Fodor) is that theories of natural language representation are so naive as to be non-starters, which is of course entirely the opposite of the conclusion to the second section of this Chapter. In fact cognitive psychology – at least North American cognitive psychology – is founded on faith in a non-conscious level of representation of which conscious verbal thought is the product.

But does not scepticism about the non-conscious level leave little for cognitive psychology to do? Indeed does it not rob us of a whole domain of investigation? No; its only negative effect is to discourage a certain kind of model-building. Positively it encourages the production of wholly a-semantic models[110] (that is, whose expressions do not state facts about the world), construed as theoretical neurophysiology. And it also encourages the marriage of data about verbal processes in adult thought to developmental questions about how such verbal representation becomes possible at all.

Indeed it is to developmental matters that we turn finally. For, as Fodor (and also Field) argued, propositional and natural language theories of representation have entirely different implications for the acquisition of language. On the former theory it is a process of mapping a pre-structured cognitive system onto the system of public language; on the latter it is the social process of *acquiring* a rule-system for thinking by a series of functional adaptations. One major implication from a natural language theory of representation would be that we cannot really divorce cognitive development from language development.

7
Meaning: the Thought of Language

If it could be said that one theorist was principally responsible for the
computational theory of the mind, then this theorist would *not* be one
of those whose work directly inspired computer-modelling in psychology (for example, Turing, Minsky, Simon, G. A. Miller) nor
Fodor, who coined the phrase. It would be Noam Chomsky.[1]

As an undergraduate in the late 1960s I read *Syntactic Structures*
and *Aspects of the Theory of Syntax* and attended Chomsky's 'John
Locke' lectures, experiences which were exhilarating and disturbing
in about equal measures. The exhilaration came from the power and
adventurousness of Chomsky's cases for mentalism and against
behaviourism, for theory-building based on deep conceptual analysis
rather than on *post hoc* generalisations from quantitive data.[2] The
disturbance came from hearing in the lectures the facile dismissal of
Wittgenstein as a 'behaviourist' and the Gricean view of meaning,
supposedly refuted by an anecdote about Chomsky himself giving a
speech against the Vietnam war in the presence of an ominous
contingent of heavily armed marines – i.e. the sentences 'meant'
whilst Chomsky's mind was otherwise engaged than using them to
mean. (Needless to say, Chomsky was privately dismissed by
philosophers sympathetic to Wittgenstein as 'philosophically naive'.)

But there was also something both exciting and disturbing at the
same time. Chomsky hinted, no more,[3] that the complex tree
diagrams which he drew to illustrate the generation of sentences out
of base structures via transformational rules could be regarded as a
model of what goes on in our heads when we produce and
comprehend language: deep structure to surface structure in production and vice versa for comprehension. The status of such rules was
formal, abstract, non-semantic and logico-mathematical; and they

were also highly complex (at least in relation to rival theories). We could *never* become conscious of such rules, and they were regarded as mechanistic in the sense of *happening in us* as we use language – just as neural processes which maintain our balance, happen in us; just as data-handling happens in a computer. *Could* it be that all this goes on in our heads as we use language? The implication was indeed that the processes which underlie not just language but all forms of ratiocination are computational in nature: rules and representations which are neither amenable to revelation in consciousness *nor* explainable in neurological terms. This was, in fact, the opening salvo of the campaign for CTM.

But there was a second and – for the purposes of this chapter – a more crucial feature of Chomsky's theorising. This was the treatment of syntactic rules as not only forming a separate epistemic 'module' from semantic functions but as actually *determining* semantic functions. Deep structure (the propositional form of a sentence) was made to contain all the information necessary for semantic interpretation. Of course the separation move had some plausibility: it restricted syntactic theories to explaining the rule-system that makes a sentence like 'Colourless green ideas sleep furiously' syntactically acceptable, and left to semantic theory the task of describing the 'selection restrictions' on the basis of which the quoted sentence does not 'make sense'. The requisite semantic theory was not developed by Chomsky himself but by his MIT colleagues Jerrold Katz and Jerry Fodor.[4]

The Katz and Fodor enterprise may seem modest enough, but in fact its philosophical assumptions were pretty far-reaching. In order for such a theory of selection restrictions to be developed they had to assume that our representation of natural language words could be in terms of abstract atoms of meaning, 'semantic markers' (for example, human, male) and 'semantic distinguishers' (terminal definitions such as 'who has never married' if the word is 'bachelor'). The semantic marker system prevented the production of anomalous sentences; but more crucially it entailed that meaning is a system of abstract conceptual features which underlie words in such as way as to be – in a deeply obscure sense – independent of our knowledge of the world and beliefs about it. Thus we represent, as it were, the finite and abstract 'essence' of a word in rather a similar way to that in which, as we saw in the previous chapter, 'propositional' theories of representation regard us as storing that which a number of semantically equivalent sentences express. To put it epigrammatically: semantic feature theory (as this is usually known) entails semantic 'essence-ism'. This was later developed by Katz and Fodor and by other linguists into the position that a conceptual language forms the basis of our natural language – which, of course, resulted ultimately in Fodor's notion of 'mental-ese' or a 'language of thought'.

In fact both these theses (rationality as a non-conscious computational activity and word-meaning as an abstract essence) are ancient; the former being associated with Plato and the latter with Aquinas. Indeed the derived notion that language-learning is the learning to map an innate language of thought (via a 'compiler') onto the corpus of natural language was first expressed by St Augustine.[5] As should be quite evident by this stage, in the computational theory of mind we see the iconoclast as archaeologist.

What is common to both theses is the assumption that *meaning and language are separable systems*. In the former thesis we understand a sentence by decoding a string of words into an abstract representation via a set of formal rules; in the latter we understand a word by translating it into our conceptual 'language'; in both we acquire language by attaching words to our innate system of proto-meanings. But what is the alternative? What is sometimes known as the 'Wittgensteinian revolution in philosophy'[6] was directed against just this bifurcation of meaning and language.

My theme in this final chapter will be the way in which this bifurcation leads to impossible accounts of language acquisition. Chomsky's and Fodor's theories of acquisition will be discussed first, and an analysis of word-meaning offered before some brief remarks are made about the way in which cognitive development becomes language development.

Sentence meaning: Chomsky's thesis

The distinctive and controversial aspect of Chomsky's work is not his thesis but the grounds on which it is put forward. A scientific hypothesis is presented, but the evidence and arguments developed are not recognisably scientific. The notion that human beings possess an innate, universal grammar and that therefore children acquire language on the basis of a program of structural rules is neither earth-shattering nor particularly original. But the assumption that such a proposal can be made not on the basis of the empirical study of language capacity, but on the basis of linguistic analysis *alone* is quite remarkable. Chomsky does not even do comparative linguistics. He does not consider evidence for the commonalities between different languages; indeed he is not even interested in commonalities between different speakers of the same language. The study of one speaker of one language is quite sufficient.[7]

So what *is* the evidence? The only evidence required comes from the speaker's judgements about the grammaticality or ungrammaticality of given sentences. Of course, in practice the 'speaker' is the linguist, that is, Chomsky. On the basis of such intuitions, a grammar of the language can be written expressing the rules that the speakers follow *tacitly*. These rules are represented in the speaker's mind.

But even before we reach the claim about innate knowledge we encounter our first conceptual difficulty – perhaps the one which has attracted most critical attention. It is one thing – the objection usually runs[8] – to *describe* performance in terms of a set of complex rules and quite another to show that these rules actually *determine* performance. An analogy: we can describe a two-year-old's ability to drink milk through a straw in terms of her utilisation of hydraulic principles (create a vacuum in the straw . . .), but the performance surely does not succeed by virtue of her knowledge of such principles. We do not have to 'know about' (in *any* sense of 'know') regularities in order to employ them. Riding a bicycle is another common example: this may be *described* in terms of the rider's knowledge of mechanics. Chomsky dismisses[9] this kind of objection on the grounds that (i) such examples are of *skills*, and language is not a skill but an object of knowledge, (ii) there may be some cases in which it *is* plausible to say that the individual 'cognises' (the term that Chomsky has recently come to use to mean 'knows tacitly') physical principles. The matter is an empirical one: the more purely skilful then the less appeal to tacit knowledge is required.

But – to remain on this theme of the status of Chomsky's evidence – how are we supposed to appeal to evidence? He gives an example. Imagine two missile systems which send rockets to the moon. One of them is run on Skinnerian lines, having several pigeons pecking at a light to keep the rocket on course. The other system

incorporates an explicit theory of the motions of the heavenly bodies and information about its position and velocity and carries out measurements and computations using its internalised theory to adjust its course as it proceeds.[10]

Both rockets may hit the same spot but only the latter system has tacit knowledge. How do we know it does? Chomsky says that 'a mere[!] investigation of behaviour might tell us little, perhaps nothing', so we must take a 'deeper look'.[11] But we are never told what form the 'deeper look' should take. The analogy strongly suggests a neurological study, but almost everything that Chomsky has ever written on the subject belies this interpretation.

Later on Chomsky gives us another celestial analogy. The position of the theoretical linguist forming hypotheses about the grammar that we have represented within us is similar to that of the solar physicist constructing theories about the thermo-nuclear reactions going on inside the sun. In neither case is it possible to get inside the object of study to collect direct evidence, so the scientists must make do with the products of the hidden processes as they are manifested 'at the periphery' – light in one case and judgements about grammaticality in the other case. It would surely be wrong to object that the hypotheses of the physicist do not have 'physical reality' because he has not been able to set up his laboratory in the heart of the sun. But, argues Chomsky, theoretical linguists are now confronted with the objection that their claims do not have 'psychological reality'[12] because they concern only linguistic intuitions not 'reaction times, recognition, recall etc.'[13] The implication is supposed to be that the accusations are equally silly. If we could *per impossibile* directly study the reactions in the sun this would be 'more evidence', not absolutely decisive evidence; just as studies of recall and the like do not give us psychological reality when theoretical linguistics gives us mere description or 'psychological fiction'. But quite apart from the fact that the analogy is an odd one,[14] Chomsky does not himself proceed as the linguist analogue of the solar physicist. For the other side of the analogy's coin is the fact that judgements about grammaticality are also 'more evidence'; whereas Chomsky treats these data as the *only* evidence. (The Chomskian solar-physicist would regard periphery data – maybe data about people's *judgements* of heat and light – as his only data.) If we look at what Chomsky does rather than what he says about what should be done we find that his proposals are almost entirely *un*influenced by data emanating from nearer the 'centre' – neurological, cognitive, developmental.[15]

Now my point here is not that linguistic analysis cannot in principle give us *arguments*[16] for some theories of grammar representation over others – and in simple cases (for example, the subject /predicate distinction) we can be quite confident that the linguist's categories do have 'psychological reality'. Indeed it may be too sweeping a dismissal of the Chomskian approach to say that rule-following must be a conscious procedure and that rules only have psychological reality if they 'cause' performance (that is, the performance would not happen unless a rule amenable to revelation in consciousness were represented). As Chomsky says, it is an empirical question whether our explanations of performance should make reference to cognised (in his special sense) rules. But if this is an empirical question then it should be investigated by empirical – that is, psychological – means, not by linguistic analysis alone. Moreover it is only to a very limited degree that we can select between grammars on the criterion of parsimony, because this notion is value-laden, and, of course, the grammar that we have represented may well not be the most parsimonious account of the regularities in the language that we use.[17]

The discussion of psychological reality brings us to the second, and still more problematic, stage of the argument. Chomsky claims that the rule-system that he has described is such that a child could never (at least in the relatively few available years) learn it from scratch. Essentially the argument is that because linguistic rules are 'structure-dependent' rather than 'structure-independent' they cannot be acquired hypothetico-deductively,[18] that is, by framing hypotheses to fit raw data, then testing and modifying them in the light of feedback. This is best illustrated by one of Chomsky's own examples.[19]

Imagine a creature new to the language system who is puzzling out the rule by which yes/no questions are formed from simple declaratives. His data are of the following kind:

> The man is here. ⟶ Is the man here?
> The man will leave. ⟶ Will the man leave?

Having given these examples Chomsky suggests structure-independent (H_1) and structure-dependent (H_2) hypotheses which might be derived from the data. On H_1 we process the declarative from left to right till we reach a word such as *is* or *will* and put that word at the beginning. This is structure-*in*dependent by virtue of treating words like beads on a string rather than as being clustered into sub-units such as 'verb-phrase', 'noun-phrase' etc. H_2 would, in contrast, 'select the first occurrence of *is, will*, etc., following the first noun phrase of the declarative.'[20] Now, H_1 is the more parsimonious hypothesis so therefore both a 'scientist observing English speakers' and an 'unstructured child' would select it. However, because H_1 ignores the abstract grammatical sub-units it will apply its rule irrespective of the presence of relative clauses. So, given sentences such as 'The man who is here is tall' and 'The man who is tall will leave' will predict 'Is the man who here is tall?' in one case and 'Is the man who tall will leave?' in the other. H_2 of course makes the correct prediction because it carries out the transposition of the auxiliary which appears *after the first noun phrase*, for example, after 'The man who is here'.

What does Chomsky conclude from this? He says that because children do not produce errors of this kind but respect the abstract grammatical structures such as 'noun-phrase', they (unlike the 'scientist') have prior knowledge of the structure-dependent or, as it is often called, the *hierarchical* nature of language. Chomsky insists that the absence of such errors is direct evidence for a universal native grammar. This is a very simple example but in essence all the cases that Chomsky cites are of this kind: children coming into the language-system do not treat words like beads on a string but process them in hierarchical units, *ergo* they have innate knowledge of these units and of their rule-bound relations. He never seriously considers alternative explanations for language learners' *not* coming out with utterances like 'Is the man who tall will leave?' and 'Each other left'.[21] This is quite extraordinary for a number of reasons but principally because it is hardly recognisable as scientific practice.

I do not believe that it is flippant to say that the Chomskian style of argument is somewhat reminiscent of the form of argument used by advocates of reincarnation. To explain: a fairly obvious sceptical reaction to the notion that we have lived before is that no real sense can be attached to the claim that egos survive bodies unless there is a thread of memory running from life to life.[22] But, says the reincarnationist, people *do* remember their previous lives, therefore reincarnation is true. The peculiarity about this as a form of theory is that the hypothesis is only *intelligible* if there is positive evidence for it; at the very least the hypothesis could never be seriously proposed without the evidence. More generally: a degree of 'distance' should exist between the hypothesis and the evidence for it such that the evidence is not *constituting* the hypothesis. In Chomsky also we find that hypothesis and evidence are not sufficiently separate. The claim that children know the basic structure of language can only seriously be put forward (maybe it goes too far to say 'is only intelligible') because we do not see children behaving like little scientists with severely restricted imaginations (who, by the way, even ignore evidence from utterances with relative clauses!). They do not behave like this kind of 'scientist' therefore they have innate knowledge. But, the fact is, there are a thousand and one possible reasons why children do not acquire language as if they were acting out some parody of Baconian science.

For Chomsky, children are like *another* kind of scientist. His arguments are supposed to show that they are scientists who already have something approximating to the correct theory.

If anything, Chomsky's critics have taken such arguments too seriously and perhaps erred on the side of generosity. Let us take the linguist Geoffrey Sampson as a case in point.[23] Although, as we shall see, Sampson's position on semantics is one very congenial to the present account, because he starts from the premiss that the child-as-little-scientist viewpoint is acceptable in principle it is inevitable that his presented alternative will be more Chomskian than not. There is nothing bizarre in the view that the child is unconsciously testing hypotheses (that is, on the basis of innate knowledge), argues Sampson, because do we not, after all, form quite unconscious hypotheses on the basis of two-dimensional retinal stimulation 'which is logically speaking quite insufficient as a basis for the decision'. Quoting Richard Gregory as a source, Sampson concludes: 'The case of perception seems to establish that the notion of unconscious theory-formulation and theory-testing makes good sense'.[24] Well *does* it? In Chapter 5 I gave some reasons why the hypothesis model of perception is very problematic. But even if it *were* a good model, the suggested parallel between unconscious inferences about material reality and unconscious inferences about a system of rules is not a very happy one. There is surely something even more troublesome in the notion of unconscious logical inferences within a rational system than in that of unconscious utilisation of perceptual cues.

Sampson dismisses the various suggestions that have been made for explaining the hierarchicality (i.e. structure-dependence) of the language system other than by the nature of the language itself. He rejects suggestions of the kind made by Stephen Toulmin[25] that a functional analysis of language will reveal that the exigencies of communication make hierarchicality inevitable. So the case for there *being* syntactic universals is accepted by Sampson; but an alternative is offered to the nativist view that the child *applies* these universals to linguistic data (what he calls 'the limited mind view'). Sampson's argument is that the genetic process is itself hierarchical because it is in the nature of complex systems to be built up from units with some degree of autonomy and that language acquisition will reflect this. The basis of the argument is the proposal of Herbert Simon[26] that successful systems (therefore, in evolutionary terms, *existing* ones) whether organs, people, or societies will have an hierarchical nature because hierarchies are better able to withstand perturbations, are more flexible and more capable of responding to selective pressures. (In fact hierarchical is only one of the things we should expect organisms to be on Piaget's account; see Chapter 4.) How may these have evolved? Sampson favours a 'symbiotic' account in which units that were initially autonomous contract relationships with other units of such a degree of interdependence that *one* new unit results from the process.

Sampson makes some interesting and plausible suggestions about how language may have evolved symbiotically. Originally one word utterances (for instance 'up' or 'tree') did a variety of jobs for our ancestors (for instance, 'up' for 'up there' or 'further up'). These kinds of utterance formed the base units of our evolved grammatical hierarchy – noun-phrase, possessive, verb, etc. The resulting hypothesis is that the base units of all human grammars will be those units which can *most plausibly stand as single utterances*. (For this reason Sampson rejects the verb-phrase, for example, 'carrying the wine' as a basic unit.)[27] The argument is not that the product of evolution retains a kind of *structural precipitate* from historical attempts to communicate, but that there is a genetic necessity (cf. Piaget) for systems of this kind.

The thesis will predict that complex sentences should be hierarchically structured, with the sub-sentential units of the hierarchy being elements that have independent uses as utterances – or which, at least, derive historically from units which once were independently useful. This is precisely what we find.[28]

The problem is that when we move to ontogeny we find that although Sampson's thesis is distinguishable from Chomsky's it is not significantly different. Where they appear to differ is on the question of whether the hierarchicality of the child's early utterances is 'contingent' or 'necessary'. For Chomsky it is contingent in much the same way that the fact that we develop feet not flippers is a contingent fact. For Sampson, on the other hand, hierarchical development is necessary given that both onto- and phylo-genetic processes of this kind will inevitably be symbiotic. (This is not a logical necessity of course, but a stochastic one: 'Simon's theses guarantee as a statistical certainty that this is how children will in fact acquire their mother tongue – the probability of their guessing one of the non-hierarchical grammars also compatible with their data before they master the data in the gradual way is so remote as to be negligible'.)[29]

But what, on Sampson's model, is the child bringing to the acquisition? Presumably there will be some predisposition to begin with the basic units and build from there – parts of speech, noun phrase, subject – predicate utterances. 'But how are we to construe the child's predisposition to do this *other* than by the application of innate knowledge of hierarchical structure?' might well be Chomsky's response. The fact is, if we accept the initial premiss that the child is essentially a tester of hypotheses about syntax then, it seems to me, Chomsky will inevitably have the last word in debates of this nature. For whenever a critic says that (i) the child is an hypothesis-tester and (ii) there is a property of language – such as symbiotic decomposition – which guarantees its learnability by beings who do not know its structure already, Chomsky can ask how it is that such beings *are able to exploit* this property. The issue is, in fact, similar to that surrounding the significance of the *recursive* nature of language rules. (Indeed, given that an hierarchical linguistic system will also be a recursive one the parallel is even closer.) It has been suggested, following Church's thesis, that a non-decidable or non-recursive language is unlearnable:[30] learnability is *conceptually related* to recursion, rather as Sampson suggests that learnability is related to symbiotic decomposition. But Chomsky denies that recursion and learnability are related conceptually 'in any empirically significant sense of this notion'.[31] Furthermore, languages may well be recursive but there is no logical necessity in this;[32] therefore the learning of language cannot be reduced to the practical ability to crack an inherently rational code. Similarly Chomsky would deny that the hierarchicality of language reflects a natural necessity: in a significant sense the structure of language is *arbitrary* and therefore the child must be prepared for its *particular* nature.[33]

In fact I would suggest that any rejection of Chomsky's thesis will tend to flounder if it shares the following two assumptions with Chomsky: (i) that the child is an hypothesis-tester engaged in a code-cracking operations, and (ii) that it is the *syntax* of the language that the hypothesis-testing concerns. (Within the Chomskian frame of reference, to deny the psychological reality of these assumptions – that is, their plausibility as developmental psychology – is to make a rather elementary error about psychological reality.) Once we accept these assumptions, nativism is practically inevitable.

Moving from (i) to (ii), Chomsky often writes as if there really are no viable alternatives to transformational linguistics with its assumption that syntax can be considered separately from semantics. Before passing on to the philosophical objections to the view that meaning and its rulebound expression are separable it is worth pointing out that there are many theoretical linguists who reject this bifurcation. As George Lackoff has written,[34] the reason why Chomsky has so radically restricted his claims about syntax over the years is that 'mountains' of linguistic evidence to the contrary have forced him to base his claim about the modularity of syntax on an ever-shrinking platform.

> Perhaps the main reason that deep structures and transformations have disappeared is that it turned out to be impossible to both keep them and maintain the principal assumption of modularity: the independence of syntax. Most of the research showing this was done by a group of the first generation of Chomsky's followers; myself, Paul Postal, John Robert Ross, James D. McCawley, Robin Lackoff, Charles Fillmore, David Perlmutter, Edward Keenan, and others. *What we found was that meaning and use (communicative function) effected virtually every rule of syntax.*[35] (my italics)

Outside this circle we have the grammatical theory of the late Richard Montague, which denies Chomskian assumptions about syntactic/semantic bifurcation from a quite different perspective. Montague's concern was with the logical formalisation of natural language, not competence models; and unlike the linguists just listed his treatment of meaning is 'extensional' (see the third section of this chapter). Nevertheless he shared with them the view that syntactic rules are not *sui generis*. As B. Partee expresses it, 'Montague offers no constraints on syntactic rules themselves; it is only in the connection between syntax and semantics that grammar is constrained.'[36]

So my point is very simply that the Chomskian separation of syntax from semantics is deeply controversial within linguistics, let alone psychology and philosophy.

To return to the child acquiring language, what Chomsky's evidence really amounts to is the undisputed fact that the child's primitive utterances are 'telegraphic'.[37] That is, if the child can say three words at a time he is likely to say things like 'Daddy drive car' where we would say 'Daddy is driving the car' and will almost certainly not say 'is driving the'. That is *all* the evidence there is for innate grammar. If we assume that the child is interested in the language system as a formal structure with tokens and rules this is indeed remarkable. But if we attend to the blinding truth that the child is a creature with beliefs, interests, emotions, and world knowledge (to give only a *modest* list) and who picks up something about word meaning (that 'Daddy' refers to his father, 'drive' is what people do when they move cars about, etc.) then this is not remarkable at all. To believe that it is, is to produce a psychological version of the following nonsense in physics: 'Isn't it remarkable and lucky that we are born obeying the laws of gravity – what chaos there would be if we were not'. As Putnam puts it:

> The child is learning and wants to learn, semantic rules, and these *cannot* be stated without the use of structure-dependent notions. There are not even plausible candidates for structure-independent semantic rules. So *of course* (given that his intelligence is high enough to learn language), *of course* the child 'internalises' structure-dependent rules.[38]

The view being supported here, in which initial syntactic ruleboundness is regarded as dependent upon a kind of semantic 'natural' necessity, must also take a radically divergent position from that of Chomsky on the relation between logic and language. It is no accident on this view that languages are hierarchical, and it reflects no evolutionary law. Given that language has to mean something by the combination of arbitrary sounds, that it must make sense and be coherent, it will be hierarchical. Language is hierarchical because it *has* to be; which is like saying that it is hierarchical because logic is or that logic is hierarchical because language has to be. Language is not separable from logic any more than is meaning from language. Unlike Sampson then, we *would* say that the hierarchical nature of language reflects a logical not a statistical necessity.[39]

The danger here, I suppose, is of treating this as an *a priori* argument for the position that the earliest utterances have the nature they do *solely* because of the child's concern with function rather than the structure of his utterances. Such an extreme functionalist position would be that the child is initially *completely indifferent* to the syntactic correctness of his utterances. But of course this is an empirical question, about the *degree* to which the child is attempting grammatical regularities as distinct from expedient and expressive words and phrases. In general, the *a priori* face of the anti-Chomskian position concerns the necessity for semantic and pragmatic interests, as it were, leading the child into the system: he cannot *essentially* be a code-cracker. The empirical face is the claim that the structural relations that early utterances do express will be more often than not explicable in functional terms. As it happens, the current evidence, as reviewed for example by Martyn Barrett,[40] does indeed suggest that holophrastic speech – early one-word utterances – expresses particular communicative functions rather than grammatical relations.

Of course, as the child enters farther into the system the degree of determination of structure by function wanes and he can use language for knowledge-orientated or 'mathetic' purposes,[41] can reflect on the system and treat it as a 'problem space'.[42] In fact it is just impossible that syntactic rules could be acquired by attention to semantic regularities alone. Where, for example, is the semantic divergence between strong and weak verbs, and where (apart from the obvious cases) is the semantic underpinning of gender categories in a language such as German or Russian? However, to say this is not, of course, to argue for innate syntactic knowledge. Although it is no easy matter, it is possible to present models of the child *coming to know* the syntactic structure of his own language. For example Maratsos and Chalkley[43] have recently described a process rather similar to the extraction of perceptual invariants[44] whereby the syntactic categories could be acquired by correlating the use of a category (for example, verb) across different 'semantic–distributional–phonetic sequences'. For example:

$$\text{————} + s = \text{present};\quad \text{————} + ed = \text{past}$$

Because this model relies on exemplar-generated learning and thus avoids reliance on prior knowledge of abstract categories it is rejected by nativists.[45]

The message in the past few pages has been this: so long as we treat the grammatical form of language and its meaning as separate entities, the acquisition of language by rulebound steps will appear so miraculous as to inspire the radical nativist thesis. But what of adult language-users? Theorists who accept the meaning/language bifurcation will also tend to accept the bifurcation between 'intending to say X' and 'X', in fact between 'thought' and 'language'. As Jerrold Katz has expressed it:

> Roughly, linguistic communication consists in the production of some external, publicly observable, acoustic phenomenon whose phonetic and syntactic structure encodes a speaker's inner, private thoughts and ideas and the decoding of the phonetic and syntatic structure exhibited in such a physical phenomenon by other speakers in the form of inner private experience of the same thoughts or ideas.[46]

But, as we have already considered (Chapter 6, second section): what is the nature of this non-verbal 'thought', or non-linguistic meaning? We considered then how Wittgenstein's account of language was directed specifically against such proposals. In fact the neo-Wittgensteinian J. F. M. Hunter has spelt out the problems for Katz's view.[47] Perhaps Hunter's most telling argument concerns the necessity for specifying the nature of the 'input', or world knowledge plus intention, about which the person will frame an utterance. We need a situation 'in which there is something to serve as input, which is pre-verbal, contains at least everything that is represented in the output, and offers no pressing problems as to its sequence, duration, repetitions or vividness'.[48] Even if *per impossibile* these conditions were fulfilled we still would have to say why it is that the situation was pre-verbally encoded in just *this* way and not another. (Cf. the interpretation of a mental image.) And there are related problems with the mapping of this a-conceptual psychic content on to the input of what Hunter calls our 'talking machine' (the Katz and Chomsky theses imply such as entity, claims Hunter – though Chomsky denies it).[49] Moreover if it were really the case that this a-conceptual input just became linguistically-encoded in a smooth mechanistic transition would we not end up saying things like, in Hunter's example, 'I believe that I believe that however perhaps I know it'.[50] The point is that even if we *accept* the metaphor of 'framing thoughts in language' this framing is to a large extent a conscious, deliberate act not something that happens to us. Hunter's conclusion is that 'thought and its expression make their appearance together'.[51]

Word meaning: Fodor's thesis

The ability to learn a word is perhaps an even deeper mystery than the ability to learn syntactic rules; particularly if we accept the view expressed above that the fundamental syntactic rules are related by a form of natural necessity to semantic knowledge at the single-word level. A nativist could therefore agree that syntactic rules may *not* be innate, but, as it were, push the process one stage further back and say that we must have innate knowledge of the conceptual categories onto which our word learning must be mapped. As we have already discussed, this is roughly the position that Fodor takes on word learning; although his view of syntactic acquisition is less clear. If Fodor's arguments for a 'central computing agency', 'brain-code', 'mental-ese' or 'language of thought' are to be sustained he *must* also argue that genuine cognitive–cum–linguistic development (*qua* the acquisition of new meanings) does not take place via learning at all. Why? Because if it can be shown that we acquire language without need for a prior language of thought (in Fodor's sense) then the case is virtually destroyed for such a language of thought underpinning the thought of the mature individual. In this case the language of thought can be regarded as an accompaniment to or even as a product of natural language processes. On the computational theory of the mind, language learning is the development of a 'compiler' between the innate 'machine code' of the brain and natural or 'programming' language.

Fodor first unveiled this thesis in a critical essay on Vygotsky's *Thought and Language*;[52] and Vygotsky's account of the development of language and of thought in language is very similar to

Wittgenstein's.[53] Vygotsky argued – though on rather slender and casually gathered evidence – that the child's meanings are radically divergent from those of the adult, and that 'word meanings evolve . . . as the child develops'.[54] He regarded the conceptual–linguistic system, as mediated in adult–child interaction, as the principal canalising agent for this development. Although there are important divergences between Wittgenstein and Vygotsky that it would not be profitable to dwell on here,[55] *vis-à-vis* Fodor their agreement on one particular issue is of great significance: that there is no significant analogy between learning a first language and learning a second language.[56] In the latter case we already understand language expressed in one system and apply this understanding to the learning of a second system; in the former case we require something that we might call a 'level of functioning' sufficient to enter the system step-by-step, but prior understanding of the system is not a prerequisite.

Now, of course, the Wittgenstein-Vygotsky thesis sets itself the empirical problem of specifying this 'level of functioning' (I shall make some speculations about this right at the end). But no matter how enormous this problem it is nothing compared with the problem that Fodor sets himself of explaining how language, how *anything*,[57] could have evolved. Be that as it may, in this 1971 paper Fodor was rehearsing the case for a language of thought. The computer analogy was aired, along with two empirical arguments: cross-modal transfer of skills implies a supra-modal 'central computing agency', as does the fact that in recall we often retain the content and forget the details.[58] He also said that the child's and the adult's thought systems could not be very different, otherwise they would not be able to communicate with each other.

In *The Language of Thought* the case is much more formal. Fodor begins with three assumptions: (i) that learning a language is a process of hypothesis-formation and testing; (ii) that this learning of a language involves learning the 'semantic properties of its predicates'; (iii) that (ii) means learning 'some generalisation which determines the extension of P[the predicate](that is, the set of things of which P is true)'.[59] Although Fodor treats them as such I do not see that (ii) and (iii) would seem contentious to anyone other than a rabid behaviourist. (i) of course is highly contentious and is based on a very simple argument: *any* theory of learning worthy of the name must assume that the learner brings to the learning experience a set of hypotheses and that the experience allows him to select one (or some) of the set and abandon the rest. For learning to be successful that which is learned must have some prior purchase in the mind of the learner and the only way to construe the conditions for this purchase is as some primitive version of that which is learned.

I do not want to spend any time on this argument, because it is little more than a reprise of Chomsky's old argument that because Chomsky cannot imagine how a child would be able to extract the deep structure of his language unless the child already knew something about the deep/surface distinction this distinction must be innate. D. W. Hamlyn presented the *reductio ad absurdum* of this some time ago:[60] if you allow this then *everything* for whose learning we do not have a solid theory must be innate. Fodor's argument is, in fact, Hamlyn's *reductio* dressed up as a profound truth about learning. His presentation is a fine example of the philosophical controversialist's art: present a *reductio* as a deep conceptual truth, so deep that we must abandon our old habits of thought which led us to regard it as a *reductio* if we are to appreciate this deep conceptual truth. And even if the argument *were* a good one, what justification have we – as I discussed above – for regarding the child as being engaged in hypothesis-testing *in fact*?

But you may say: 'Well, the fact that Fodor's argument for the developmental *necessity* of a brain-code and for language-development being compiler-development is a poor one, does not allow us to exclude the *possibility* that language-development could happen in something like the way Fodor says it does'. But for the thesis to be even possible, the argument for the possibility of a brain-code must, independently of developmental considerations, be shown to be sound. If a brain-code – as Fodor understands it – is an inherently confused notion then the developmental thesis *has* to be mistaken. To consider the inherent plausibility of the brain-code notion I will reconsider two of the sceptical points I made in Chapters 4 and 6, sharpening one and extending the other with the help of some borrowed arguments.

First, the analogy that Fodor draws between non-conscious mental processes and a computer machine-code is just that – an analogy; and not only does Fodor offer no justification for the analogy, it is actually a bad one. Putnam has neatly expressed the reasons why.[61] For Fodor to present the machine-code in his arguments as if it were capable of expressing functions containing the logical quantifiers 'all' and 'some' and having word definitions is seriously to misconstrue what the machine-code is actually capable of.

> Machine language does not contain (nor can one introduce into it by definition) such notions as 'tree', 'cow', 'jumps', 'spontaneous', 'pert', and so on – it only contains such notions as 'add', 'subtract', '0', '1', 'put result in address 17', 'go back instruction so-and-so', and 'print out contents of address blah – blah'.[62]

The second difficulty to be reconsidered (p. 189 above) is that despite the care that Fodor takes in the early part of his book to refute a version of psycho-physical reductionism, his language-of-thought argument may actually require the assumption of a lawlike relationship between states of the computational system in the physical brain and thoughts expressed in natural language. Additionally, as J. Heil has argued in a recent paper,[63] Fodor must assume that machine-codes have lawlike relationships to states of affairs in the *world* that are independent of the relationship that we as interpreters of the world give them. The computational theory of the mind makes a parallel between the way our minds represent the world and the way in which we might say that the internal states of a digital computer represent or symbolise, but in order for the machine to represent the world in its machine-language, it must have been given a programming language and a compiler by a human being. (Cf. my earlier remarks about a computer's data-structures being 'put there'.) It is therefore a programmer who 'provides the essential link' between world-states and machine-states. But where is the programmer in human cognition? Is it an homunculus? Heil is not arguing against the possibility (as would, say, Malcolm) that such codes can be said to represent:

> rather that such states have meaning, if at all, roughly in the same way that marks on paper have meaning: they have to be *given* a meaning by human beings.[64]

(And cf. my remarks there about data structures lacking, in a sense, what words in a book lack.)

In order for Fodor to escape the necessity of an homunculus – an interpreter to mediate between innate code and material reality – he must, as did *Gestaltists* such as Köhler (world–brain 'isomorphism'), claim that there is a natural, *casual*, relation between brain-representations and their possible extensions. Much of Heil's paper is taken up with arguments to show that no such causal relation can exist because there is no *natural* way of categorising the material world. The world does not have a structure over and above the application of concepts to it. This is not a solipsistic view but rather a statement about the deeply anthropocentric nature of 'structure'.[65] If Fodor were to reply that in fact his conception of an innate brain code *is* that of a kind of innate conceptual system, not merely a set of states which correspond to natural categories, then this would be tantamount to abandoning the computer analogy. This is because: (i) machine languages are not in any sense like concepts – as we discussed immediately above, and (ii) the task of the 'compiler' would then be reduced to little more than that of simple correlation.

Is there a more empirical and modest version of the Fodor thesis that might still be viable despite all this? Despite, that is, (i) the failure of the claim about impossibility of genuine, *de novo* learning given the dependence of all learning upon hypothesis-testing; (ii) the failure of the machine-language/brain-code analogy and (iii) the problems with the assumption about the lawlike nature of psycho-physical relations and of brain–world relations. A proponent of the thesis might say that so long as it is *intelligible* to say that the acquisition of a word requires a kind of proto-concept (not necessarily innate) and so long as there is no viable alternative theory, had we not better stick with the intelligible theory? It is probably the case that we find it easier to appreciate this than the claim that words somehow evoke concepts or that concepts and words arrive together.

Let us approach this restricted version from a little distance. Fodor quotes with approval Peter Bryant's discussion of the old claim of Kuenne[66] that children come to perform 'far' relational transposition tasks through learning words like 'bigger' (the word, in classic neo–behaviourist style, is an internal mediator between Ss and Rs).[67] Quite rightly, Bryant points out that this 'leaves unanswered the very awkward question of how they learned the meaning of the words in the first place'.[68] But Bryant's point applies, and was only meant to apply, to the claim that the word is *all* the child needs – that having the word is a *sufficient* condition for learning. It is an argument against the crude position that language acquisition *causes* new concepts out of nothing; which is a logical non-starter.

But one may still say that linguistic experience canalises the acquisition of concepts, that pre-verbal functioning and language-competence are mutually dependent. Indeed recent data collected by Linda Siegel[69] suggest that although the emergence of a simple perceptual skill like discriminating between two circles in terms of their area is not aided by verbal competence in young children, anything more complex such as one-to-one correspondence, conservation, spatial ordering, seriation, certainly does appear to be greatly facilitated by, if not actually dependent on, verbal competence.

Indeed, should we not look very closely at the claim that the child's behaviour (whether guided by reinforcements in Siegel's experiments or evolving from naturalistic encounters in Piaget's) evinces understanding of 'concepts' like size-relation, transitive relation or class inclusion? In what sense are these 'concepts'? Alternatively, consider the evidence that if rats are overtrained by one hundred trials they will respond in terms of abstract dimensions such as size and shape in a transfer-of-learning experiment.[70] Does this mean that rats have potentially abstract concepts like ours except that they are not verbalisable? Yet, most people who would recognise the ridiculousness of an affirmative answer to this question are quite happy to accept that pre-verbal children have concepts of this kind that are ready to be attached to the appropriate verbal labels. To say that there is something special in the human case because the infant will eventually acquire language is to commit a cardinal error of developmental logic:[71] explaining the course of development in terms of its product or *telos*. Now, almost certainly, there *is* a fundamental difference between the rat's non-verbal 'concepts' and the child's pre-verbal 'concepts'[72] but these differences must be illustrated by qualitative differences in the evincing behaviours not in terms of what is to come. Of course there is nothing wrong with the use of the expression non-verbal or pre-verbal 'concept' as a *facon de parler*,[73] but these do have a nasty habit of become entrenched dogmas.[74]

In general it is a mistake to view a verbal concept as equivalent to 'core concept plus sign', as if the sign were the icing on the cake. One way of expressing the divergence is by saying that a verbal concept is a concept *for the subject*: the subject applies the concept on his own behalf. But a non- or pre-verbal concept is only a concept for the *other* – for the describer of it. To that extent it is not in the mind of the user. Let us now consider Fodor's further argument for the view that verbal concepts must grow out of proto-concepts.

Fodor argues that learning a word must involve learning a bi-conditional truth rule of the kind: '*y is a chair* is true iff Gx',[75] where 'G' would be something like 'is a portable seat for one'. Later on he says that when 'trying to learn the concept C' we must 'learn the conditions under which something is an instance of (falls under) C. So presumably, you have to learn something of the form (x)[76] (x is C iff x is F) where F is some concept that applies whenever C does'.[77] Our concern is with the nature of F and G in these formulations. What sense can be attached to the claim that a child has or does not have the concept of 'portable seat for one' or any thumbnail definition of 'chair' that you care to produce? The fact is, almost *any* behaviour could or could not serve as evidence for possession of such a concept. Did the little mouse whom the cat frightened under the chair have something approaching this concept? Is the concept complete for the child who behaves as if any seat of a certain size is portable by men at least as strong as her father? More generally, in Wittgensteinian terms[78] the meaning of a word or rule does not express an essence and words are infinitely and unpredictably extensible on the basis of human interests. Therefore there is no sense to the claim that the language-learning child must have this essence as part of his cognitive armoury before he can acquire the word. This objection is predictable and Fodor claims to answer it thus:

> All it shows is that *if* the truth condition on 'is a chair' is expressed by 'is a portable seat for one', then 'is a portable seat for one' must be open-textured, undefined etc., for just those cases where 'is a chair' is.[79]

But it is difficult to see how this is supposed to be an answer to the Wittgensteinian objection, particularly as it says 'for just those cases where . . .': anti-essence-ism[80] insists that in *principle* and without exception it is impossible to lasso the intension (roughly here: definition) by formulae, at least by something strong enough to support Fodor's *a priori* argument that the essence of a concept must be cognised before the word can be acquired.

I hope now that we have reached a clearing in this tangle of claims and counter-claims in which the profundity of Vygotsky's statement that 'word meanings evolve . . . as the child develops' stands forth. The point is this: when the child comes to use a word the intension of that word is determined by his cognitive life not by some 'essence' that the word possesses (and of course the word will itself go on to determine cognitive life). *It need not be* at all close to the intesion of the word for the average adult. Once we accept this the *necessity* for prior knowledge of an essence or possession of a proto-concept (Fodor's *F* and *G*) simply disappears: what the acquisition of the word has achieved is a toe-hold in the linguistic system on the basis of *an* not *the* intension. This is indissociable from the view that there is no such entity as *the* intension of a word, because words have an inherent potential for assimilation and accommodation. Or to put it another way: word-meanings evolve as the *culture* develops.

But would not Fodor remind us at this point that adults and children, in fact, succeed rather well in communicating with each other? He calls Vygotsky's attempt to deal with this kind of objection 'simply hopeless'.[81] Vygotsky's claim was that the child's 'usage of words coincides with that of adults in its objective reference but not in its meaning'.[82] That is to say, children's and adults' words may share extensions whilst having different intensions. But Fodor's answers to Vygotsky are themselves unsatisfactory. First, he says that we discuss with children such things as witches and goblins which have the same extension (that is, the null set) quite successfully, so our communication cannot be being mediated by a common objective reference. But – in answer – they do have a form of objective reference which is their material representation in books, cartoons etc., and which is enough to secure a reference around very different intensions (many children, but few adults, believe they are real). A similar case: my daughter at four years old refused to believe that Elvis Presley had just died because she could watch his films on television. What we can regard as the objective reference (stretching it: 'extension') in this case was filmed representations of Presley not the Presley ashes. The refusal to believe in the death highlighted what (despite 'successful' communication as in: 'No, we're *not* having that Elvis record on again') was communication, with profoundly different intensions, because the child believed what she saw on the television was necessarily a creature living at that point of time.

Fodor's second argument is deeply puzzling. It is roughly that if Vygotsky puts so much faith in the meaning-securing properties of objective reference then he must be an old-style philosophical empiricist who

thinks that concepts are severally related to experience by necessary and sufficient conditions for their application so that whether a given concept applies is, at least in principle, independent of any fact about the world except those mentioned in its definition.[83]

In other words Vygotsky is being interpreted as exactly what he is arguing against: a supporter of semantic essence-ism. Finally, Fodor puts much weight on the claim that he interprets Vygotsky to be making about the difference in *kind* between child and adult meanings. This is not my reading of Vygotsky, although a Piagetian would certainly take the view that Fodor attacks.

I suspect that Vygotsky had very young children in mind when he wrote of communication being carried forward on the basis of common extensions and divergent intensions. Indeed, let us take as an illustrative case *pre*-verbal child–adult communication. Studies have confirmed that there is a period in the baby's life (roughly at eight months) when he becomes fascinated by objects and their relations,[84] sometimes to the exclusion of the mother. Successful mother-managed communication must therefore take place via the object so that mother, object and baby become enmeshed in what Werner and Kaplan called the 'primordial sharing situation'.[85] Clearly the object, be it, teddy, cup or rattle, 'means' something different to the mother and to the child, but their interaction is nevertheless sustained through this common reference. The early verbal exchanges between adults and children are often in the nature of elaborations of this.[86]

Good and bad alternatives to semantic essence-ism

It is now time to consider rather more carefully, and from a *non*-Wittgensteinian perspective, some of the problems with semantic essence-ism (henceforth: 'semanticism'), and in particular to cover objections implied against it through the work of the logician W. V. O. Quine. But first we will consider two less formal difficulties.

The first problem is that if we know the meaning of a word by virtue of knowing an essence or set of semantic features, then this must contain an infinity of negative information. (Cf. previous chapter where I note the problem encountered by propositional theories of belief that they entail people having beliefs of the kind that 'paint is not a refreshing drink'.) At some point the Katz and Fodor theory must say that if we are prevented by restrictions on selection rather than knowledge of the world from saying things like 'The cathedral flew to New Zealand' then we would need to have as part of our stored knowledge of being a 'cathedral' that it does not fly – and the same goes for our knowledge of water taps, fields etc. Of course we would also have to store the fact that cathedrals do not float, crumble like cake and so on. Where might such a process stop? As Johnson-Laird has pointed out,[87] probably the only kind of negative information that we store is information such as that spiders are not insects and whales are not fish.

A second problem flips up on the other side of the same coin. How is it that we *do* get meaning, indeed often heightened meaning, from word-combinations that flout the selection-restrictions? Symbolist poetry is not a very persuasive example, but what about just good, if not very plain, prose; such as Peter Tinniswood's description of a face as being 'a morass of lumbering puzzlement'.[88] Semantic feature theory only seems to work for the most literal speech and, as socio-linguistic research has shown,[89] a very high proportion of our language is figurative.

We will now approach the matter by way of the general imposs-ibility, noted above, of giving a fixed, absolute and formal definition of a word so successfully that every apple, house, act of mendacity, and prelim year, undergraduate registration card has a defining property P such that statements that 'the thing/quality/act/whatever has this property', *have* to be true. Even if we give a finite *list* of properties there are radical difficulties with what is necessary to the list and when it is sufficient. To put the matter more technically: it is not possible to have *analytic* truths of the form that (say) an apple has property P. Analytic judgements have been defined somewhat differently by different philosophers but essentially they are the judgements that are true in virtue of what their words mean rather than because of the way the world is. Kant defined an analytic truth as one whose predicate is included in its subject and whose negation is therefore contradictory: 'Their son is a boy', for example. *Synthetic* judgements on the other hand, tell us something about the way things are, so their truth depends on empirical fact, e.g. 'Their son is a prodigy'. To return to semanticism then, if it is not the case that linguistic terms express fixed essences then the distinction between analytic and synthetic truths looks rather shaky, or at least it looks to be a matter of degree. If we take the case of 'son' in our example, it is very easy to envisage conversational exchanges in which our analytic example would be genuinely informative or synthetic (e.g. a chromo-some test on the offspring, or the statement being made with the implication that 'boys will be boys'). This is the thesis of 'radical empiricism': every statement that is claimed to be analytic in virtue of the definition of its terms has some empirical content.

The other direction from which to approach the problem is from logic itself, as did Quine in his famous paper 'Two dogmas of empiricism'.[90] Quine's case was not directed against formalised logical truths, such as $p \rightarrow q$, p, therefore q, but against purportedly analytic truths that are a mixture of the purely logical and the definitional, as in our above example. Definitions (for example, 'a son is a male offspring') depend upon synonymity (that is, 'son' and 'male offspring' have the same meaning). The problem is that if we want to define analytic truth in terms of synonymity we find that the only way we have of construing synonymity is in terms of analytic truth; hence there is a kind of 'intensional circle'. Here is the gist: we start with a purportedly analytic judgment (such as 'the son is a boy') express this as a truth in logic dependent on a definition (for example, 'p is q' when p is defined as q), express this as the self-evident truth p is p because p can be substituted for q, then show that this substitution works because p and q are synonymous – they 'mean the same thing'. But the only analysis of equivalent meaning here is that p means q because 'p is q' yields an analytic truth. Every judgement whose truth rests on the meaning of its terms is caught in this intensional circle. For our purposes, what the intensional circle shows about the dependency of analytic truths upon synonymity is less important than the converse dependency of synonymity upon the notion – *itself* dependent – of analyticity. Analyticity is leaning on as well as being leant on, so synonymity lacks the logical prop that semanticists wish it to have.

Quine's sceptical case against synonymity is closely related to his scepticism about the translation of terms from one language into another. In pairing the words and sentences of one language with those of another language there are *in principle* many ways of succeeding: many schemes of translation will 'fit'. The only 'evidence' we can have about the meanings used by a native speaker of a foreign language, consists of the sentences he will accept or reject in given circumstances (or 'stimulus conditions' as Quine calls them). All we can do here is assimilate the foreigner's meanings to our own (cf. Chapter 1 and Davidson's comments on 'warping the evidence to fit the frame'). For Quine – a behaviourist – meaning is nothing more than dispositions to assent to, or dissent from, sentences. However, we do not have to be behaviourists to appreciate the problems that the 'indeterminacy of radical translation' set for semanticism. Essentially, Quine's point is similar to Wittgenstein's regarding the ultimate dependency of the understanding of pictures, rules, words, etc. upon an *interpretation*: the empirical evidence for one translation scheme could always be interpreted in favour of another scheme.[91] If we do reject behaviourism in this context we can still say that in meaning something in language L_1 person X has something in mind, and that person Y in language L_2 also has something in mind that may be treated as equivalent to person X's meaning in some circumstances. And we can do this whilst denying that there is any sense to the claim that what they have in mind could ever be the *same* thing – the same intension. Certainly, the equivalence is not strong enough to support logical truths. (Cf. the problems with type-identity monism that were discussed in Chapter 2.) So the problem of translation between languages is only the problem of translation within languages (that is, synonymity) writ large. Quine has, in fact, set down the verbal theory of thought to which these theses commit him.[92]

For many people the implication from this line of argument that the 'same thought' is never expressed in different words or indeed that thoughts can never be type identical even when expressed in the same words is a very uncomfortable one. But perhaps it is possible to make this conclusion seem a little more palatable by considering an obvious case and then trying to appreciate how the differences between the obvious case and the other cases may indeed be differences of degree. Here is an obvious case: imagine that the great bad poet William McGonagall, on top of all his other problems, became blind and in ignorance of John Milton's earlier effort wrote a poem about it. The final lines of this poem might have been:

For no one can gainsay/
the usefulness of those who stand in readiness out of the way.

Now I do not think that many people would want to claim that this expressed the same thought as Milton's:

They also serve who only stand and wait.

But where is the difference in kind between this case and one in which we suppose that 'there is no more wine left' and 'the drink is finished' express the same thought?

Before passing on to review how some logicians have tried to break out of the intensional circle, let us consider the implications of the Quinean analysis of meaning for Fodor's developmental claims. Indeed it is interesting to note that G. Harman anticipated the Fodor thesis and compared it with the broadly Wittgensteinian/Quinean approach in a paper published as early as 1970.[93] There he contrasted a 'code-breaking' (CB) view of language acquisition with the 'incorporation view' (IV) (see the earlier discussion of Field's thesis for the same distinction). On CB:

> one's inner language, which one thinks in, is distinct from one's outer language, which one speaks. Communication involves coding or translation between inner and outer languages. Learning language is a matter of learning an outer language and involves acquiring the ability to do such coding or translation.

The contemporary theorist with whom Harman associates this thesis is Jerrold Katz. On IV:

> Knowledge of a language is the ability to use that language; and the primary use of language is in thought. Knowing a language is being able to think in it. Learning an outer language involves the incorporation of that language into one's inner language.[94]

Quine and Wittgenstein are the main contemporary proponents cited here.

One particularly interesting facet of Harman's discussion involves the recognition that this is an empirical divergence as well as a philosophical divergence – or at least that the two kinds of issue run together. He recognises that on IV, comprehension cannot far precede production, that is, the language that the child understands should be, more or less and allowing for the odd extreme case, the language he is competent in using. The conclusion of an empirical study by Shipley, Smith and Gleitman[95] is quoted in favour of the opposite view that comprehension *does* run well ahead of production. However, some fourteen years later, with evidence at our disposal of the kind marshalled by Barrett,[96] this conclusion looks very shaky indeed. And even if further evidence led us once more to favour the position that comprehension runs far ahead of production, it is still open to IV, as Harman says, to regard thoughts not as sentences with 'deep structures' (that is, not hierarchical syntactic units in a fit state to be said) but as 'simply the deep structures without the sentences (but with the relevant words)',[97] that is, a string of inner words, or perhaps only one word, which carries the propositional form of a possible sentence *for the subject* which the subject is unable to frame as an utterance.

But whether or not supporters of CB accept such a proposal they *must* claim that, for communication to be possible on their model and for translation between inner and outer language to take place in acquisition, two different sentences or codes can express the 'same thought', that is, different forms of words can be type-identical, or identical in intension. Here, of course, is where Quine's indeterminacy of radical translation thesis' comes in. Much hinges on whether his argument is a good one or not. By and large Harman supports the Quine thesis and concludes that IV is probably in better shape than CB. What clinches the argument in favour of the Quine thesis, for Harman, is that the inevitability of translation being a matter of *degree* can be shown up by its *non-transitive* nature. That is, 'if *x* is the translation of *y* and *y* is the translation of *z*, *x* need not be the translation of *z*'.[98]

Clearly, Quine's intensional circle threatens to undermine the whole basis of semanticism, and by extension that of code-breaking theories of language acquisition. So not surprisingly there have been a number of concerted efforts to break out of it. These have been of two main varieties (i) the 'empirical' challenge from linguists such as Katz that people regard the analytic/synthetic distinction as one of kind not of degree;[99] (ii) a principled objection from linguists such as David Lewis,[100] J. Hintikka[101] and Richard Montague[102] who attempt an 'extensional' treatment of meaning and necessity. The latter is by far the more serious.

Broadly, if meaning can be related in a principled way to objective reference or extension then analyticity can be made independent of its subjective, psychological embedding, can be made a fact of reality rather than a fact of mental convention. Thus, 'Their son is a boy' is analytic because the extension of 'son' will *in fact* be a male child. 'All fathers are (or have been) men' is analytically true because the extension of 'fathers' is included in that of 'men'. But things are not *this* easy because words only have extensions by virtue of the fact that they, as it were, 'point to reality' and this matter of 'pointing to' is intension. This is the problem.

Given this, let us then attend to the role which such an extensional approach assigns to the intension/extension relationship. An extension of a sentence, for Lewis, is its truth-value, and the extension of a common noun is the set of things to which it applies. The extension depends on the meaning of words but also 'on other things as well: on facts about the world, on time of utterance, on place of utterance, on the speaker, on the surrounding discourse, etc.' Lewis calls the latter set, *indices*. The intension of a sentence is a *function* which relates such indices to an extension or truth-value. 'An *appropriate intension* for a sentence is any function from indices to truth-values'.[103] The decision to regard intensions as the functions which determine extensions originated with Carnap.[104]

The above quotation from Lewis mentioned 'facts about the world' as one of the extra things (in addition to word meaning) on which truth-value of sentences depends. (Essentially, Carnap concentrated on these facts alone ignoring time of utterance, place, context etc.) To see how this works I must introduce the technical expression 'logically possible worlds' which Carnap, after Leibniz, employed. 'Snow is white' is true in a world in which snow *is* white and false in worlds in which snow is black, green, etc. There are an infinity of logically possible worlds in which a sentence can be true or false. Therefore we need to know at least two things if we are to determine the truth value of a sentence: (i) the possible world in which it is supposed to hold, and (ii) the meaning of the words. A 'possible world co-ordinate' for Lewis and Montague is one feature of the index, but the total index for a sentence must include a number of further facts about context, speaker, audience, time, etc. On this theory, therefore, intensions are not semantic essences but the functions which relate indices to extensions: the 'pointers at' reality.

Moreover, on this account logical necessity is not dependent upon analyticity, thus upon synonymity, thus upon semantic essences. A sentence which is necessarily true is *true in all possible worlds*. On this basis a form of 'modal' logic[105] (that is, a logic of necessity and possibility) has been developed whose semantics are purely extensional, in which intensions are functions from possible worlds to truth-values. Montague claimed that in producing a semantics for English of this nature 'we have been able to do with denotation (i.e.

objective reference) alone',[106] and so establish a rigorous *science* of semantics in which the embarrassing dependency upon essences has been eradicated.

Now, my task in a book of this nature is not to assess critically possible worlds semantics. I have mentioned it here because the picture would be seriously incomplete without it. But the picture would actually be distorted if I left the impression that possible world semantics has established a sound basis for scientific semantic theory in the face of Wittgensteinian and Quineian scepticism. Indeed the success of such a theory would vitiate most of the assumptions and arguments of this book, because 'intension' as I have been using it is a sloppy version of the traditional (and itself quite sloppy) notion of meaning-for-the-subject. Does this traditional notion of intension have to be jettisoned and replaced by the notion of a 'function'?

There have been three kinds of objection to possible world semantics. First, it is evident that its proponents cannot agree about the ontological status of these possible worlds.[107] Second, as Putnam has pointed out,[108] it is simply false to claim that knowing (i) a description of a possible world and (ii) the meaning assigned to the words in a sentence is sufficient for a person to judge truth-value. Even if the characterisation of the logically possible world is clear to him the problem *still* remains of *what is going to count* as a chair, apple, act of cunning and so on. This still depends upon a particular 'theory' as Putnam calls it. That is to say, it is dependent upon an interpretation of the word. Words like 'chair' have meanings of course, but they are not connected with extensions in such a simple way, whether the extensions are in the real world or in logically possible worlds.

Third, proponents of semanticism have argued, rather as did Putnam, that possible world semantics cannot be established without some dependency upon the very notion that they wish to eradicate – that of 'sense' or meaning. (The terms which Montague tends to use, 'sense' and 'denotation', are closer to the ones originally used by Frege – '*Sinn*' and '*Bedeutung*' – and they are equivalent to 'meaning of an expression' versus 'objective reference'.) Katz and Katz[109] discuss Montague's theory in particular. Although it would not be fruitful to investigate their argument in any detail its flavour can be given. They discriminate between what they call Montague's 'advertised' position and his 'real' position. The advertised position is encapsulated in the quotation I gave above: semantics can be purely extensional. The 'real' position, however, involves a commitment to the sense as distinct from the denotation of a sentence. This comes through Montague's use of 'analysis trees', which are graphic representations of the steps in the construction of a sentence from a finite set of syntactic expressions. Katz and Katz argue that such a notion is as near as makes no difference to the traditional concept of the represented sense or meaning of a sentence. (For example, two analysis trees are said to represent the same sense when they are logically equivalent, and an expression is ambiguous if and only if it has two analysis trees which are not logically equivalent – not a million miles in fact from transformational grammar's 'deep structures'.) If Katz and Katz are correct, Montague grammar, despite its pretensions to the contrary, has not escaped a commitment to the traditional notion of intension.

But where does all this leave psycho-linguistics? Recently there has been an attempt by some psycho-linguists to develop a psychological theory of language out of some of the intuitions of possible world semantics within the context of the computational theory of mind. This is 'procedural semantics' which deals, in Johnson-Laird's[110] words 'with the meaning of the procedures that computers are told to execute'.[111] In general, compiling and executing a program is supposed to be strongly analogous to a person comprehending an utterance. There are two stages in this comprehension process, according to Johnson-Laird: (i) translating the sentence into 'a program in [the subject's] internal mental language',[112] (ii) then deciding whether to 'run it' (that is, to pass the salt, to believe the proposition). It is not at all clear as to how Johnson-Laird regards this 'internal mental language' in the *human* case. The empirical face of procedural semantics is a research strategy which disposes of abstract deep structure,[113] proposes that comprehension and production is sequential (left-to-right) and, most importantly, tries to change the point of emphasis from understanding and producing declarative utterances to the *process* of understanding and producing a range of communicative moves (question, answer, request – in addition to making statements). Many psychologists would regard these as healthy developments.

But the *conceptual* face of procedural semantics is something rather different. Johnson-Laird parallels the 'model theoretical' (that is, possible world) semantics with procedural semantics by virtue of the fact that just as the former has intensions as the functions from possible worlds (plus other things) to truth values so, for the latter, 'the intension of a program [is] the procedure that is executed when the program is run, and the extension of a program [is] the result that the program returns when it has been executed'.[114] So 'a truth-value is but one of the possible results of executing a program; others include answers to questions, compliance with requests, additions to knowledge'.[115]

This seems wholly bizarre. How can an answer to a question be an extension? If so, we may well ask where the truth or otherwise of the answer is supposed to enter the picture. How, indeed, can the cognitive procedures involved in understanding or framing an utterance *be* an intension? Is it not the worst kind of psychologism to equate contingent, a-semantic processes with the meaning of words and their reference to the world? But, more seriously, how can it be possible to lump 'truth-value' in with answering questions, passing the salt and the like? Every utterance takes its meaning at least in part from its relationship to the world: what 'pass the salt' means is dependent in *some* way upon what is true of the world. This (i.e. the dependency of a theory of meaning on a theory of truth) is what philosophers such as Davidson have insisted as we discussed in Chapter one. What Johnson-Laird's application of procedural semantics to psychology seems to want to avoid at all costs is any commitment to a theory of representation. It is as if, as a means of avoiding the problems with a computational theory of representation on the one hand and commitment to a natural language theory of representation on the other, nothing about representation is being suggested. Thus we have a theory that is all process and no state.

It is notable that a critique of procedural semantics – including a version of this argument – has been undertaken by Jerry Fodor.[116] It makes strange reading indeed; not because of the content, which is highly sympathetic to the present account, nor because of the style, which is Fodor at his most bantering, but because of who is writing it. Fodor interprets Johnson-Laird's references to an 'internal mental language' – in the absence, as I said, of any clear evidence to the contrary – as meaning that understanding language involves translation into our machine-language. After all, procedural semantics is a computational theory. Explaining the human capacity to extract meaning from language as 'translation into the *S*'s machine language' is essentially, of course, Fodor's *own* theory, or if not exactly that then

Fodor is committed to something as near to this as makes no difference. The strangeness resides in the fact that it is *this* which Fodor spends most of his time attacking; and his refutation is a splendid job. He even fields the Wittgenstein/Quine view that there is a sense in which every word of a language should be regarded as a semantic primitive. Of course Johnson-Laird points this out with relish in a reply,[117] together with some well-chosen quotations from *The Language of Thought* to illustrate just what Fodor's target is. Moreover many of Fodor's arguments for the traditional truth-based semantics also go directly against the thesis which he expressed in the 'methodological solipsism' paper. But then in the same year in which *The Language of Thought* appeared Fodor had co-authored an essay attacking the notion of a conceptual language,[118] so maybe Fodor's ambivalence should come as no great surprise.

But it seems to me that the way the issues have been covered in this section also leaves *us* with a rather ambivalent orientation to meaning. For neither Wittgenstein nor Quine in their arguments against semanticism were at all sympathetic to the notion of meaning being 'in the head' or of an intension being the meaning-for-the-subject. Wittgenstein gave no positive thesis and seemed to doubt the prospects for one, and Quine's positive thesis was behaviourist. Nevertheless there is a way of accepting Wittgenstein's denials that meaning is a private mental act conveying an essence, whilst allowing that the intension of an utterance can be said to be what the speaker has in mind.

We can begin by asking the question: what is it that needs to be conveyed to somebody (child or adult) for him to know the meaning of X? What has to be conveyed is a definition of some kind, which can be regarded in the case of common nouns as a set of facts about the extension – for example, that lemons have a yellow skin, a tart taste and so on. If the subject understands this definition sufficiently well to use the word as we do then he can be said to know the meaning. But how are we to regard the definition if not as the expression of a fixed semantic essence? One answer might be that what is necessary for conveying an intension is the expression of a prototype or exemplar – the typical chair, tiger, lemon etc.[119] In reality of course the extensions often vary far and wide from the exemplar that we may have 'in mind' and may even be poised on the border between the magnetic fields of two different exemplars (for instance, we may come across a new kind of fruit with an orangey-yellow skin, the size and shape of an orange, but with a taste as bitter as a lemon). But all this is in the nature of the relation between words and the world. The relation cannot really be called 'loose' (loose compared with what?) but it is not the kind of relation that a science of semantics requires.

Prototype theory,[120] as it is usually known, is nowadays very popular in psychology, especially in developmental psychology, but that is not sufficient reason to distrust it. It has, after all, very good connections (Wittgenstein's notion of family resemblance) and it has an advantage that can hardly be overemphasised: it enables us to dispose of the notion that learning a word *must* require prior abstract knowledge of a category. It does not, of course, dispose of the process of abstraction because understanding the relation between an exemplar and an instance is certainly characterisable as an abstraction process. But it enables us to understand how an abstract entity need not determine word-learning at the outset. In general, prototype theory can be preferred over essence-ism for the same kinds of reason that I argued in the previous chapter the notion of representation in natural language is preferable to that of representation in propositions: the advantage of concreteness.

Predictably, because prototype theory blunts the edge of the radical nativist thesis, the MIT nativists have loosed their formal logical battalions against its very possibility.[121] Less formally, but from the same stable, Keil[122] has recently argued that prototype theory fails because at some point we must propose that the child is 'constrained' to categorise experience in given ways. Indeed we must; and in fact a supporter of prototype theory must assume this if he is to explain how the process of word-learning gets off the ground. But his scepticism is about the prior necessity for something characterisable as abstract knowledge of conceptual categories not about *any* constraints.[123] Obviously the human child's brain is different from (say) that of the chimpanzee; and nobody would seriously propose that development was 'unconstrained' by native propensities.

Let us consider, in passing, how Keil produces a variation on the familiar Chomskian theme. Keil has collected some interesting and original data on the child's developing ability to attach predicates to appropriate subjects (such as, to judge 'The rabbit is awake' as sensible and 'The milk is awake' as not). But what is still more interesting is the way in which Keil derives support for nativism from his data. Because the philosopher Fred Sommers[124] has characterised knowledge of ontological categories in terms of something called the 'M constraint',[125] and because children (at least those old enough to be tested) almost without exception do not make gross category mistakes (for example, judging 'The idea is hungry' as sensible) they are therefore naturally predisposed, runs the argument, to obey the 'M constraint'. This is even more like the 'reincarnation' (see p. 222 above) form of argument than Chomsky's own! And, as with Chomsky, the possibility is never seriously considered that there may be other explanations for the fact that children are quite good at discriminating sense from nonsense.

Last, and by no means least, prototype theory has the considerable advantage of according rather well with what we know about infant's[126] and children's[127] concept acquisition. But unfortunately, to say that words are learned by communicating prototypes is not to say very much simply because we also have to say something substantial about the conditions for the subject's understanding the definitions. Minimally the definer and the subject must share something: certain common interests, assumptions about significance and appropriateness, maybe emotional ties,[128] and certainly a common biological nature. Wittgenstein used the term 'forms of life' (*Lebensformen*) to refer to what needs to be shared if any learning is to take place. Some would, of course, dismiss this notion as obscurantist or as a mere formula; but it is only so if taken as a *terminating* point in a philosophical discussion . . . 'ah the form of life, of course' and we sit back with our problem dissolved by a bromide. In fact it is the *semanticist* notion that we need protoconcepts for verbal concepts that is the convenient formula. To claim that no theory of language acquisition can be developed without a pretty substantial theory of human interests, endowments and social life . . . what could be more inconvenient than that! Language regarded as a 'module', [129] as in Chomsky, is one of the most seductively convenient formulae imaginable.

It was considerations such as these which lead Vygotsky to say that 'a word is a microcosm of human consciousness',[130] and, of course, consciousness, as Brentano tells us, is transitive: it necessarily takes an object. So this 'sharing' between the language-learner and the language-knower can only take place in a shared physical world. To put it another way, there cannot be intensions without extensions, meaning without world *knowledge* (that is, *true* beliefs, not just beliefs). This was, in fact, the main burden of the second section of Chapter 4, and one road towards the more or less Davidsonian approach to truth in meaning that I supported in Chapter 1. So to put the matter empirically: despite the fact that the evidence for the development of an 'object concept' determining the *timing* of linguistic development is weak,[131] no theory of language acquisition can be complete without a theory of the child's knowledge of the furniture of the world.

From intentions to intensions

In this final section I will make a few speculative suggestions about the nature of the 'level of functioning' that I cryptically referred to earlier as being necessary for the acquisition of word meaning. A few hardly less cryptic remarks will be produced about the developmental roots of intensions in sensory-motor inten*t*ions; because, to put it grandly, this seems to be the point at which our biological form of life filters into our cognitive form of life.

A theory which seeks to explain the growth of word meaning in terms of the abstraction of common properties will stress the fact that one word (such as 'red') can be applied to a great number of objects (strawberries, Santa Claus, Sunsets, etc.). But what is the consequence of attending to the fact that, conversely, many words can be applied to the *same* object? For nothing can be referenced in only *one* way. Now, it is this property of language which principally defines for us the 'intensional context': that in such contexts the substitution of a co-referential term can change truth-value. This is so because in contexts in which propositional attitudes are implicated, truth is not independent of what the speaker has 'in mind'. Given this, is it not of some importance to study the child's abilities in *pre-verbal* behavioural reference in terms of the referencing of one thing/event/person in a variety of ways?

It is not recognised as such, but the classic study of the infant's co-referential capacities has already been undertaken – by Piaget. Although there are alternative construals of the data, Piaget regarded his studies of the development of object knowledge[132] (necessarily including space, time, and causality) as describing the course of self–world dissociation through action. As we have discussed (Chapter 4), at the outset the infant can be regarded as essentially *re*active rather than active: pre-adaptive behavioural packages are triggered by the environment. Piaget would have been very unimpressed by the recent

broadly Gibsonian evidence[133] for perceptual pre-adaptations to
existence constancy, self/world differentiation and the like, because,
on his terms such behaviour is reactive rather than accommodatory.
What being accommodatory means here is changing action in the
light of new data, resulting in a gradual differentiation of actions
themselves (including perceptual accommodations such as eye-
movements) from the world – of intentions from extensions. Coming
to appreciate that there is a datum independent of our actions means
knowing that there need not be a one–to–one relationship between
an action and a datum. Indeed co-reference is almost 'built in' to
sensory-motor development in the form of sensory co-ordinations.
For example, the ability to co-ordinate visual accommodations and
manual accommodations sufficiently well to grasp a seen datum is
one of the earlier forms of co-reference. Indeed all forms of inter-
sensory co-ordinations are forms of co-reference: turning towards a
sound is another case. So we may speculate that co-reference of
action sets the infant on the road towards defining 'a something'
outside itself.

But, as Piaget's other observations show, for much of the first year
of life the object is defined by *an incompletely differentiated* co-
ordination between sight and touch. So if the object cannot be seen it
is assumed not to be *graspable* and so the infant will cease to retrieve
objects once they become completely occluded behind others. But
once the infant can retrieve completely occluded objects he can be
judged as being able to differentiate modes of reference – visual from
motor – and thus as being able to apply a range of distinct sensory-
motor references to objects. If the infant knows that his rattle may be
neither seen nor felt; seen and not felt; not felt, and not seen but
heard, and so on, these sensory modes of reference are becoming
differentiated from the object. In this way a new autonomy of each
mode of sensory reference is evolved.

But not until around the age of twelve months is a range of actions
differentiated from the object's *location*. As the perseveration error of
eight to twelve months demonstrates (the infant habitually finds
something behind one occluder, the object is transferred to another
hiding place in the sight of the infant, and the infant returns to the
original location to search) objects are still defined by actions at
specific locations. As Bremner's data tell us,[134] in some circumstances these are purely egocentric actions (for example, searching
exclusively on the left hand side of his body) and less often they are

allocentric actions (such as always looking for the object under the *white* cover). In both cases, we might interpret Piaget as saying, the perseveration error is made by virtue of the fact that the infant cannot appreciate that a *range* of perceptual accommodations can define an extension. For example when the object is moved from *A* to *B* (the new hiding place) the infant does not take this in as being a movement of that object because a visual accommodation to that movement is not yet 'regarded' as an action co-referential with that of manual retrieval at location *A*.

We may interpret the failure of older infants (roughly twelve to eighteen months old) to cognise invisible displacements of objects in much the same way. (Here, for example, the adult shows the infant a coin being hidden in his – the adult's – hand; the hand is moved behind a cushion and the coin deposited there, the hand is brought forth still closed and shown to the infant, the infant searches in the hand and finding nothing but does *not* go on to search behind the cushion.) In this case Piaget's explanation is that the development of the ability to form mental images of absent objects and processes (which, for Piaget is derived from imitation) enables the invisible displacement to be recorded. Expressed in the present referential terms: the range of actions which may define an object is broadened so as to include *unwitnessed* but *inferred* actions, which is tantamount to saying that objects can be referenced in *thought* as well as action. In this way the basis for intensions is laid.

What we have been considering up to now is *intra*-individual co-reference. But, of course, there also is, and has to be, *inter*-individual co-reference – particularly between mother and baby. I will not dwell on this as it has already been discussed.[135]

I am proposing therefore that, just like intensions, intentions are definitively co-referential, and that it is in *this* sense that the roots of meaning are to be found in action. But so far, so little. What is the bridge that must be crossed into the language system, the bridge that object-knowers as sophisticated as chimpanzees do not cross? So late in the day I can merely indicate two related answers to this question that are open to us (apart from the obvious vocal–auditory pre-adaptations) – one of them is depressingly general and the other all too hackneyed. The first would be to point to a research strategy: look at the differences between the human and the chimpanzee forms of life, in particular at chimpanzees' *lack* of interest in objects relative to people,[136] and to humans' capacity for ascribing intentions to others, relative to that of chimpanzees. The second form of answer would be that it is in the nature of human beings to symbolise their intentions as motoric or vocal gestures. Here perhaps the Piagetian notion of the 'symbolic functions' really is too broad to be of much use: the adaptation of arbitrary signifiers is what we require here. And surely this symbolising of intentions is something that infants *bring* to the process of language acquisition: it is hardly likely to require teaching. (Goldin-Meadow and Feldman's evidence of deaf children's *invention* of rulebound signing systems is very notable in this context.)[137] This is why it is reasonable to translate early one-word utterances such as 'car', as 'there is a car', or 'give me the car': as is the case for early actions on objects, the car and the mental orientation towards it are not differentiated so one word includes both extension and an intension. And this is why such early utterances do not – *pace* the structural theorists – express 'underlying grammatical relations' such as 'demonstrative + article + noun' or 'verb + indirect object + direct object'. And, finally, this is why the child's early syntactic units are modular or hierarchical – because actions are.

Postscript

Needless to say, the mystery about 'the relation between thought and language' is not dispelled simply by being sceptical about the division between thought and language. Although I believe that an essentially verbal theory of human thought is the appropriate one I must admit that such a belief does little to clarify how it is that language and thought seem to have a kind of mutuality relationship: beliefs may be determined by language and language by beliefs. Our implicitly 'causal' model of the relationship seems to be deeply wrong in *some* way; if only we could say in *what* way! But then, at least such a view saves us from the paradoxes created by semanticism.

Yet there are still paradoxes aplenty in the verbal theory of thought. Truly creative thought, for example, needs to break clear from language and yet this can only be achieved on the basis of some form of symbolising activity. This is a problem for the verbal theory; but it is still more problematic to view Shakespeare and Einstein and Matisse as having better machine languages in their brains than the rest of us.

A verbal theory of thought will tell us only some of the story, maybe even as little as half of it, given that we have two halves to our brain. But, in mitigation, it *is* in the context of the rational rather than the inspirational that the 'thought and language' debate has traditionally been played out – and half a story is better than the wrong story.

I will end with just one more paradox from the verbal theory of thought: more words, more distinctions, more concepts does not necessarily mean better thought, and it may mean worse. This is nicely illustrated in a passage from the Martin Amis novel *Other People*:

> 'But what was bad about her?' Mary asked.
> 'Insecurity, I think. For all her brains and looks, I think she was desperately insecure . . .'
> Big deal, thought Mary as Michael chatted contentedly on.
> Insecure. Is that all. Who isn't? What did people do and say about what they said and did before that kind of word came along?[138]

The word 'insecure' as used here is derived partly from depth psychology and partly from existentialism (ontological insecurity) through the usual distorting channels of human talk and now emerges as a bedraggled banality. It is the kind of word that taken by itself is little more than a tautology about human life – as the Amis character says – and harmless in itself. But its dangerous combination of the empty and the spuriously clinical makes it a prime tool for pseudo-thought and self-deception. In the passage, a man too vain to have any real psychological insight makes an implicit claim to such insight, whilst at the same time protecting himself from the memory of the woman who obliterated him in a battle of wills. Thus by the use of that word to describe her he can hide from himself the fact that he was proved to be the weaker: now he is merely the victim of her 'insecurity'. This immunises him, also, from having to regard himself as an object worthy of her contempt.

Maybe when we used terms like 'unhappy', 'mentally ill', 'vulnerable' or – most important – *said nothing on the subject* where now we say 'insecure' we were forced to be more honest because we were, paradoxically, nearer reality.

We should never blame the *words*; words are only as good or as bad as the people using them.

Notes and References

Introduction: Setting the Scene

1. Functionalism in cognitive *developmental* psychology means something quite different. For example, a functionalist explanation of language development is one that implicates the child's extra-linguistic intentions. See my book, *The Acquisition of Knowledge* (London: Macmillan, 1978).

1 Philosophy and the Science of Human Nature

1. For example, T. Trabasso, C. A. Riley and E. Wilson, 'Spatial strategies in reasoning: a developmental study', in R. Falmagne (ed.), *Psychological Studies of Logic and its Development* (Hillsdale, New Jersey: Erlbaum Associates, 1976).
2. R. J. Sternberg, 'Representation and process in linear syllogistic reasoning', *Journal of Experimental Psychology: General*, 1980, 109, pp. 119–59.
3. N. R. F. Maier, 'Reasoning in white rats', *Comparative Psychology Monographs*, 1929, 29.
4. See H. Werner and B. Kaplan, *Symbol Formation* (London: John Wiley, 1963).
5. See: D. Klahr, and J. G. Wallace, *Cognitive Development and Information Processing* (Hillsdale, New Jersey: Erlbaum Associates, 1976) and Trabasso's recent work (see note 1) passim.
6. J. Russell, 'The status of egocentric errors in children's performance of allocentric placement tasks', *Educational Psychology*, 1981, vol. 1, pp. 159–71.
7. This example comes from J. A. Gray's *Elements of a Two-process Theory of Learning* (London: Academic Press, 1975).
8. By this I mean that it is standard practice to study structures such as the striate cortex by developmental studies – with kittens for example.
9. For an expression of this view see D. W. Hamlyn's *Experience and the Growth of Understanding* (London: Routledge & Kegan Paul, 1978) p. 109.
10. See K. Nelson, 'Structure and strategy in learning to talk', *Monographs of the Society for Research in Child Development*, 1973, 38, no. 149.
11. See J. H. Flavell, 'Metamemory' In R. V. Kail and J. W. Hagan (eds), *Perspectives in the Development of Memory and Cognition* (Hillsdale, New Jersey, Erlbaum Associates, 1977).
12. This is not strictly a prelude. Rather, the processes of object–concept development and the acquisition of the kind of causal knowledge discussed here are indissociable.

13. See S. Körner, *Kant* (Harmondsworth: Penguin, 1955) p. 85.
14. See T. Mischel, 'Scientific and philosophical psychology: an historical introduction', in T. Mischel (ed.) *Human Action* (London: Academic Press, 1968). Also: S. Toulmin in T. Mischel (ed.), *Cognitive Development and Epistemology* (London: Academic Press, 1971).
15. See F. Jacob, *The Logic of Living Systems: a History of Heredity* (London: Allen Lane, 1974).
16. See A. Moszkowski, *Conversations with Albert Einstein* (London: Sidgwick & Jackson, 1972).
17. See my article 'The status of genetic epistemology', *Journal for the Theory of Social Behaviour*, 1979, vol. 9, pp. 53–70, for a detailed discussion of how philosophical theses are affected by psychological data.
18. See T. Mischel, reference in note 14.
19. This view is present in Aristotle in that he analysed 'wanting' causally; but is definitively in David Hume.
20. L. Wittgenstein, *Philosophical Investigations* (Oxford: Blackwell, 1953) paras 611–60.
21. Principally Gilbert Ryle, G. E. M. Anscombe, Anthony Kenny.
22. A. I. Melden, *Free Action* (London: Routledge & Kegan Paul, 1961).
23. J. Shotter, *Images of Man in Psychological Research* (London: Methuen, 1975)
24. C. Taylor, 'Interpretation and the sciences of man', *Review of Metaphysics*, 1971, 12, pp. 3–52.
25. See note 17.
26. B. F. Skinner, *About Behaviourism* (New York: Alfred A. Knopf, 1974), p. 14. This gives a clear exegesis of radical behaviourism.
27. In *The Acquisition of Knowledge* (Macmillan, 1978) pp. 240–8, I examined how the related Wittgensteinian notion that mental states are not 'private' provides a justification for the researcher's reference to the mental states of his subject.
28. J. Shotter, 'The development of personal powers', in M. P. M. Richards (ed.), *The Integration of the Child into the Social World* (Cambridge University Press, 1974).
29. See M. E. Lamb, 'A re-examination of the infant social world', *Human Development*, 1977, no. 20, pp. 65–85.
30. The philosopher-psychologist G. H. Mead (1863–1931), who provided the philosophical framework within which such theorising is carried on, referred to his position as *social behaviourism*.
31. J. Shotter, 'Conference overview' (read by John Newsom) at the Annual Conference of the Developmental Section of the British Psychological Society, 1979, held at Southampton University.
32. See R. D. Laing, *Sanity, Madness and the Family* (Harmondsworth: Penguin, 1964).
33. Routledge & Kegan Paul, 1958.
34. Peters has, in fact, stated such a viewpoint more recently in S. C. Brown (ed.), *Philosophy of Psychology* (London: Macmillan, 1974) Chairman's remarks, pp. 53–9.
35. Ibid, p. 10.
36. Ibid, p. 12.
37. For further comments on the notion of the hermeneutical circle see my 'The status of genetic epistemology' (note 17 for reference).
38. S. Toulmin, 'Rules and their relevance for understanding human behaviour', in T. Mischel (ed.) *The Self* (Oxford: Blackwell, 1977).
39. S. Toulmin, 'Reasons and causes', in R. Borger and F. Cioffi (eds), *Explanation in the Behavioural Sciences* (Cambridge University Press, 1971).

40. See principally: A. J. Ayer, *Man as a Subject for Science*, Lecture 6 (London: Athlone Press, 1964). Also, D. Pears, 'Are there reasons for active causes?', in A. Stroll (ed.), *Epistemology* (London: Harper & Row, 1967).

41. D. Davidson, 'Actions, reasons and causes', *Journal of Philosophy*, 1963. Reprinted in A. R. White (ed.) *The Philosophy of Action* (Oxford University Press, Oxford, 1968).

42. Ibid, p. 86.

43. See Toulmin (note 36). Also T. N. Chopra, 'Explaining and characterising human actions', *Mind*, 1979, 88.

44. See note 36, quote from p. 5.

45. P. Pettit, 'Rationalisation and the art of explaining action', in N. Bolton (ed.) *Philosophical Problems in Psychology* (London: Methuen, 1979).

46. Ibid, p. 11.

47. See review by Betty A. Levy, 'Speech processing during reading', in A. L. Lesgold *et al., Cognitive Psychology and Instruction* (New York: Plenum Press, 1977).

48. At a seminar given at Liverpool University, May 1980.

49. C. McGinn, 'Action and its explanation'. In N. Bolton (ed.); see note 45.

50. In S. C. Brown (ed.). See note 34.

51. Ibid, p. 42.

52. Ibid, p. 42.

53. Conducted with Merrill Carlsmith.

54. A. J. Marcel, 'Conscious and pre-conscious recognition of polysemous words: locating the selective effects of prior verbal context', in R. S. Nickeson (ed.), *Attention and Performance: VIII* (Hillsdale, New Jersey, Erlbaum Associates, 1980).

55. This is a meaningless jumble of lines, usually cut-up pieces of upper-case letters. The same effect is *not* found with energy masking (which is just white noise) for some reason.

56. Shallice, T., 'Dual functions of consciousness', *Psychological Review*, 1972, vol. 79, pp. 383–93.

57. As note 54, p. 456.

58. I intend here the Cambridge human performance tradition which originated with Craik.

59. As note 51, p. 43.

60. Monism, contrary to 'dualism', holds that the mental world is identical to the physical world; thus mental events are brain events.'Anomalous' is being used *literally* here to mean 'unlawful'.

61. J. Piaget, *Psychology and Epistemology* (Harmondsworth: Penguin, 1972) pp. 81–4.

62. Referred to by Piaget in his *Genetic Epistemology* (New York: Columbia University Press, 1970).

63. As note 51, p. 62.

64. Some would take the view that the physical sciences do not deal in causes at all. The classic presentation of this view was by Bertrand Russell in 'On the notion of cause', *Proceedings of the Aristotelian Society*, 1912.

65. See Introduction, note 1.

66. D. W. Hamlyn, *Experience and the Growth of Understanding* (London: Routledge & Kegan Paul, 1978).

67. D. W. Hamlyn, 'Folk psychology and cognitive psychology', *Cognition*, 1981, p. 117.

68. See my article, 'The interpretation of conservation instructions by five-year-old children', *Journal of Child Psychology and Psychiatry*, 1975, vol. 16, pp. 233–44.

69. Reviewed in my 'Propositional attitudes', in M. Beveridge (ed.) *Children Thinking through Language* (London: Edward Arnold, 1982).

70. Most of these are collected in D. Davidson, *Essays on Actions and Events* (Oxford University Press, 1981).

71. All quotations will be from the 'Psychology as philosophy' paper. See note 34 for reference. This and next two are from p. 51; the fourth, p. 52.

72. Again, I must point out the crucial role of David Hamlyn's writings in this regard. See note 66.

73. J. Russell, 'Cognitive structures and verbalised beliefs', in S. Modgil (ed.) *Jean Piaget: A British Tribute* (London: Routledge & Kegan Paul, 1983).

74. In all conservation problems the child is presented with two identical arrays or substances (e.g. rows of sweets, drinks, balls of plasticine): Standard s and Variable v_1. Variable v_1 is then perceptually transformed in some way to make Variable v_2. The child is asked whether Standard s = Variable v_2.

75. J. Russell, 'Non-verbal and verbal judgements of length invariance', *British Journal of Psychology*, 1979, 70, pp. 313–17. Also J. Russell, 'Nonverbal abilities in number conservation', *Educational Psychology* 1983, vol. 3, pp. 43–53.

76. See note 68 for reference.

77. E.g. M. D. S. Braine, and B. L. Shanks, 'The development of the conservation of size', *Journal of Verbal Learning and Verbal Behaviour*, 1965, vol. 4, pp. 227–42.

78. Unpublished data.

79. See note 68 reference. Also papers by Russell in *Journal of Genetic Psychology*, 1982; *Child Development*, 1981; *Educational Psychology*, 1981; *Journal of Experimental Child Psychology*, 1981.

80. 'The preference for deductive over perceptual story completions', Paper presented to the Annual Conference of the Developmental Section of the British Psychological Society, September, 1982. Durham University. To be published. See BPS Bulletin for abstract.

81. See M. Donaldson, *Children's Minds* (Fontana, 1978) for a similar approach.

82. See B. McGee, *Popper* (London: Fontana, 1976) for a clear account of Karl Popper's philosophy of science.

83. This should not be confused with *solipsism*. Solipsism is the claim that we are logically debarred from knowing the mental states (*qua sensations*) of others. As Wittgenstein has shown, such a position rests on a misconstrual of sensation language. What I am talking about here is the testing of hypotheses about belief systems, not questions about whether people have pains or not.

84. H. P. Grice, 'Meaning', *Philosophical Review*, 1957, 66, pp. 377–88.

85. D. Davidson, 'Belief and the basis of meaning', *Synthese*, 1974, 27, pp. 309–29.

86. Ibid. What Davidson is talking about here is the everyday ascription of meaning to individuals by individuals, not developing philosophical theories of meaning. As we have already discussed, Davidson claims that the latter enterprise can never result in certainty (see p. 43 last paragraph).

87. M. de B. Platts, *Ways of Meaning* (London: Routledge & Kegan Paul, 1980) Ch. 3.

88. See note 30.

89. A. Denkel, 'The speaker's communicative intent', *Journal for the Theory of Social Behaviour*, 1980, 10, pp. 19–38 (extract from p. 23).

90. In *Philosophical Investigations* (see note 20) Wittgenstein gives what he assumes to be the impossible instruction: 'Say "It's cold in here"' and mean "It's warm in here"' (para. 520).

91. See: M. A. K. Halliday, *Learning how to Mean* (London: Edward Arnold, 1975) p. 48.

92. Davidson, 'Belief and the basis of meaning', p. 21 (see note 84).
93. For example P. M. Greenfield, and J. H. Smith, *The Structure of Communication in Early Language Development* (New York: Academic Press, 1976).

2 Brain and Mind

1. See, for example, R. Rorty, 'In defence of eliminative materialism', *Review of Metaphysics*, 1970, 24, pp. 112–21.
2. See Eysenck's discussion of the status of his theory in R. Borger and F. Cioffi (eds) *Explanation in the Behavioural Sciences* (Cambridge University Press, 1970).
3. Austen Clark, *Psychological Models and Neural Mechanisms* (Oxford: Clarendon Press, 1980).
4. For a useful introduction to the literature on neurotransmission see R. M. Julien's *A Primer of Drug Action* (San Francisco: Freeman, 1981).
5. See the review by J. Maj, 'Antidepressant drugs: will new findings change the present theories of their action?' *Trends in Pharmacological Studies*, 1981, pp. 80–3.
6. J. Vetulani, R. J. Stawarz, J. V. Dingell and P. Surser, 'A possible common mechanism of action of antidepressant drugs', *Naunyn Schmiedebers Arch Pharmak*, 1976, 293, p. 109.
7. A. R. Green and D. W. Costain (eds) *Pharmacology and Biochemistry of Psychiatric Disorders* (New York: Wiley, 1981) p. 87.
8. For research on second order systems see D. C. U'Prichard, D. A. Greenberg, P. P. Sheehan, S. H. Snyder, 'Tricyclic antidepressants: therapeutic properties and affinity for alpha-noradrenergic receptor binding sites in the brain', *Science*, 1978, 199, pp. 197–8. And for work on 'downstream' neural activity see W. Kostowski, 'Brain noradrenaline, depression and antidepressant drugs: facts and hypotheses', *Trends in Pharmacological Studies*, 1981, pp. 314–17.
9. For a review of the evidence see R. Finlay-Jones, 'Showing that life events are a cause of depression – a review', *Australian and New Zealand Journal of Psychiatry*, 1981, 15, pp. 229–38.
10. M. Seligman, *Helplessness* (San Francisco: Freeman, 1975).
11. Moreover there are also suggestions from the animal literature that the observed behavioural deficits are due to the stress (shock) not to learned helplessness. See J. M. Weiss, H. I. Glazer, J. A. Pohorecky, J. Brick, and N. E. Miller, 'Effects of chronic exposure to stressors on avoidance–escape behaviour and on brain norepinephrine', *Psychosomatic Medicine*, 1975, 37 pp. 522–34. In the human literature see the special issue of *The Journal of Abnormal Psychology*, 1978, vol. 87, no. 1, which was devoted to learned helplessness.
12. H. S. Akiskal and W. T. McKinney, Jr., 'Depressive disorders: towards a unified hypothesis', *Science*, 1973, 182, pp. 20–9.
13. J. J. Schildkraut and S. S. Kety, 'Biogenic amines and emotion', *Science*, 1967, vol. 156, pp. 21–30.
14. See my trilogy of papers: 'Action from knowledge and conditioned behaviour: Part One: the stratification of behaviour', *Behaviourism*, 1980, 8, pp. 87–98. 'Action from knowledge and conditioned behaviour: Part Two: criteria for epistemic behaviour', *Behaviourism*, 1980, 8, pp. 133–48. 'Action from knowledge and conditioned behaviour: Part Three: the human case', *Behaviourism*, 1981, 9, pp. 107–26.
15. For conditioning see: J. A. Gray, *Elements of a Two-Process Theory of Learning*

(London: Academic Press, 1975). For a review of his position on anxiety see J. A. Gray, 'The neuropsychology of anxiety', *British Journal of Psychology*, 1978, 69, pp. 417–34, and also Gray's new book *The Neuropsychology of Anxiety: an Enquiry into the Functions of the Septo-Hypocampal System* (Oxford University Press, 1983).

16. From Gray, 1975, p. 347.
17. Jerry Fodor, *The Language of Thought* (Brighton: Harvester, 1976).
18. As expressed for example by L. Stein and C. P. Wise, 'Amphetamine and noradrenergic reward pathways' in E. Usdin and S. H. Snyder (eds) *Frontiers in Catecholamine Research* (Oxford: Pergamon, 1973).
19. *British Journal of Psychology* (see note 15).
20. Although learned helplessness begins from a form of stimulus-stimulus pairing (shock and stimuli signalling one half of the chamber) the situation is clearly instrumental. Learned avoidance is instrumental learning and learned helplessness the other side of the same coin: learned *una*voidance. Moreover the problem of learned helplessness is explaining why the animal *fails to take action*; in contrast the kind of behavioural breakdown with which Gray's theory of anxiety is concerned is that of the *disruption of ongoing behaviour* by stimuli classically associated with anxiety-causing stimuli as he defines them.
21. As we discussed above Davidson produced this theory in his 'Psychology as philosophy' paper (see Chapter 1 note 46). A more formal statement of the thesis is given in his 'Mental events' in his collection *Essays on Action and Events*. (Oxford: Clarendon Press, 1980).
22. Intensionality is one of the most difficult notions in philosophy to define. One distinction which it would be well to make here is that between intensionality as it will be defined in the text and Franz Brentano's revival of the scholastic notion of 'intentionality'. Brentano referred to this as a necessary feature of consciousness. Mental events are intentional because, like actions, they are necessarily directed towards objects. All consciousness if *of* something, even if that something doesn't exist or is defined as the object of subject's cognitive perspective on a physical object (intentional object). This may be illustrated through the verbs which implicate consciousness: believe, hope, intend, know, perceive, notice, remember, forget, imagine, decide . . . (Though this is also true of some non-mental verbs such as 'own' and 'accompany'; so this property of taking an object is a *necessary* not a *sufficient* condition for a verb's being mental.) Some (for example John Searle in *Mind*, 1979, 87, pp. 74–92) have taken the view that the two notions are quite distinct and should be kept separate. However, in what follows I will be working on the assumption that there is a basic commonality between the two terms; after all not only do mental verbs take objects, they create intensional contexts.
23. In Brown (ed.), *Philosophy of Psychology*, p. 43.
24. T. Honderich, 'Psychophysical lawlike connections and their problem', *Inquiry*, 1981, pp. 277–303, at p. 292.
25. Ibid, p. 286.
26. Ibid, p. 288.
27. S. P. Stich, 'On the relation between occurrents and contentful mental states.' *Inquiry*, 1981, pp. 353–8.
28. J. L. Mackie, 'The efficacy of consciousness: comments on Honderich's paper', *Inquiry*, 1981, pp. 343–51. (Extract from p. 350.)
29. See note 22.
30. *Philosophical Investigations*, para. 304.
31. In Honderich, 'Psychophysical lawlike connections', p. 279 (the 'individual correlation thesis').

32. See D. W. Hamlyn's 'Conditioning and behaviour' in Borger and Cioffi (see note 2).
33. For an early example of this see Valenstein *et al.*, 'Re-examination of the role of the hypothalamus in motivation', *Psychological Review*, 1970, 77, pp. 16–31.
34. 'Philosophy and our mental life' in Putnam's collection *Mind, Language and Reality. Philosophical Papers Vol. 2*. (Cambridge University Press, 1975).
35. Ibid, p. 291.
36. Ibid, p. 292.
37. Ibid, p. 293.
38. Just two examples of such macro-theorising might be the suggestions made by A. R. Luria about the existence of three main functional units of the brain in his *Working Brain* (Penguin, 1973), and the 'group selective theory' of the higher brain functions presented by G. M. Edelman and V. B. Mountcastle in *The Mindful Brain* (Cambridge, Mass: MIT Press, 1978).

3   The Computational Theory of Mind

1. From an interview with its creator Bill Chamberlain in the *Guardian* newspaper, 14 November 1981.
2. For an excellent digest of AI systems along with a spirited advocacy of the computational theory of mind see M. A. Boden, *Artificial Intelligence and Natural Man* (Brighton: Harvester, 1977). For a more technical account of how computers achieve some of the things described in Boden's book see B. Raphael, *The Thinking Computer: Mind Inside Matter*. (San Francisco: Freeman, 1976). For a good textbook on AI see P. H. Winston, *Artificial Intelligence* (Reading, Mass.: Addison-Wesley, 1980).
3. J. Searle, 'Mind, brains and programs', *The Behavioural and Brain Sciences*, 1980, 3, pp. 417–57.
4. See for example Richard Young's model of how children fail seriation tasks: R. M. Young, 'Strategies and the structure of a cognitive skill', in G. Underwood (ed.), *Strategies and Information Processing* (London: Academic Press, 1978).
5. The phrase 'computational theory of the mind' was coined by Jerry Fodor in his important paper 'Methodological solipsism considered as a research strategy in cognitive psychology', *The Behavioural and Brain Sciences*, 1980, 3, pp. 63–109. In fact Fodor uses the term in a somewhat more specialised sense than I shall be using it. A detailed discussion of Fodor's views will be given in Chapter 4.
6. In developing their General Problem Solver (GPS) Newell, Simon and Shaw employed introspective reports of how people solve means–end problems. The GPS is a system for achieving goals by step-by-step means. It has two 'objects' – the initial problem state and the goal state – and turns the former into the latter by a series of operations performed by 'operators', having first identified the differences between the two objects. See A. Newell and H. A. Simon, 'GPS – a program that simulates human thought', in E. A. Feigenbaum and J. Feldman (eds), *Computers and Thought* (New York: McGraw-Hill, 1963). For description of CONNIVER program see note 2, Boden, p. 371.
7. This is a term derived from Wilhelm Wundt's mammoth work *Völkerpsychologie* (translation by L. Schaub, *Elements of Folk Psychology: Outlines of a Psychological History of the Development of Mankind* (London: George Allen & Unwin, 1916)) and is now taken to mean our everyday, unsystematic knowledge of psychology.
8. See G. Boudreaux, 'Freud and the nature of unconscious mental processes', *Philosophy of the Social Sciences*, 1977, 7, pp. 1–32.

9. There have been some efforts in this direction (see Boden, note 2). One practitioner, K. M. Colby, seemed to have regarded his system ironically as a *reductio ad absurdum* of the incautious claims originally made on behalf of strong AI.

10. Ryle and Wittgenstein have both argued that it is wrong to regard thought as something going on 'in the head' (see end of Chapter 4). However brain-processes certainly do, and these support thought. The force of the Ryle–Wittgenstein objections do not apply to non-conscious thought as it is intended here.

11. M. Polanyi, 'The logic of tacit inference' *Philosophy*, 1966, 41, pp. 1–18. Also: Polanyi, *Personal Knowledge* (New York: Torch Books, 1964).

12. R. Dreyfus, *What Computers Can't Do: a Critique of Artificial Intelligence* (New York: Harper & Row, 1972).

13. For a discussion see Raphael, Chapter 4 (note 2).

14. For example: L. Uhr and C. Vossler, 'A pattern recognition program that generates, evaluates and adjusts its own operators' in Feigenbaum and Feldman (see note 6).

15. For a discussion of the relation between computer simulation and neurological investigation see D. Marr, *Analysing Natural Images: a Computational Theory of Texture Vision* (Cambridge, Mass.: MIT AI Lab. 1975). For a good discussion of the relation between Roberts' vision program and neurological work on vision, see L. G. Roberts, 'Machine perception of three-dimensional solids', in I. J. T. Tippett *et al.* (eds) *Optical and Electro-Optical Information Processing* (Cambridge, Mass.: MIT Press, 1965) and K. Oatley, *Perceptions and Representations* (New York: The Free Press, 1979), ch. 7.

16. One form of answer has been that consciousness need not be explained at all because it is nothing more than a by-product of mental function as, for example, exhaust fumes are the product of the functioning of an internal combustion engine. The philosophical position associated with this view is known as 'epiphenomenalism'. The classic statement of this was Thomas Huxley's 'On the hypothesis that animals are automata, and its history', in T. H. Huxley. *Method and Results: Essays* (London: Macmillan, 1893) pp. 199–250. Huxley claimed that consciousness is the epiphenomenon of molecular changes in the brain, thus always an effect and never a cause.

17. For a useful discussion of the hidden/open division see Robin Campbell's 'Cognitive development and child language', in P. Fletcher and M. Carman (eds) *Language Acquisition* (Cambridge University Press, 1979).

18. See M. A. Boden, *Purposive Explanation in Psychology* (Brighton: Harvester, 1972).

19. More of this later. I have already dealt with the criterion for intensionality that truth-value of intensional sentences may be changed by the substitution of co-designates. To the extent that a representation is necessarily *partial* this criterion will be fulfilled because characterisation of the representation cannot be in terms of what is represented (the extension). This quality is also known as 'referential opacity'. Another criterion is that of 'existential generalisation': an intensional occurrence of a term does not entail that there is an extension for the term (i.e. that the 'whatever is being referred to' exists). For example, 'John is thinking about unicorns' is intensional, whereas the extensional 'John is riding a unicorn' implies that these animals exist. Again, a computer may certainly have a representation of an object which does not exist. Indeed, as we shall be discussing at length in Chapter 4, there is a sense in which nothing exists for the computer. For further criteria of intensionality see R. M. Chisholm, 'Intensionality' in *The Encyclopaedia of Philosophy* (London: Macmillan, 1967).

20. It makes sense to say that someone has a false belief that he is in pain and that

264 Notes and References

20. presenting him with evidence (e.g. that it was an ice cube not a knife that was scraped down his back) may change this belief.

21. L. Wittgenstein, *Philosophical Investigations* (Oxford: Blackwell, 1953) para. 293.

22. That is, that there is a relationship between two things: the observer/describer on the one hand and the object on the other. This matter is discussed at length in Chapter 6.

23. D. C. Dennett. *Content and Consciousness* (London: Routledge & Kegan Paul, 1969) p. 94.

24. D. C. Dennett. 'Why you can't make a computer that feels pain', *Synthese*, 1978, 3, pp. 415–56.

25. Not all computers are of this 'digital' type: 'analogue' computers have physical continua such as the brightness of a light beam or the velocity of a mechanical shaft as their data (see note 2, Raphael, pp. 10–12;). However analogue computers are not adapted to abstract, verbal and logico-mathematical tasks.

26. See the debate between S. M. Kosslyn and Z. W. Pylyshyn on this matter. For example: S. M. Kosslyn, 'Information representation in visual images', *Cognitive Psychology*, 1975, 7, pp. 341–370; and Kosslyn's book *Image and Mind* (Cambridge, Mass.: Harvard University Press, 1980). For the sceptical position on imagery see Z. W. Pylyshyn, 'What the mind's eye tells the mind's brain', *Psychological Bulletin*, 1973, 80, pp. 1–24; and Pylyshyn's 'The imagery debate: analogue media versus tacit knowledge', *Psychological Review*, 1981, 88, pp. 16–45. (See Chapter 6 section 4 for a full treatment.)

27. For example Karl Pribram presents the case against the view that motoric and kinaesthetic information could be represented by a symbolic code: K. Pribram, 'Some comments on the notion of the perceived universe'., in R. Shaw and J. Bransford (eds) *Perceiving, Acting and Knowing: Toward an Ecological Psychology* (Hillsdale, New Jersey: Erlbaum Associates, 1977).

28. R. E. Fikes and N. J. Nilsson. 'STRIPS: a new approach to the application of theorem proving to problem solving', *Artificial Intelligence*, 1971, pp. 189–208.

29. The predicate calculus enables us to formalise what is present *within* propositions. As distinct from the propositional calculus, it can quantify ('all' rendered ( ) and 'some' rendered $\exists$), refer to individuals $(x, y, z \ldots)$ and describe properties of individuals (e.g. $Fx, Gx \ldots$). For example, $(x)(Fx \rightarrow Gx)$ means that everything with quality F also has quality G; $\exists x(Fx \rightarrow Gx)$ means that some things with F also have G.

30. See note 6.

31. See note 18.

32. See Chapter 2, note 34.

33. Wittgenstein pointed out that terms need not be applied to instances on the basis of some property that the instances have in common. Common properties are implicated in some concepts (e.g. the colour words), but in other cases such as 'bread' and 'game' there may be no property common to all instances. The term 'family resemblance' was used to describe such concepts because there can be a 'Smith family face', for example, without all the people who have this kind of face *necessarily* sharing one particular facial feature on the basis of which their face can be said to be of the Smith type. This will be discussed later. See Wittgenstein, *Philosophical Investigations*, paras 66–8.

34. *Philosophical Investigations*, para 304 (see note 21).

35. For a discussion see D. C. Dennett, *Brainstorms* (Brighton: Harvester, 1979), pp. 30–3.

36. In 'modal' contexts (see note 28, Chapter 4 and p. 65 above) it is not at all nonsensical to claim that different kinds of belief may have different phenomeno-

logies. For example, to believe 'necessarily *p*' should have a different phenomenology from believing 'possibly *p*'. For this reason I think it may be incorrect (*pace* Chisholm note 19) to claim that because modal contexts are intensional therefore this is a case of non-psychological intensionality: putting 'necessarily' or 'possibly' before a proposition *does* imply a mental orientation on the part of somebody.

37. J. Fodor, 'The mind–body problem', *Scientific American*, Jan 1981, pp. 124–32. The inverted spectrum is associated with the work of N. Block (*Philosophical Review*, 1980) and S. Shoemaker (*Philosophical Studies*, 1975). Although I have presented Putnam as a functionalist I should say that in his *Reason, Truth and History* (Cambridge University Press, 1981) he regards the inverted spectrum problem as showing the impossibility of functionalism as a complete theory of mind.

38. Ibid, p. 130.

39. Descartes proposed that the mind affects the 'flow of animal spirits' (roughly: neural impulses) via the pineal gland: an organ chosen for this important job primarily because it is in the very centre of the human brain.

40. The best source for Pylyshyn's position is his 'Computation and cognition: issues in the foundation of cognitive science', *The Behavioural and Brain Sciences*, 1980, vol. 3, pp. 111–69. This is the source on which I am drawing here. For a briefer statement see 'Psychological explanation and knowledge–dependent processes', *Cognition*, 1981, vol. 10, pp. 267–74; and for a longer one: *Computation and Cognition* (Cambridge, Mass.: MIT Press, 1982).

41. See P. H. Winston. *The Psychology of Computer Vision* (New York: McGraw-Hill, 1975).

42. Subjects are presented with a pair of equal lines. One of the lines has 'arrows' at the ends and the other has 'forks'. They typically judge the line with the forks to be longer.

43. *Cognition*, 1981, see note 40.

44. See note 26.

45. See note 40, first reference, p. 129.

46. Z. W. Pylyshyn, E. W. Elcock, M. Marmor, and P. Sander, 'Explorations in perceptual–motor spaces', *Proceedings of the Second International Conference of the Canadian Society for Computational Studies of Intelligence* (Toronto: University of Toronto, 1978).

47. For a similar distinction as applied to animal-learning studies (also made on the basis of three criteria) see my trilogy of papers in *Behaviourism*, 1980–81 (ch. 2, note 14, for reference). The terms used there were 'regulative' and 'mandatory' for 'cognitively penetrable' and 'impenetrable' respectively.

48. Ibid, p. 118. Also see Pylyshyn, 'Validating computational models: a critique of Anderson's indeterminacy of representation claims', *Psychological Review*, 1979, vol. 86, pp. 383–94, discussed at length in Chapter 6.

49. See note 26.

50. See note 3, p. 419.

51. R. Schank and R. Abelson, *Scripts, Plans, Goals and Understanding* (Hillsdale, New Jersey: Erlbaum, 1977).

52. For application of this notion to children's cognition see Katherine Nelson, 'How young children represent knowledge of their world in and out of language', in R. S. Siegler (ed.), *Children's Thinking: What Develops?* (Hillsdale, New Jersey: Erlbaum, 1978).

53. T. Winograd, *Understanding Natural Language* (New York: Academic Press, 1972).

54. Ibid, p. 418.

55. Comment on Searle's paper (see note 3) p. 428.
56. See note 16.
57. George Miller considers (and rejects) this as a possibility in 'Trends and debates in cognitive psychology', *Cognition*, 1981, vol. 10, pp. 215–25. See the end of Chapter 4 for a brief discussion of Miller's own position on this.
58. Comment on Searle's paper. See note 3, p. 446.
59. (See note 2) Boden, *Artificial Intelligence*, 1977, pp. 442–43.
60. See S. Schachter and J. E. Singer, 'Cognitive, social and physiological determinants of emotional states', *Psychological Review*, 1962, 69, pp. 379–99.
61. Ibid, p. 44.
62. Such as Bernard Harrison, *Form and Content* (Oxford: Blackwell, 1973).
63. (See note 2) Boden, 1977, p. 442.
64. See note 24.
65. Ibid, p. 422.
66. Ibid, p. 423.
67. For a clear exposition of Skinner's functionalism see Brenda Mapel, 'Philosophical criticism of behaviourism: an analysis', *Behaviourism*, 1977, vol. 5, pp. 17–35.

4   Conditions for Belief and Knowledge

1. This is my gloss, not Pylyshyn's.
2. There will be a full discussion of this matter in Chapter 7.
3. For a clear exposition: R. A. Boakes and M. S. Halliday, 'The Skinnerian analysis of behaviour', in. R. Borger and F. Cioffi (eds), *Explanation in the Behavioural Sciences* (Cambridge: Cambridge University Press, 1970).
4. N. Chomsky, *Rules and Representations* (Oxford: Blackwell, 1980). Also in *The Behavioural and Brain Sciences*, 1980, 3, pp. 1–61.
5. For a discussion see D. C. Dennett, *Brainstorms* (Brighton: Harvester, 1979) pp. 122–4.
6. Associationism is the psychological/philosophical doctrine that 'the process by which individual atoms of consciousness come to be associated with each other is the fundamental principle of thought'. Aristotle and Hobbes had laws of association, but they were not 'associationists' because they did not regard this process as the basic principle of thought. The British Empiricist Philosophers – Locke, Berkely and Hume – were all associationists in one form or another, but it was Hume who made the principle explicit. The importance of associationism to the development of British psychology can hardly be overestimated. The 'Scottish School' formed the bridge between Humean mental philosophy and the associationistic theoretical psychology of J. S. Mill. Mill's writings strongly influenced W. Wundt's construal of psychological explanation, and so we may say that associationism was a major theoretical impulse towards experimental psychology. See R. Thomson, *The Pelican History of Psychology* (Harmondsworth: Penguin, 1968) for a useful account of this progression. Associationism is still with us in the employment of classical conditioning-based models of mental function and personality.
7. Hume argued that the self is 'nothing but a bundle or collection of different perceptions'. See D. G. C. McNabb, *David Hume* (Oxford: Blackwell, 1966) pp. 146 ff. for an attempted refutation of this.
8. Dennett, *Brainstorms*, p. 122.
9. For arguments in favour of homunculi in the sense that the term is being used here see: F. Attneave, 'In defense of homunculi', in W. Rosenblith, *Sensory*

Communication (Cambridge, Mass.: MIT Press, 1960); R. de Sousa, 'Rational homunculi', in R. Rorty (ed.), *The Identities of Persons* (University of California Press, 1976).

10. For example: D. Bobrow 'Dimensions of representation', in D. Bobrow and A. Collins (eds), *Representation and Understanding* (New York: Academic Press, 1975).

11. Boden, *Artificial Intelligence*, p. 432.

12. Artistotle's principles of association (contiguity, similarity and contrast) were the processes on which recollection was supposed to function.

13. See note 6.

14. H. A. Simon, *Models of Thought* (New Haven: Yale University Press, 1979) pp. 63–4.

15. H. Beilin, 'Piaget and the new functionalism', an invited address to the Eleventh Symposium of the Jean Piaget Society, Philadelphia, May, 1981.

16. D. C. Dennett, *Brainstorms*, p. 112, for example: 'I want to claim that AI is better viewed as sharing with traditional epistemology the status of being a most general, most abstract asking of the top-down question: how is knowledge possible?'

17. A. Newell, 'You can't play Twenty Questions with nature and win: projective comments on papers of this symposium', in: W. G. Chase (ed.), *Visual Information Processing* (New York: Academic Press, 1973) p. 296.

18. Beilin, *Piaget*, p. 23.

19. I must point out that Margaret Boden, a proponent of CTM, takes the opposite view. In her monograph, *Piaget* (Fontana, 1979) ch. 7, she argues that Piaget's theory is highly congruent with AI for four reasons: (i) both are formal-algebraic, (ii) Piaget has written in approval of AI's attempt to offer a 'realisation' of abstract psychological theories of which his own is an example, (iii) both are structuralist, (iv) both are concerned with 'mind' and 'representation' not behaviour and physiological realisations. She backs this up with some examples of Piaget's general support for 'cybernetics'. (I briefly touch on the cybernetic aspects of Piaget's theory below.) But there is an alternative interpretation of each of these four points: (i) Piaget *describes* mental structures in algebraic terms; he does not – as does strong AI – claim that the counters of thought *are* symbolic in this sense. (ii) It makes more sense to say that Piaget was regarding realisation in the weak AI sense here – as testing the internal coherence of a theory/description. (iii) AI systems give general accounts of 'structures' but Piaget's is quintessentially an organic theory that does not rely on associative links (see below for full discussion of this point). (iv) There are places where Piaget *is* reductionist (e.g. 'The problems of consciousness in child psychology', in: *Conference on Problems of Consciousness* (New York: Josiah Macy Foundation, 1954) p. 146); also, as I discuss later, the representational media for Piaget are analogue not formal – symbolic. These are not *answers* to Boden: they merely show how complex the issue is.

20. For a thorough exposition of this see F. Jacob, *The Logic of Living Systems* (London: Allen Lane, 1974).

21. Leibniz regarded the world as an organisation of hierarchically arranged 'monads'. Monad is an obscure concept (which Leibniz inherited from Giordano Bruno), and for him it meant something like a unit of motive energy. Leibniz's inspiration for the re-drafting of Bruno's concept was definitely biological: he saw through one of the earliest microscopes that water droplets teemed with life. This led to the concept that within each unit of life there are smaller units with their own motive energy which go to make up the organisational structure of the larger unit. The way in which Leibniz deployed the term 'monad' in some contexts

suggested the notion of a cell. It was the pragmatist philosopher John Dewey, who originally indicated (in Leibniz, *New Essays Concerning Human understanding – a Critical Exposition* (Chicago: C. C. Grigg, 1888)), how Leibniz's notion of embryonic development as differentiation plus gradual integrative organisation of units (monads) was the first statement of the biological theory of epigenesis as against the older pre-formation theory.

22.　The work of Heinz Werner (e.g. *The Comparative Psychology of Mental Development* (Chicago: Follet, 1948)) should also be located in this tradition. Also the 'organismic' approach of Overton and Reese: see W. F. Overton and H. W. Reese's 'Models of development: methodological implications', in J. R. Nesselroade and H. W. Reese (eds) *Lifespan Developmental Psychology: Methodological Issues* (New York: Academic Press, 1973).

23.　Again, in contrast, Boden (see note 19) emphasises the commonalities between cybernetics and Piagetian theory. Admittedly, Piaget does also.

24.　Clearly CTM would reject this, however, in so far as it equates thought with non-conscious processes.

25.　For a similar argument see R. Harris, 'Discussion', in: S. C. Brown (ed.) *Philosophy of Psychology* (London: Macmillan, 1974) pp. 274–6.

26.　The logical principle that something either is or is not the case.

27.　E. Sober in 'Psychologism', *Journal for the Theory of Social Behaviour*, 1980, 8, pp. 165–91, argues (on p. 189) for a more liberal interpretation of the thesis:

> Although logical truths are not true *because* we think in a certain way, they nevertheless may have psychological reality. This version of psychologism avoids the abdication of normative inquiry that is implicit in some psychologistic views; it also acknowledges a certain empirical possibility – that the principles of right reason which philosophy seeks to discover are used in the information-processing systems of thinking organisms.

One may accept Sober's position, however, whilst still insisting (see next section) that computational systems of the kind considered by CTM do not have beliefs in that way that Sober's analysis requires.

28.　See also Chapter 3 note 19. A number of expressions create modal contexts in addition to 'necessarily' and 'possibly': the auxiliaries 'can', 'must', 'may', 'should', 'ought' carry modality, and it is also introduced by the suffix '-able' plus certain past participles and by 'certainly', 'surely', and 'probably'.

29.　Fodor 'The mind–body problem', *Scientific American*, Jan. 1981, p. 131.

30.　See Dennett on 'the intentional stance' with regard to programs (see note 5).

31.　See Chapter 3, note 19.

32.　Fodor, 'Methodological solipsism' *Behavioural and Brain Sciences*, 1980, vol. 3.

33.　Ibid, p. 64.

34.　This phrase is one used to describe the phenomenologist Husserl's methodology of *epoche* in which the essence of psychological states is supposed to be revealed by a systematic suspension of one's belief in the existence of objects 'beyond' the phenomenal field. The similarities between Fodor's 'methodological solipsism' and phenomenology are too complex and contradictory to go into here. For a discussion of the relevance of phenomenology to psychology see N. Bolton's 'Phenomenology and psychology', in: N. Bolton (ed.), *Philosophical Problems in Psychology* (London: Methuen, 1979).

35.　Fodor, 'Methodological solipsism', p. 64

36.　Ibid, p. 67.

37.　See Chapter 3, note 19.

38.　Fodor, 'Methodological solipsism', p. 67.

39. Ibid, p. 67.
40. Ibid, p. 67.
41. See my 'The status of genetic epistemology', *Journal for the Theory of Social Behaviour*, 1979, 9, pp. 53–70.
42. I gave an extensive summary and critique of Baldwin's genetic epistemology in my book *The Acquisition of Knowledge* (London: Macmillan, 1978). (The definitive statement of Baldwin's genetic epistemology is to be found in his *Thought and Things*. *Vols. I–III* (London: Swann and Sonnenschein 1906–1911). Dr. Wolfe Mays has pointed out to me that I underestimated the Hegelian aspect of Baldwin's genetic epistemology (see Mays's review in *Philosophical Books*, 1980). This is certainly true; and I tried to repair some of the damage in 'Baldwin, Hegel and the dialectic of personal growth'. (Paper presented to the Annual Conference of the British Psychological Society, Aberdeen, April, 1980.)
43. In *The Origin of Intelligence in the Child* (London: Routledge & Kegan Paul, 1937) Piaget actually begins with something very similar to Kant's table of categories. See my 'Piaget's theory of sensorimotor development: outlines, assumptions and problems', in G. Butterworth (ed.), *Infancy and Epistemology an Evaluation of Piaget's Theory* (Brighton: Harvester, 1981).
44. Kant's mind-dependent example is that of standing before a house and viewing it; and his mind-independent example is that of watching a ship sailing downstream. One of the earliest critics of Kant's account was Schopenhauer who pointed out that the condition was inadequate as it stood. The house and the ship example are not sufficiently different because we have sequences of perceptions produced by the relative movements of a body and an object in both cases: eye to object for the example of the house and object to observer's body in the example of the ship. (In a sense, Schopenhauer argues, we observe the movements of our eyes.) Yet, as D. W. Hamlyn has shown (*Schopenhauer* [London: Routledge & Kegan Paul, 1980] pp. 47–8) Kant may be defended against this criticism up to a point; and one can disagree with the details of Kant's argument whilst agreeing with the conclusion. Indeed Schopenhauer did.
45. S. Körner, *Kant* (Harmondsworth: Penguin, 1955) p. 85.
46. J. W. von Goethe, *Faust*, part 1, lines 1224–37.
47. By 'adual' I refer to Baldwin's term 'adualism' – the initial state in which the neonate has no self–object division. In fact subjectivity is something of a misnomer here because there is no co-relative objectivity.
48. I am just stating this as a fact. It is difficult to see on what grounds it could be questioned.
49. T. Nagel, 'What it is like to be a bat', *Philosophical Review*, 1974, 83, pp. 435–51.
50. Ibid, p. 436.
51. In a footnote Nagel (see note 49 above) would appear to be saying just this: 'perhaps anything complex enough to behave like a person would have experiences'. (p. 436). But there is an ambiguity here: the statement can be interpreted to mean 'would *have to have* experiences' rather than 'would have experiences as a consequence of this degree of complexity'.
52. Vitalism is not a very clear doctrine. It is rooted in Aristotle's claim that there is some non-material quality in animate bodies not present in inanimate bodies. Its prime nineteenth-century proponents were Hans Driesch and Henri Bergson. It is Bergson as an advocate of the vital principle ('*elan vital*') that Piaget appears to be arguing against in his references to vitalism, despite Piaget's Bergsonian insistence that organisms are creative not passive in evolution and development.
53. A term derived from Aristotle to mean, roughly, purposefulness. Driesch employed this (see note 52) in his vitalism.

54. See note 21.
55. Which even Piaget does (e.g. in *Origins of Intelligence in the Child*, [London: Routledge & Kegan paul, 1953]).
56. Searle, 'Mind, brains and programs', p. 424.
57. See D. W. Hamlyn, 'Human learning' in S. C. Brown (ed.) *Philosophy of Psychology* (London: Macmillian, 1974).
58. D. W. Hamlyn suggests the former in 'Epistemology', *The Encyclopaedia of Philosophy* (London: Macmillan, 1966) and J. Bennett *Kant's Analytic* (London: Cambridge University Press, 1966) the latter.
59. P. F. Strawson, *Individuals* (London: Oxford University Press, 1959).
60. Solipsism is the position that we can attain certainty only of our own existence. Knowledge is private on this view, so knowledge of 'other minds' cannot be attained.
61. P. L. Berger and T. Luckman, *The Social Construction of Reality* (Harmondsworth: Penguin, 1971).
62. A. C. Danto in *Nietzsche as Philosopher* (London: Collier-Macmillan, 1967) has highlighted Nietzsche's Wittgensteinian views of language and 'public' consciousness. Nietzsche's position is set out in *The Gay Science (Die fröliche Wissenshaft) Nietzsche's Werke in Drei Bände* (Munich: Carl Hanser Verlag, 1958). As Berger and Luckman (*Social Construction of Reality*, p. 19) point out Nietzsche also influenced the sociology of knowledge by virtue of materialism and the notion of 'false consciousness' to be developed later by Marx.
63. D. W. Hamlyn, 'Person perception and understanding others', in T. Mischel (ed.), *Understanding Other Persons* (Oxford: Blackwell, 1974).
64. D. W. Hamlyn, 'Cognitive systems, folk psychology, and knowledge', *Cognition*, 1981, 10, pp. 115–18, extract from p. 118.
65. For example, G. A. Miller, E. Gallanter and K. H. Pribram, *Plans and the Structure of Behaviour* (New York: Holt, Rinehart & Winston, 1960).
66. G. Miller, Comments on Pylyshyn's paper, *The Behavioural and Brain Sciences*, 1980, 3, p. 146.
67. See note 16, Chapter 3.
68. G. Miller, 'Trends and debates in cognitive psychology', *Cognition*, 1981, 10, pp. 215–25, extract from p. 222.
69. H. C. Longuet-Higgins, 'Artificial intelligence – a new theoretical psychology?', *Cognition*, 1981, 3, pp. 197–200.

5   Perception

1. The account of the theory will be taken from Gibson's last book: *The Ecological Approach to Visual Perception* (Boston: Houghton Mifflin Company, 1979).
2. For a discussion of this matter see the final chapter of D. W. Hamlyn, *Sensation and Perception* (London: Routledge & Kegan Paul, 1961). Also see his *Psychology of Perception* (London: Routledge & Kegan Paul, 1957).
3. For an elaboration of this point see G. E. M. Anscombe, 'Comment on Professor R. L. Gregory's paper', in S. C. Brown (ed.) *Philosophy of Psychology* (London: Macmillan, 1974).
4. G. Ryle, *The Concept of Mind* (London: Hutchinson, 1949).
5. U. Neisser, *Cognition and Reality* (San Francisco: Freeman, 1976) p. 17.
6. There were, of course, exceptions, principally Spinoza and Leibniz.
7. Hegelian idealism is another matter. As Charles Taylor put it:

Hegelian idealism, far from being a denial of external material reality, is the strongest affirmation of it; it not only exists but necessarily exists (*Hegel* [Cambridge: Cambridge University Press, 1975] p. 109).

Nevertheless Hegelian philosophers have tended to emphasise mind's responsibility for nature. For example, T. H. Green wrote: 'The consciousness through which alone nature exists *for us* is neither natural nor the result of nature' (my italics) (Quotation taken from D. B. Klein, *History of Scientific Psychology* (London: Routledge & Kegan Paul, 1974)).

8. Gibson, *Ecological Approach*, p. 239 (the metaphor comes from David Hume).
9. Ibid, p. 245.
10. Ibid, pp. 160–2.
11. For example: E. J. Gibson and R. Bergman, 'The effect of training on absolute estimation of distance over the ground', *Journal of Experimental Psychology*, 1954, 48, pp. 473–82.
12. J. J. Gibson, J. Purdy, and L. Lawrence, 'A method for controlling stimulation for the study of space perception: the optical tunnel', *Journal of Experimental Psychology*, 1955, 50, pp. 1–14.
13. G. A. Kaplan, 'Kinetic disruption of optical texture: the perception of depth at an edge', *Perception and Psychophysics*, 1969, 6, pp. 193–8.
14. D. N. Lee and E. Aronson, 'Visual proprioceptive control of standing in human infants', *Perception and Psychophysics*, 1974, 15, pp. 529–32.
15. W. Schiff, 'Perception of impending collision', *Psychological Monographs*, 1965, 79, no. 604, relevant section, pp. 16–18.
16. K. von Frieand and J. J. Gibson, 'The sensitivity of the eye to two kinds of continuous transformation of a shadow-pattern', *Journal of Experimental Psychology*, 1959, 57, pp. 344–47.
17. Gibson, *Ecological Approach*, p. 310.
18. U. Neisser, 'Gibson's ecological optics: consequences of a different stimulus description', *Journal for the Theory of Social Behaviour*, 1977, 7, p. 24.
19. Gibson, 'New reasons for realism', *Synthese*, 1967, 17, pp. 162–72.
20. For example: J. Hintikka, 'Information, causality and the logic of perception' in *The Intentions of Intentionality and Other New Models for Modalities* (Dordrecht: Reidel, 1975); D. W. Hamlyn, 'The concept of information in Gibson's theory of perception', *Journal for the Theory of Social Behaviour*, 1977, 7, pp. 5–16.
21. For example: U. Neisser (see note 18); S. Ullman, 'Against direct perception', *The Behavioural and Brain Sciences*, 1980, 3, pp. 373–415; A. Costall, 'On how so much information controls so much behaviour: James Gibson's theory of direct perception', in G. Butterworth (ed.) *Infancy and Epistemology* (Brighton: Harvester, 1981).
22. For example: D. Marr and T. Poggio's analysis of stereo disparity (*Science*, 1976, 194, pp. 283–7) owes something to Gibson's notion of ecological properties despite the author's theoretical divergence from Gibson on the nature of perception.
23. This is why Gibson is sometimes mistakenly called a phenomenologist. The view is mistaken because the notion of there being a 'phenomenal field' was one of the main things Gibson continued to argue against.
24. See my 'The status of genetic epistemology', *Journal for the Theory of Social Behaviour*, 1979, 9, pp. 54–70.
25. J. A. Fodor and Z. W. Pylyshyn, 'How direct is visual perception? Some reflections of Gibson's "ecological approach"', *Cognition*, 1981.

26. Ibid, p. 168.
27. Gibson, 'New reasons for realism', p. 162.
28. Ullman makes this point usefully: 'Against direct perception', p. 378.
29. Hamlyn, Neisser, Ullman (see notes 20 and 21).
30. See J. J. Gibson, 'The concept of the stimulus in psychology', *American Psychologist*, 1960, 115, pp. 694–703.
31. See note 21; Ullman, 'Against direct perception', p. 375.
32. Gibson, *Ecological Approach*, p. 147
33. See E. J. Gibson, *Principles of Perceptual Learning and Development* (New York: Appleton-Century-Crofts, 1969).
34. For a critique of the Gibson theory of perceptual development in these terms see p. E. Bryant, 'Cognitive development', *British Medical Bulletin*. 1971, 27, pp. 200–5.
35. D. Marr and T. Poggio, 'From understanding computation to understanding neural circuitry', *Neuroscience Research Program Bulletin*. 1977, 15, pp. 470–88.
36. Ullman, 'Against direct perception', p. 380
37. See note 20, Hamlyn, 'Concept of information', p. 16.
38. See note 3, R. L. Gregory, 'Perceptions as hypotheses' in S. C. Brown (ed.).
39. Six from a list of nine.
40. This was originally a drawing of an 'impossible triangle' which at first glance looks as if it is made of three pieces of wood of square cross-section. However the upper face of each piece at one angle is drawn so as to be the lower face of another angle, thereby giving contradictory distance cues. A wooden model of this can be constructed.
41. Gregory, 'Perceptions as hypotheses', p. 209.
42. *Mind in Science* (London: Weidenfeld & Nicolson, 1981) pp. 375–8.
43. The 'Electric Brae' near Girvan in Ayrshire is a good example of a visual illusion that is at least partly natural. The alignment of the hills against the road makes travelling downhill seem like travelling uphill. If you take a photograph of one person standing in front of another on the road it looks as if the person behind has risen a little in the air.
44. See Chapter 3 note 37, Fodor's replies to comments on his paper, 'The mind–body problem', p. 107.
45. See note 3, Anscombe 'Comment on Professor Gregory's paper'.
46. Gregory mentions this criticism (see note 42) but dismisses it.
47. Kant, Bartlett, Piaget, and many others, though each used it somewhat differently of course.
48. G. E. M. Anscombe, 'The intentionality of perception: a grammatical feature', in R. J. Butler (ed.), *Analytical Philosophy* (Oxford: Blackwell, 1965).
49. There is some similarity between what I am calling extensional perception and Dretske's notion of 'non-epistemic seeing', but it is not worth indicating the similarities and differences. See F. Dretske, *Seeing and Knowing* (London: Routledge & Kegan Paul, 1969).
50. This intuition seemed to have played a role in the so-called 'new look in perception'. For example studies were done which showed that poor children perceived coins as heavier than did other children. See J. S. Bruner and C. C. Goodman, 'Value and need as organising factors in perception', *Journal of Abnormal and Social Psychology*, 1947, 42, pp. 33–44.
51. J. Hintikka, 'On the logic of perception', in *Models for Modalities* (Dordrecht: Reidel, 1969).
52. V., C. Aldrich, 'Aesthetic perception and objectivity', *British Journal of Aesthetics*, 1978, 18, pp. 209–16.
53. Ibid, p. 212.
54. See note 20. Hamlyn, 'The concept of information', p. 13.

55. Gibson, Ecological Approach, p. 129
56. See note 25, Fodor and Pylyshyn, Some reflections . . .
57. These are Kant's examples. See note 44. Chapter 4.
58. See note 19. Gibson, 'New reasons for realism', p. 166.
59. Duchamp exhibited a urinal signed 'R. Mutt' (the name of a firm of sanitary engineers) in 1915. He called it 'Fountain'.
60. This is the usual translation of Heidegger's term '*Dasein*'. It means something like 'a particular mode of conscious existence relative to other things'.
61. Aldrich makes first-order extention capable of carrying an 'intentional content' (p. 212). Obviously it would not be illuminating to compare the present taxonomy with Aldrich's very closely.
62. See J. Hopkins, 'Visual geometry', *Philosophical Review*, 1973, for an analysis of this concept.
63. J. Piaget, *The Mechanisms of Perception* (London: Routledge & Kegan Paul, 1969).
64. See Chapter 4, note 44.
65. That is, perception necessarily involves a point of view.
66. D. W. Hamlyn, 'Epistemology and conceptual development', in T. Mischel (ed.), *Cognitive Development and Epistemology* (London: Academic Press, 1971).
67. See for example E. Vurpillot, in *Journal of Experimental Child Psychology*, 1968.
68. See David Elkind's review paper in the *American Scientist*, 1975.
69. T. G. R. Bower, 'The visual world of infants', *Scientific American*, 1966.
70. G. E. Butterworth and L. Hicks, 'Visual proprioception and postural stability in infancy: a developmental study', *Perception*, 1977, 6, pp. 255–62.
71. See note 14. Lee and Aronson, 'Visual proprioceptive control . . .'.
72. G. E. Butterworth and E. Cochran, 'Towards a mechanism of joint visual attention in human infancy', *International Journal of Behavioural Development*, 1980, 3, pp. 253–72.
73. See T. G. R. Bower, *Development in Infancy* (San Francisco: Freeman, 1974).
74. See my *The Acquisition of Knowledge*, Part 3, Section 1, for a discussion of this point.
75. See Chapter 4 note 42, Baldwin, *Thought and Things*, vol. 1.
76. This may happen very early. See for example, L. B. Cohen *et al.*, 'Infant habituation and generalisation to differing degrees of stimulus novelty', *Journal of Experimental Child Psychology*, 1971, 14, pp. 435–76.
77. H. Werner and B. Kaplan, *Symbol Formation* (London: Wiley, 1963).
78. For a discussion of this point see my 'The subject–object division: implications for language acquisition and ego development', *New Ideas in Psychology*, 1984.
79. Indeed this is not even accurate because perception is perspectival whereas reality of course is not. For qualifications about the status of mental 'objects' see Chapter 1, p.
80. A. Hannay, 'The "what" and the "how"', in D. F. Gustafson and B. L. Tapscott (eds), *Body, Mind and Method* (Dordrecht: Reidel, 1979) p. 26.
81. This would not be true of perception₁ *qua* observation.
82. See note 42 Chapter 4. In the final volume of *Thought and Things* Baldwin develops the theory that the aesthetic mode is the highest level of understanding. It resolves the dualisms mind/body, ego/alter, singular/general and objective/subjective that characterise thought.

6 Representation

1. N. Malcolm, *Memory and Mind* (Ithica: Cornell University Press, 1977).
2. Bertrand Russell also suggested that we gain information from the order in

which the images appear and the degree to which they have 'faded'; Russell, *Analysis of Mind* (New York: Humanities Press, 1921) pp. 162–5.

3. Wittgenstein, *Philosophical Investigations*, paras 82–6, 143–150, 172–8.
4. Malcolm, *Memory and Mind*, p. 105.
5. E.g. H. H. Price, *Thinking and Experience* (New York: Hutchinson University Library, 1953). pp. 235–6.
6. See discussion of Kosslyn's work in section 5.
7. *Memory and Mind*, p. 115.
8. Ibid, p. 115.
9. In *The Concept of Mind* (London: Hutchinson, 1949).
10. Malcolm, *Memory and Mind*, p. 221.
11. N. S. Sutherland, 'Outlines of a theory of visual pattern recognition in animals and man', *Proceedings of the Royal Society*, B, 171, 1968.
12. Ibid, p. 209.
13. J. Fodor, *Language of Thought* (New York) (Thomas Y. Crowell Co. 1975).
14. Ibid, p. 57.
15. Ibid, p. 60.
16. *Philosophical Investigations*, paras 244–64, 293–317.
17. Fodor, *Language of Thought*, p. 70.
18. For Wittgenstein no disputes were *merely* terminological. Anyone holding a 'verbal' theory of thought would have to agree.
19. Fodor, *Language of Thought*, p. 71.
20. Wittgenstein would in fact deny that a split between the intention and the term could be made in this way.
21. In logic this is short for 'if and only if'. For example 'a figure is a square if and only if it has four equal sides'; but 'the garden is wet if it has been raining' is not 'iff' because the garden could have become wet by the lawn sprinkler having been turned on.
22. Fodor, *Language of Thought*, p. 75.
23. Ibid, p. 77.
24. Fodor, *Language of Thought*, p. 64.
25. H. H. Field, 'Mental representation', *Erkenntniss*, 1978, 13, pp. 9–61.
26. What makes the belief true is a situation in a 'possible world'. For discussion of this concept see the next chapter.
27. Ibid, p. 18.
28. See W. V O. Quine, *From a Logical Point of View* (New York: Harper Torchbooks, 1953). See next chapter for a discussion of Quine's views.
29. See D. Davidson, 'Truth and meaning', *Synthese*, 1967, 17, pp. 304–23.
30. A token is an instance or specimen of a type. For example 'tree' is a token of the type noun.
31. Field, 'Mental representation', p. 41.
32. Ibid, p. 30.
33. Field argues that the type-identity of thought tokens could be demonstrated by physiological data, 'Mental representation', p. 43.
34. D. M. Armstrong, *Belief, Truth and Knowledge* (London: Cambridge University Press, 1973).
35. Ibid, p. 46.
36. 'Critical notice: *The Language of Thought* of Jerry Fodor', *Mind*, 1973.
37. Fodor, *Language of Thought*, p. 63.
38. J. M. Baldwin, *The Dictionary of Philosophy and Psychology* (New York: Macmillan, 1901–5).
39. J. Russell, 'Propositional attitudes', in M. Beveridge (ed.), *Children Thinking Through Language* (London: Edward Arnold, 1982).

40. A term coined by J. Searle after J. L. Austin's term 'illocutionary act' – e.g. question, statement, promise, demand, and so on: the communicative 'act' achieved in speaking.
41. See *Philosophical Investigations*, especially paras 327–44.
42. Ibid, para. 335.
43. Ibid, para. 337.
44. For a clear, useful review of the literature see J. T. E. Richardson's *Mental Imagery and Human Memory* (London: Macmillan, 1980).
45. In *The Concept of Mind*.
46. See Chapter 1 and note 30.
47. Dennett, *Content and Consciousness* (London: Routledge & Kegan Paul, 1969). Also see his 'Two approaches to mental images' in *Brainstorms* (Harvester, 1979). There he is still sceptical but distinguishes between 'metaphysical' and 'scientific' iconophobia, the first being certainly justified and the second probably true.
48. A. Hannay, *Mental Images: a Defence* (George Allen & Unwin, 1971) pp. 166–74.
49. Ibid, pp. 187–91.
50. For an extensive critique of this see Hannay, *Mental Images*, ch. 6.
51. Much of Wittgenstein's scepticism about imagery and introspection in general was inspired through his acquaintance with William James' use of phenomenological data. It was perhaps this kind of practice which stimulated his famous comment about the 'conceptual confusion' of psychology.
52. Wittgenstein, *Philosophical Investigations*, para. 167.
53. This is the example used by E. Wolgast in 'Wittgenstein and criteria', *Inquiry*, 1964, 7.
54. Hannay, *Mental Images*, p. 201.
55. Ibid, pp. 199–204.
56. Ibid, p. 203.
57. J. P. Sartre, *The Psychology of Imagination* (London: Methuen, 1972). This is a translation of *L'imaginaire* which appeared in France in 1940.
58. Ibid. See Mary Warnock's introduction to the book for a useful discussion of the background.
59. In his later work this became the distinction between the being-in itself ('en-soi') of the material and the being-for-itself ('pour-soi') of the mental.
60. That is, with its own laws of function, with the independence from reality that imagination exemplifies, a lack of reliance upon objects in the world.
61. This is the 'nothingness' in Sartre's later work that is supposed to make judgement possible. It is perhaps related to Hegel's claim that every idea contains its negation.
62. Note that much of Sartre's argument is phenomenological: he refers to the features of introspective experience as much as, or more than, the features of the concept of imaging.
63. Wittgenstein, *Philosophical Investigations*, para. 389. Wittgenstein imagines someone saying: 'The image must be more like its object than any picture. For, however like I make the picture to what it is supposed to represent, it can always be the picture of something else as well. But it is essential to the image that it is the image of *this* and of nothing else'. And he comments: 'Thus one might come to regard the image as a super-likeness'.
64. Sartre, *The Psychology of Imagination*, p. 61.
65. Ibid, p. xiii. Also see M. Warnock, 'Imagination in Sartre', *British Journal of Aesthetics*, 1970, 10.
66. Ibid (Sartre), p. 109.

67. Ibid, p. 142.
68. This only appears to hold for human adult consciousness. See my earlier comments on consciousness as *un*selfconscious.
69. Ibid, p. 19.
70. Ibid, pp. 110–14.
71. Ibid, p. 119.
72. For example, J. S. Bruner's view that young children's thought is iconic although they can use words to communicate; *Studies in Cognitive Growth* (New York: Wiley, 1966). See Fodor, *Language of Thought*, pp. 176–79 for a conceptual argument against this view.
73. *Philosophical Investigations*, p. 112.
74. *Language of Thought*, pp. 178–82.
75. For a discussion of developmental issues in motoric representation see P. Mounoud and A. Vinter 'Representation and sensorimotor development' in G. Butterworth (ed.), *Infancy and Epistemology* (Brighton: Harvester, 1981).
76. This was originally put forward by A. Paivio. See his *Imagery and Verbal Processes* (New York: Holt, Rinehart & Winston, 1971).
77. In *Brainstorms* – see note 47 above.
78. This roughly corresponds to the way Kosslyn *et al.* classify the supporting data. See S. M. Kosslyn, S. Pinker, G. E. Smith, and S. P. Swartz, 'On the demystification of mental imagery', *Behavioural and Brain Sciences*, 1979, 2, pp. 535–81.
79. R. N. Shepard and J. Metzler, 'Mental rotation of three-dimensional objects', *Science*, 1971, 171, pp. 701–03.
80. S. M. Kosslyn, T. M. Ball, B. J. Reiser, 'Visual images preserve metric spatial information: evidence from studies of image scanning', *Journal of Experimental Psychology: Human Perception and Performance*, 1978, 4, pp. 47–60.
81. Ibid.
82. S. M. Kosslyn, 'Measuring the visual angle of the mind's eye', *Cognitive Psychology*, 1978, 10, pp. 356–89.
83. S. M. Kosslyn, 'Can imagery be distinguished from other forms of internal representation? Evidence from studies of retrieval time', *Memory and Cognition*, 1976, 4, pp. 291–7.
84. Z. W. Pylshyn, 'The imagery debate: analogue media versus tacit knowledge', *Psychological Review*, 1981, 88, pp. 16–45.
85. Ibid, p. 25:

A function was said to be cognitively impenetrable if it could not be altered in a way that exhibits a coherent relation to the meaning of its inputs. For example, although a function might still count as being cognitively impenetrable if it varied with such things as practice or arousal level or ingestion of drugs, it would not be viewed as cognitively impenetrable if it changed in rationally explainable ways as a function of such things as whether a subject believes that the visually presented stimulus depicts a heavy object (and hence visualises it as moving very slowly) or whether the subject views it as consisting of one or two figures, or as depicting an old woman or a young lady (in the well-known illusion), and as a consequence behaves in a way appropriate to that reading of the stimulus.

86. Ibid, p. 31.
87. Quotes in B. Ghiselin, *The Creative Process* (New York: New American Library, 1952), p. 45.

88. S. M. Kosslyn, 'The medium and the message in mental imagery', *Psychological Review*, 1981, 88, pp. 46–66.

89. Ibid, p. 57.

90. Ibid, p. 62.

91. Ibid, p. 40.

92. See note 78.

93. Comments. See note 78.

94. See Chapter 3.

95. See the review by R. A. Finke, 'Levels of equivalence in imagery and perception', *Psychological Review*, 1980, 86, pp. 113–32.

96. For example the 'associative network' theory of Quillian, the 'conceptual dependency' theory of Schank, and Winograd's SHRDLU data base – these are, in fact, the examples that Anderson (see note 99) gives and discusses.

97. Note that all the examples given in note 96 are based on computational systems.

98. This was expressed in Pylyshyn's first critique of imagery theories: 'What the mind's eye tells the mind's brain', *Psychological Bulletin*, 1973, 80, pp. 1–24.

99. J. R. Anderson, 'Arguments concerning representations for mental imagery', *Psychological Review*, 1978, 85, pp. 249–77.

100. See note 99.

101. 'Computable' here means that it is in principle possible to state the inverse of the encoding process *with sufficient precision* to allow its accurate translation into another form of representation. In particular all relevant categories and distinctions in the original encoding have to be maintained for it to be accurate (see Pylyshyn's comments – note 103). 'Precise' is a value-laden word and theories of AI take great care to express it in mechanical terms, i.e., terms which employ only Turing machine concepts. See M. L. Minsky, *Computation: Finite and Infinite*, (Englewood Cliffs, New Jersey: Prentice-Hall, 1967) ch. 5.

102. F. Hayes-Roth, 'Distinguishing theories of representation: a critique of Anderson, "Arguments concerning mental imagery"', *Psychological Review*, 1979, 86, pp. 376–82.

103. Z. W. Pylyshyn, 'Validating computational models: a critique of Anderson's indeterminacy of representation claims', *Psychological Review*, 1979, 86, pp. 383–94.

104. See note 78, *Behavioural and Brain Sciences*, 1979, no. 2, pp. 545–6.

105. Also see note 101. This is a derivation of the claim originally made by Alonzo Church that any effective (or algorithmic) procedure in mathematics can be performed on a computing machine, defining an effective procedure as a set of rules that tells us, from moment to moment, exactly what to do. The more famous version of this pronouncement was that of Turing. Minsky paraphrases Turing's thesis as: 'Any process which could naturally be called an effective procedure can be realised on a Turing machine': Minsky, *Computation: Finite and Infinite*, p. 108. Thus if some behaviour can be described as sets of effective procedures then it can be performed by a computer.

106. This is *primitive* as opposed to *general* recursion. Primitive recursive functions are those which are *predictably terminating*, unlike general recursive functions which might continue to infinity. Recall Anderson's function f (see also note 101). If the computability of f was generally recursive then it would be useless for the task of providing an inverse between one representation and its mimic: we could never determine when the translation and decoding were complete.

107. As argued by S. M. Kosslyn and J. R. Pomerantz, 'Imagery proposals and the form of internal representations', *Cognitive Psychology*, 1977, 9, pp. 52–76.

108. Hayes-Roth, 'Distinguishing theories . . .', p. 380.

109. J. R. Anderson, 'Further arguments concerning representation for mental

imagery: A response to Hayes-Roth and Pylyshyn', *Psychological Review*, 1979, 86, pp. 395–406.

110. As we discussed earlier computational models use a-semantic sequences. Therefore they are best regarded as models of brain function with no foothold in the intensional domain.

7   Meaning: the Thought of Language

1. This does not at all imply that Chomsky is sympathetic to computer-modelling in psycholinguistics. Quite the reverse; his opposition to modelling is part of his general distrust of empirical approaches to the issues he is discussing. See Chomsky's comments on Seymour Papert's paper in M. Piattelli-Palmarini (ed.), *Language and Learning: the Debate Between Jean Piaget and Noam Chomsky* (London: Routledge & Kegan Paul, 1980). Here the distinction is very clear between AI within experimental psychology and the computational theory of mind: the latter is a metatheory with a distrust of 'grass roots' AI. See also Jerry Fodor on 'procedural semantics': note 116 below for the reference.

2. The same theme emerges in Chomsky's writings on foreign affairs: study of the 'deep structure' of imperialists' intentions (e.g. USA, Israel) as opposed to a pragmatic/empirical explanation of their actions in terms of immediate contingencies. I think it is important to maintain a degree of 'cognitive complexity' sufficient to applaud this whilst remaining sceptical about the linguistic theory!

3. J. M. Greene refers to this principled ambivalence about the empirical implications of his theory as the 'competence–performance slip' (Greene, *Psycholinguistics: Chomsky and Psychology* (Harmondsworth: Penguin, 1972). When faced with negative data there is always the possibility of a retreat or a 'performance–competence slip'. This reverse slip took place some time ago and Chomsky now denies that we need to give linguists' proposals 'psychological reality'.

4. J. J. Katz and J. A. Fodor, 'The structure of semantic theory', *Language*, 1963, 39, pp. 170–210.

5. Wittgenstein explicitly opposed the Augustinian view of language acquisition in *Philosophical Investigations* (e.g. para. 32 onwards); whilst Fodor has claimed in a number of places that it is precisely the correct kind of theory.

6. Somewhat misleading because this underplays the influence of J. L. Austin and Ryle. We now appear to be in a state of post-revolutionary backlash.

7. See S. E. Toulmin, 'Brain and language: a commentary', *Synthese,* 1971, 22, pp. 369–95.

8. See Toulmin (previous note); T. Mischel in S. C. Brown (ed.), *Philosophy of Psychology* (Macmillan, 1974); J. Searle, in *The Times Literary Supplement*, 10 Sept. 1976, and his commentary on Chomsky's paper in *Behavioural and Brain Sciences*, 1980, 3, pp. 37–8.

9. Chomsky, *Rules and Representations* (Oxford: Blackwell, 1980) pp. 101–03.

10. *Rules*, p. 103. The analogy is an odd one because, in addition to the pecking pigeons, the behaviouristic rocket would have to include some quite sophisticated 'rules and representations' in order to translate the results of the key pecks into regulations of the rocket's course.

11. Ibid.

12. It was the linguist Edward Sapir who introduced this concept in 'The psychological reality of the phoneme' reprinted in D. G. Mandelbaum (ed.), *Selected Writings of Edward Sapir* (Berkeley: University of California Press,

1949). He derived the notion of a 'phoneme' from purely linguistic evidence and then went onto ask whether this is really a unit of speech perception – i.e. whether it has 'psychological reality'. Chomsky asserts that Sapir shouldn't have bothered: the linguistic evidence is sufficient (*Rules*, p. 108).

13.   Ibid, p. 192.
14.   This is because, for Chomsky, the analogy is between the sun and the *mind*, not between the sun and the brain. We *can*, to a limited extent, study the neurological determinants of language; but nothing *physical* prevents us from looking 'directly' at the unconscious or non-conscious (tacit) linguistic rules that we employ.
15.   Richard Cromer – a development psychologist sympathetic to the nativist position – comments on *Rules and Representations* as follows: 'Chomsky does himself a disservice by stating too much of his case in the form of assertions frequently not backed up with supporting evidence and therefore open to criticism . . . There is a good deal of empirical evidence to support Chomsky's position'. *Behavioural and Brain Sciences*, 1980.
16.   John Morton distinguishes between an 'idealisation' (abstract description of the structure of language) and 'models of potential' (theories of how the brain actually represents linguistic processes). The former *may or may not* be relevant to the latter. (In 'The use of natural and linguistic concepts in psychological explanation' in S. S. Brown (ed.) – see note 8.) This allows us to be clearer about the competence/performance distinction – see note 3.
17.   This is Searle's position (note 8 above). Robin Campbell, 'Cognitive development and child language', in P. Fletcher and M. Garman (eds) *Language Acquisition* (Cambridge University Press, 1979) has argued that there are two distinct but interacting aspects to language-acquisition: that to which the child can have no conscious access ('cryptic'), and that which has to be open to consciousness ('phenic'). The principal object of cryptic access is the grammar; the main phenic aspect is the process of communication. It is unclear, though, whether Campbell regards grammar as non-consciously represented or whether it is an abstract idealisation from linguistics, something to which we need have no *access*. His statement (p. 430) that linguistics is not part of cognitive psychology would tend to support the latter interpretation were it not for the fact that Campbell regards 'cognitive psychology' as the study of exclusively phenic or consciously accessible processes, not of cryptic or tacit processes. Nevertheless, the reader is encouraged to consult this paper as a serious treatment of the central issues.
18.   See the first chapter of *Aspects of the Theory of Syntax* (MIT Press, 1965) for Chomsky's earliest arguments against this viewpoint.
19.   In M. Piattelli-Palmarini (ed.) (see note 1) p. 39.
20.   Ibid.
21.   Ibid, p. 42.
22.   It was David Hume who stated most clearly the view that the unity of the ego is only guaranteed by memory.
23.   G. Sampson, *Making Sense* (Oxford: Oxford University Press, 1980).
24.   Ibid, p. 170.
25.   See note 7.
26.   H. A. Simon, 'The architecture of complexity', *Proceedings of the American Philosophical Society*, 1962, 106, pp. 467–82. Reprinted in Simon's *The Science of the Artificial* (MIT Press, 1969).
27.   Sampson, *Making Sense*, p. 160.
28.   Ibid, p. 158.
29.   Ibid, p. 172.

30. See W. J. M. Levelt, *Formal Grammars in Linguistics and Psycholinguistics: Vol. 2. of Applications in Linguistic Theory* (The Hague: Mouton, 1974) pp. 39–41.

31. *Rules and Representations*, p. 171.

32. Ibid, p. 122.

33. Sampson does, in fact, (pp. 149–54) attempt to show why his position is radically different from Chomsky's.

34. G. Lackoff, 'Whatever happened to deep structure?' (Comments on Chomsky's paper), *Behavioural and Brain Sciences*, 1980, 3, pp. 22–3.

35. Ibid, p. 23.

36. Barbara Partee, 'Some transformational extensions of Montague grammar', in B. Partee (ed.), *Montague Grammar* (London: Academic Press, 1976) p. 55.

37. For further discussion in the same vein see my book *The Acquisition of Knowledge* (Macmillan, 1978) pp. 172–4.

38. H. Putnam, in M. Piattelli-Palmarini (see note 1), p. 294.

39. The Piagetian position would be different again: logic and language are hierarchical because action is necessarily hierarchical (see Piaget, *Genetic Epistemology* [Columbia University Press, 1971]).

      Sampson's argument as to why hierarchicality is not a logical necessity is unconvincing. He says that it is easy to invent non-hierarchical systems of formal logic whose rules are structure-independent, but that logicians do not work with these because they are 'uninteresting' (*Making Sense*, p. 128). But *why*, we may well ask, are they uninteresting? Because they are not really logics at all.

40. M. Barrett, 'The holophrastic hypothesis: conceptual and empirical issues', *Cognition*, 1982, 11, pp. 47–76.

41. See M. A. K. Halliday, *Learning How to Mean* (London: Edward Arnold, 1975).

42. Annette Karmiloff-Smith, *A Functional Approach to Child Language: A Study of Determiners and Reference* (Cambridge: Cambridge University Press, 1979).

43. M. P. Maratsos and M. A. Chalkley, 'The internal language of children's syntax: the ontogenesis and representation of syntactic categories', in K. E. Nelson (ed.), *Children's Language*, Vol. 2 (New York: Gardner Press, 1980).

44. See E. J. Gibson's *Principles of Perceptual Learning and Development* (New York: Appleton-Century-Crofts, 1969).

45. F. C. Keil, 'Constraints on knowledge and cognitive development', *Psychological Review*, 1981, 88, pp. 197–227 (see pp. 218–19).

46. J. Katz, *The Philosophy of Language* (New York: Harper & Row, 1966) p. 98.

47. J. F. M. Hunter, 'On how we talk' in his *Essays after Wittgenstein* (London: Allen & Unwin, 1973).

48. Ibid, p. 159.

49. *Rules and Representations*, p. 77.

50. Ibid, p. 161.

51. Ibid, p. 169.

52. Fodor, 'Some reflections on L. S. Vygotsky's "Thought and Language"', *Cognition*, 1972, 1, pp. 83–95.

53. For possible historical influences between Vygotsky and Wittgenstein, via the child-psychologists Karl and Charlotte Bühler, see S. E. Toulmin's 'Ludwig Wittgenstein', *Encounter*, 1969, 32, pp. 58–71.

54. L. S. Vygotsky, *Thought and Language* (MIT Press, 1965) p. 124.

55. One of Vygotsky's main themes was the ontogenetic and phylogenetic distinctness of the roots thought and language – this is not Wittgensteinian. Additionally, Vygotsky's version of Marxism led him to a kind of social transmission view of knowledge development, which is not particularly

congenial to the view which is derivable from Wittgenstein, that the sharing of 'forms of life' (see below) is the main developmental necessity.

56. St Augustine viewed language acquisition as essentially equivalent to the learning of a second language. (See note 5 above.)

57. If what comes later is necessary inherent in what went before, it is difficult to explain the evolution of new forms: how might a human being be implicit in our fishy ancestors. Piaget (in M. Piattelli-Palmarini (ed.) [see note 1], p. 150) makes this point against Fodor with particular regard to the evolution of mathematics: the previous structure may contain something of a subsequent one but 'as a possibility' not as the structure itself.

58. The evidence for this view that Fodor covers in *The Language of Thought* is mainly of the following kind: he reviews data which show that the processing strategies we adopt (e.g. in speech perception – surface processing but no semantic processing or vice versa) depend on the task variables. Therefore we are able to manipulate our internal representations intelligibly. In general, (i) there are representations of representations and (ii) lower level representations depend on higher level computations. But, true as this seems to be, it is difficult to see how this makes the language of thought proposal (that is, why this must be an abstract, conceptual language similar to that of a computer) any more plausible. If anything, evidence of this kind demonstrates the importance of conscious 'metacognitive' processes.

59. Ibid, p. 59.

60. 'Human learning' in S. C. Brown (ed.); see note 8.

61. In M. Piattelli-Palmarini (see note 1).

62. Ibid, p. 305.

63. J. Heil, 'Does cognitive psychology rest on a mistake?' *Mind*, 1981, XC, pp. 321–42.

64. Ibid, p. 332.

65. Ibid, p. 339. Heil writes:

> The upshot is that to say that two things have the same structure is to say very little about them. It is to say that it is possible to divide them up in a certain way so that their parts and the relations among them may be matched. But this can be done, with a little ingenuity, for *any* two complexes.

66. M. R. Kuenne, 'Experimental investigation of the relation of language to transposition behaviour in young children', *Journal of Experimental Psychology*, 1946, 36, pp. 471–90.

67. The transposition paradigm is a test of relational learning. For example, we might reinforce an *S* for responding to a 4″ square and ignoring a 2″ square. We then give the *S* a 4″ square together with a 6″ square and he chooses the 6″ square. Here *S* has performed a relational response: responding in terms of the relation 'bigger'. Sticking with the 4″ square would be an absolute response. This is what Kuenne calls a 'near test'. A 'far test' might be giving the *S* a 10″ square and a 14″ square. If the child picks the 14″ square then the response is still more relational. Kuenne claimed that language competence (e.g. use of the word 'big') was necessary for 'far' test performance.

68. P. E. Bryant, *Perception and Understanding in Young Children* (London: Methuen, 1974).

69. L. S. Siegel, 'The development of quantity concepts: perceptual and linguistic factors', in C. J. Brainerd (ed.) *Children's Logical and Mathematical Cognition* (New York: Springer-Verlag, 1982).

70. B. E. Shepp and P. D. Eimas, 'Intradimensional and extradimensional shifts in

the rat'. *Journal of Comparative and Physiological Psychology*, 1964, 57, pp. 357–62.

71.   J. M. Baldwin (see Chapter 4, note 42) called this the 'Fallacy of the Implicit'.

72.   Whether there is such a 'fundamental difference' between this and the *chimpanzee*'s concepts is another question of course.

73.   For example no one would want to stop reference to 'the infants–object *concept*' and the like.

74.   Such talk of pre-verbal concepts seems to·encourage theorists (e.g. T. G. R. Bower in his *Development in Infancy* [London: Freeman, 1974] ch. 7) to overintellectualise the infant's achievements, such that data from (say) heart rate decrease after the removal of an occluder is supposed to tell us something about the infant's 'beliefs' about a thing's continuing existence when unperceived. For elaboration see my book *The Acquisition of Knowledge* (London: Macmillan, 1978) pp. 125–31.

   Peter Geach has been one of the severest critics of the view that there are non-verbal 'concepts'. See his *Mental Acts* (London: Routledge & Kegan Paul, 1957).

75.   Fodor, *Language of Thought*, p. 62 (notation slightly modified here for clarity).

76.   Parentheses of this kind indicate the 'universal quantifier', meaning 'for all x'.

77.   Fodor, *Language of Thought*, p. 79.

78.   See previous comments in this book on family resemblance and on rule application.

79.   Fodor, *Language of Thought*, p. 79.

80.   See G. Sampson, *Making Sense*, ch. 3 (note 23). Also see W. Labov, 'The boundaries of words and their meanings', in C. J. N. Bailey and R. W. Shuy (eds), *New Ways of Analysing Variation in English* (Washington D.C.: Georgetown University Press, 1973). Also: G. Lakoff, 'Hedges: a study of meaning criteria and the logic of fuzzy concepts', Papers from the eighth regional meeting, Chicago Linguistics Society, 1972, pp. 182–228.

81.   Fodor, *Language of Thoughts*, (see note 52) p. 87.

82.   Vygotsky, *Thought and Language*, p. 130.

83.   Fodor *Language of Thoughts*, p. 87.

84.   C. Trevarthen in A. Locke (ed.), *Action, Gesture and Symbol* (London: Academic Press, 1980).

85.   H. Werner and B. Kaplan, *Symbol Formation* (London: Academic Press, 1963).

86.   See papers in Locke (ed.); cited in note 84, Also. J. S. Bruner, 'The ontogenesis of speech acts', *Journal of Child Language*, 1975, 2, pp. 1–19.

87.   P. Johnson-Laird, 'Procedural semantics', *Cognition*, 1977, 5, pp. 189–214 (p. 209).

88.   In Peter Tinniswood, *Tales from a Long Room* (Arrow Books, 1981).

89.   E.g. H. R. Pollio, J. M. Barlow, H. J. Fine and M. R. Pollio, *Psychology and the Poetics of Growth* (Hillsdale New Jersey: Erlbaum Associates, 1977).

90.   Originally 1951. Reprinted in W. V. O. Quine, *From a Logical Point of View* (Cambridge, Mass.: Harvard University Press, 1953).

91.   In his *Word and Object* (MIT Press, 1960) Quine imagines the case of a linguist in the field trying to decide whether the word *gavagai* which natives say when a rabbit appears means the same as our 'rabbit'; or could it mean 'rabbit segment' or . . .

92.   Quine, 'Mind and verbal dispositions', in S. Guttenplan (ed.), *Mind and Language* (Oxford: Clarendon Press, 1975).

93.   Gilbert Harman, 'Language learning', *Noûs*, 1970, 4, pp. 33–43.

94.   Ibid, p. 34. Harman has his IV proponent leaving open the question what inner

'language' precedes inner verbal language. See the fourth section of this chapter for some speculations.

95. 'A study of the acquisition of language', *Language*, 1969, XIV, pp. 322–42.
96. See note 40.
97. Harman, 'Language learning', p. 39.
98. Ibid, p. 98.
99. But, as Sampson indicates (*Making Sense*, p. 68) the experiment that might decide the issue is only *described* by Katz, *not performed*. See also J. J. Katz, *Semantic Theory* (Harper & Row, 1972) pp. 249–51.
100. D. Lewis 'General semantics'. *Synthese*, 1971.
101. J. Hintikka, 'Semantics for propositional attitudes', in his *Models for Modalities* (New York: Humanities Press, 1969) pp. 87–111.
102. R. Montague, in R. H. Thomason (ed.), *Formal Philosophy* (New Haven: Yale University Press, 1974).
103. D. Lewis, in Partee (ed.) *Montague Grammar*, p. 6 (see note 36).
104. Rudolf Carnap, *Meaning and Necessity* (Chicago University Press, 1942).
105. For a clear account of modal logic see Susan Haack, *Philosophy of Logics* (Cambridge: Cambridge University Press, 1978).
106. R. Montague in Thomason (ed.), *Formal Philosophy*, p. 217.
107. See Haack, *Philosophy of Logics*, p. 191 onwards for a discussion of these difficulties.
108. H. Putnam, 'Is semantics possible?', in his collection *Mind, Language and Reality: Philosophical Papers, Vol. 2* (Cambridge University Press, 1975).
109. F. M. Katz and J. J. Katz, 'Is necessity the mother of intension?', *Philosophical Review*, 1977.
110. Johnson-Laird, 'Procedural semantics'.
111. Ibid, p. 190.
112. Ibid, p. 191.
113. For Johnson-Laird's much earlier thoughts on the eliminability of deep structure see his chaper in J. Lyons (ed.), *New Horizons in Linguistics*, (Harmondsworth: Penguin, 1970).
114. Ibid, p. 192.
115. Ibid, p. 193.
116. J. A. Fodor, 'Tom Swift and his procedural grandmother', *Cognition*, 1978, 6, pp. 229–47.
117. P. N. Johnson-Laird, 'What's wrong with grandma's guide to procedural semantics: a reply to Jerry Fodor', *Cognition*, 1978, 6, pp. 248–60.
118. J. D. Fodor, J. A. Fodor and M. F. Garrett, 'The psychological unreality of semantic representation', *Linguistic Inquiry*, 1975, 6, pp. 515–31. Sampson points this out.
119. See note 108 for reference.
120. See E. Rosch and C. B. Mervis, 'Family resemblances: Studies in the internal structure of categories', *Cognitive Psychology*, 1975, 7, pp. 573–605.
121. D. N. Osherson and E. E. Smith On the adequacy of a prototype theory as a theory of concepts. *Cognition*, 1981, 9, 35–58.
122. See note 45. Keil, 'Constraints on knowledge . . .'.
123. Robin Campbell (see note 17) makes a similar point about prototype theory.
124. F. Sommers, 'Types and ontology', *Philosophical Review*, 1963, 72, pp. 327–63.
125. Only for homophones are *M*-shaped relations possible between predicates and subjects. As an illustration let us take the case of 'bat' (the animal and the tennis implement). The predicates 'is made by hand' and 'was dead' may be applied, respectively, to the subjects 'chair' and 'cow'; these being the outer strokes of the

M with the predicates at the top vertices and the subjects at the end points. The predicates may be joined at the downward vertex by 'bat' which, *solely by virtue of meaning two things at once* can be covered by both predicates. But for words which have one meaning or for homophones on *one* of their meanings, no such linkage is possible: there is nothing of which we can say both that it was dead and that it was made by hand. In general the human conceptual system does not have linkages across divides such as animate–inanimate: there are natural *discontinuities*.

126.   See Paul Harris, 'Infant cognition', in M. M. Haith and J. J. Campos (eds), *Handbook of Child Psychology*, vol. 1 (New York: Wiley, in press).

127.   N. E. Kossan, 'Developmental differences in concept acquisition strategies', *Child Development*, 1981, 52, pp. 190–298.

128.   See, for example, D. W. Hamlyn, 'Person perception and understanding others', in T. Mischel (ed.) *Understanding Other Persons* (Oxford: Blackwell, 1974).

129.   This is the term Chomsky employs in *Rules and Representations*.

130.   In *Thought and Language*, p. 153.

131.   See Paul Harris, 'Cognitive prerequisites to language', *British Journal of Psychology*, 1982, 73, pp. 187–95.

132.   See Piaget, *The Child's Construction of Reality* (London: Routledge & Kegan Paul, 1955).

133.   See George Butterworth in G. Butterworth (ed.), *Infancy and Epistemology* (Brighton: Harvester Press, 1981).

134.   Gavin Bremner, 'The infant's understanding of space', in M. V. Cox (ed.), *Are Young Children Egocentric?* (London: Batsford Academic, 1977).

135.   I give this account in more detail and follow the speculations through to include early grammatical development elsewhere. See note 78 in Chapter 5 for reference.

136.   See Jane Goodall, *In the Shadow of Man* (Boston: Houghton Mifflin Company, 1971).

137.   S. Goldin-Meadow and H. Feldman, 'The development of language-like communication without a language model, '*Science*', 1977, 197, pp. 401–2.

138.   Published by Jonathan Cape, 1980.

Index